FOOL

OTHER BOOKS BY
ANDREW BARD SCHMOOKLER

The Parable of the Tribes:
  The Problem of Power in Social Evolution

Out of Weakness:
  Healing the Wounds that Drive Us to War

Sowings and Reapings:
  The Cycling of Good and Evil in the
  Human System

The Illusion of Choice:
  How the Market Economy Shapes Our Destiny

FOOL'S GOLD

The Fate of Values in a World of Goods

Andrew Bard Schmookler

HarperSanFrancisco
A Division of HarperCollinsPublishers

FOOL'S GOLD: *The Fate of Values in a World of Goods.*
Copyright © 1993 by Andrew Bard Schmookler. All rights reserved.
Printed in the United States of America. No part of this book may be used
or reproduced in any manner whatsoever without written permission except
in the case of brief quotations embodied in critical articles and reviews.
For information address HarperCollins Publishers, 10 East 53rd Street,
New York, NY 10022.

FIRST EDITION

Library of Congress Cataloging-in-Publication Data
Schmookler, Andrew Bard
    Fool's gold : the fate of values in a world of goods /
Andrew Bard Schmookler.
        p. cm.
    Includes bibliographical references.
    ISBN 0-06-250828-8
    1. Social values. 2. Consumption (Economics)—
Moral and ethical aspects. 3. Consumers—United States.
4. Wealth—United States. I. Title.
    HM216.S298 1993
    303.3'72—dc20   91-58894
                                          CIP

92 93 94 95 96 ❖ HAD 10 9 8 7 6 5 4 3 2 1

This edition is printed on acid-free paper that meets the American
National Standards Institute Z39.48 Standard.

To my wife
April Moore
My soulmate
In her sense of the sacred.

CONTENTS

OVERTURE

Nothing Sacred

"Nothing sacred." The phrase used to be part of a question: "Is nothing sacred?" It was not the existence of a sacred realm that the question put in doubt, but the moral and spiritual condition of one's interlocutor. The question might be restated, "Have you no sense of your proper limits?" or "Are you blind to the meaning of things?" The question expressed not skepticism but outrage.

Nowadays, "nothing sacred" fairly well describes our predominant metaphysics. The universe is but matter and energy following impersonal laws; society, in one view that has shaped much of our social universe, is but a collection of social atoms energetically pursuing their own narrow interests. The idea of the sacred seems worn out, obsolete. We have traded it in for a new model of the cosmos as an indifferent mechanism.

How different is the universe of "Anything goes" from the earlier cosmic vision of "Thou shalt not." That older worldview was defined by stories that suggested that one could not help but understand—or painfully discover—the boundaries of the sacred. The sacred was equipped to defend itself from trespass.

In the Old Testament, Lot's wife turns to see what she is not supposed to see, and instantly she is turned to a pillar of salt. The Lord responds to the rebellion of Korah: "And the earth opened

1

her mouth and swallowed them up, and their homes, and all the men appertained unto Korah, and all their goods"(Numbers 16:32, KJV). When the Philistines abducted the ark of the Lord, bringing it to the city of Gath, "the hand of the Lord was against the city with a very great destruction: and he smote the men of the city, both small and great, and they had emerods in their secret parts" (1 Samuel 5:8, KJV).

Even good intentions are no protection. Consider the case of Uzzah, who reached out to steady God's ark. "And when they came to Nachan's threshingfloor, Uzzah put forth his hand to the ark of God and took hold of it; for the oxen shook it. And the anger of the Lord was kindled against Uzzah; and God smote him there for his error; and there he died by the ark of God" (2 Samuel 6:6–7, KJV).

A person incapable of reading the sign on the fence that reads "Danger! High Voltage" might have no sense that the equipment within holds a special charge. But ignorance is no defense. If our illiterate explorer thoughtlessly intrudes inside the fence and improperly handles the high-voltage equipment, he or she will be electrocuted. There will be no need for us to challenge such a person with the question, "Is nothing electrified?"

The ancient Greeks, like the Jews, had stories about the high-voltage domain of the sacred. Actaeon is out hunting in the forest with his dogs when he unexpectedly comes upon Artemis, goddess of the hunt, in a state of undress. Artemis sees how he sees her, sees in his face that Actaeon's response to her female form takes no account of her sacred status as a goddess. To punish him for seeing her with mundane eyes, the goddess transforms him into a stag, whereupon the hunter's own dogs turn on him and tear him to pieces.

"It's not nice to fool Mother Nature," say our commercials, as a goddess figure in the woods makes thunder and lightning to show how wroth she has become because the margarine tastes so much like butter.

We laugh at her comic wrath, and then proceed to clear-cut whole forests. In the grandeur of the redwoods reaching into the heavens, we see only so many board feet. (If not we, then our agents, those who procure for us our picnic tables and siding.) There is no thunder and lightning, no matter how crassly mundane the lust in our eyes, no matter how brutally we rape the earth. If whatever is sacred would be protected by high-voltage wires, our civilization has concluded, there's nothing sacred here.

Where was the high-voltage fence to block humanity's creation of an Auschwitz? There the camp sat quietly in the woods. The "cargo" was delivered in boxcars, unloaded, and processed. Like the factories our civilization has built across the world in the centuries since the smokestacks of the Industrial Revolution first started darkening the skies, Auschwitz was efficient. And the sun still shone on the woods. It did not matter that what this factory produced was death, the death of innocents. The earth did not crack open to swallow the showers and the ovens and those who ran them.

Like Sherlock Holmes's famous dog that did not bark, the silence of the cosmos as the matter-of-fact, mundane process of extermination goes forward—whether it be the gassing of human beings in the camps or the ongoing holocaust of the tropical forests—seems a telling clue to the nature of our case. Time just keeps ticking in Newton's clockwork universe. Nothing is sacred, we deduce. We can create a hell on earth, and the universe yawns in its indifference.

If we conclude this, we misread the case. We fail to grasp the real mystery in the human condition. The error may be in looking for the realm of the sacred as something that is just "out there," like cosmic radiation that can mutate our genes, even if we were in a coma, or that can be read as clues to the origins of the universe. Perhaps a better approach would be to envision the sacred in terms of the quality of the human instrument that registers it.

Imagine people who look upon the world and see it only in the shades of gray of a black-and-white TV. They will be bewildered by the excitement of others in their midst who see the world in color. It might seem that they live in the same world, that they are seeing the same things. But to the color-blind, those who go on and on about the lusciousness of that red rose seem fools. The technicians at Auschwitz saw in black and white things that were happening in color.

When a musical instrument is sounded, if it is intact, its vibration will be rich with overtones. All of our experiences sound us in this way—the sun rising over the waters, the sharing of a meal, the death of a member of the family. What it means to me to attend the birth of my child—whether I am attuned to the sacredness of the event—depends on how open is my being, how accessible my sounding board to the deepest resonances.

Perhaps the question is not, "Is there a realm of the sacred?" but rather, "Is there a realm of the purely mundane?"

Are those people fools who experience the breaking of bread as a sacrament? In this swirling universe, the appearance of this evolving film of life on our floating grain is itself a miracle. Each morsel that sustains us, each breath that moves through us, is part of that miracle. Are those who experience the presence of the divine in each encounter of daily life more deluded than the practical people of merely mundane matters, or are they more aware?

Did the butchers of Auschwitz prove that there is nothing sacred in the fabric of human life they so brutally and callously tore? People who experience the world as a place where nothing is sacred, I would say, are telling us less about the nature of the cosmos than about their own damaged capacities. The fingers were still moving across the keyboard, but some of the strings inside the case had snapped.

With none of us is the instrument altogether intact. We may be born with the potential to be grand pianos, but we end up with debris strewn across our strings. One can still play the keyboard, but the instrument may plunk dully when it should resound.

The experience of the sacred vibrates the deepest parts of our being; it brings our realization of just how rich is the music of our lives. In my own life, those moments when my instrument has opened up to the reverberations of the sacred stand almost as a different state of being from my more usual, more narrow band of receptivity. As if music that one had heard only on a little car radio were suddenly encountered in live performance. As when Dorothy lands in Oz and we suddenly see her and her surroundings in color.

But, for me, it is not as though I am not in Kansas anymore. Rather, I realize that I never was there—not as I perceived it. Even after I return to my more mundane—that is, truncated— baseline state, I try to remember the colors, the rich sounds, that I now know are always there. Just as one who really knows Beethoven's Seventh can "hear" the full grandeur of the piece even when listening to it on a tinny radio, I try not to forget what I know about the sacred: about the vital channel that can open between a man and a woman; about the awesome upsurgence of the life force in a grove of trees; about the way two friends can open each other like morning glories in the new sun.

There are many divisions one can discern among the people of our society. Sometimes it seems to me the most essential divide is between those who experience the world as having a sacred dimension and those who do not.

Last summer, as I traveled with my family in the American South, we encountered another family on a wooded trail near Tallulah Falls in Georgia. We entered into friendly conversation, and it was clear to me that in many ways we were on different sides of a great cultural divide. I don't know how they vote on the issues, but my guess is that the votes of that couple cancel out ours in national elections. It was not their politics, however, but their spiritual consciousness that they spontaneously and unself-consciously displayed. Even here, ideology and belief would divide us. Their speech was marbled with quotations from texts that they—unlike we—regard as uniquely divine truth. All their decisions and crises they saw in terms of the workings of a Christian Lord that my wife and I do not believe in—not, at least, in terms they would recognize. As for our beliefs about the sacred, I imagine that if we had spelled them out they would have seen us as pagans. And yet. . . And yet we felt an uncommon tie with this family. (Whether that feeling was reciprocated I do not know.) The light in their faces revealed them to contain what we, too, seek. The music of their lives drew us to them as kindred spirits. Their lives were in touch with the sacred, and our contact with them felt special for that.

I have seen that same light in the faces of very different people: an eighty-two-year-old Cambodian Buddhist monk and healer, an Orthodox rabbi, a Hindu spiritual leader. The lamp of belief and tradition that refracts the light is different in each case. But the light always seems the same. It suggests they have touched the same source of luminescent, living understanding. They have established contact with the sacred source of our being, and their lives are similarly aglow from that.

(Not that the differences are trivial. Like the blind man with the elephant in the Sufi story, different cultural and subcultural streams are in touch with different aspects of the sacred's universal realm. In the United States, the cultural left seems more sensitive to the sacredness of the natural systems of the biosphere, whereas the cultural right may be more cognizant of the sacredness of the family. Followers of different aspects of the sacred can collide. On an issue like abortion, where the best representatives of each side are seeking to serve elements of the sacred—human liberty and unborn life—that are here in opposition, the different parts of the elephant different people grasp seem to lead to unbridgeable chasms of political disagreement. Fallible human instruments are not alike attuned to the whole range of life's sacred vibrations.)

What need have we to talk of any of this in terms of the sacred? Why not confine our discourse to terms of *value?* I regard human creativity as sacred; friends of mine also value it highly but would never use the freighted religious term. I resonate with the ancient (pagan) concept of sacred groves; others I know, while rejecting the idea of sacredness, also care deeply about the fate of old-growth forests in the Pacific Northwest. Love within the family, I say, is sacred—a concept that would be rejected by many I know who are nonetheless committed to tending their family bonds. Could I not use such words as *valuing, caring, commitment*—less likely to spark controversy, to open gulfs in the way of mutual understanding—without losing anything of consequence?

My valuing Bach's creativity and my experiencing its sacredness are similar, but there remains an essential difference. My loving my child is akin to my sensing how sacred is the bond between us. But the loving does not seem large enough to contain my experience of the sacredness of our link, while the second does seem to embrace the first. What is added in recognizing the realm of the sacred is something that goes beyond me as the container of the feeling, beyond the immediate relationship between me and that which I appreciate deeply.

In the recognition of the sacred, my consciousness experiences itself as a part of the entire vibrant and seething whole.

It is not just that things matter. They matter so much that their mattering cannot be contained within my little vessel. I feel small in relation to the enormous value I have glimpsed, and my body may register its encounter with the so-much-biggerness of it by bristling out in goose bumps. The stripping of the tropical forest can seem like bad news, but sometimes the picture on the screen shakes my bones and makes me tremble as I recognize the *desecration* this damage represents.

The love I have for my child is something in itself, but it is also part of something that goes beyond him and me. When I experience this, my comprehension of this child's "value" makes my cup run over. When I see my youngest child nursing his mother, I realize that his ancestors have been sucking on her ancestors for 50 million years. Their bond is so elemental that it is not just what is happening between the two of them. It is part of a whole stream. The love between one parent and a child is part of the whole human story going back to when we were furry creatures. Apprehending the thread of that continuous story, I am moved closer to the mystical experience of oneness. It does not seem adequate to describe something as "light" once one has seen that it is luminous.

So where are we with the mystery of the dog that did not bark, that is, with the cosmos that did not open up and swallow the butchers of Auschwitz, with a Mother Nature who does not strike down with bolts of lightning those who fool around with vital balances?

If, in describing the sacred, we put the emphasis on our experience, on the deeper resonance of our instrument, does this not imply that the sacred is merely like the beauty that is merely in the eye of the beholder? Without the high-voltage lines of the Lord, is not the sacred squeezed out of the "really real" realm of "objective" reality?

To say that something is "merely in the eye of the beholder" is to misunderstand the nature of the beholder's eye. It took the evolution of life on earth billions of years to create an eye like yours or mine, and many millions more to create the mind that completes the beholding. Our seeing did not develop in a vacuum, but in continuous interaction with our mother, the earth, and with the exacting requirements for survival she imposes. If our eye beholds beauty, that is because our apprehension of beauty served the sacred cause of our survival.

Just as mathematics is not merely a mind-game but also helps unlock the mysteries of the universe, so also does the delight we take in form and order, in light and color, in mists and melodies, speak about the nature of living as a human being on planet earth.

The sacred may be in the eye of the beholder in the same sense that beauty is. But hardly "merely." We have been molded by a patient, wonderfully ingenious process that founds its entire empire upon one rock of value: life and its continuation. We are crafted to survive—and more than that, to serve the survival of those wholes of which we are part. The deeper vibrations of our experience of the sacred are deep precisely because the instrument is enlarged. The resonance extends beyond us into that connection with the larger whole: family, tribe, humankind, life, Gaia, cosmos, God/Brahman.

The mystic returns, saying all is One. The One speaks to us through our experience of the sacred. Maybe the sacred is also "out there." Maybe, like the astronomer's cosmic radiation, the radiance of the sacred affords some clue to the mystery of our origins.

Over many years, I have been visited by a series of dreams that have come as gifts. Like many gifts, they have their burdensome aspects. These dreams fill me with the anguish of seeing the sacred realm eroded, endangered. Their theme is the destruction of sacred trees. In one, a whole forest of trees as big as gods is reduced to a ribbon in a remote valley. Living stumps a mile across, in another such vision, stand to be uprooted to make way for a shopping center.

The anguish is a small price to pay for the way my cup runs over with a nectar of feeling, sweeter and richer than any words of mine might convey. What a privilege to live in a world where things of such beauty exist, where values of such magnitude are at stake! These dreams help enlist me in the cause of saving the green mantle of our imperiled planet.

A friend of mine dreams often, and in terror, of concentration camps. He never was in one, and his parents fled in time, but he is connected to the camps by the many relatives who made the one-way trip into the death camps to leave only via chimney around the time my friend was born.

My friend may make mistakes in life. But those errors that helped expose the living tree of European Jewry from which he has flowered to being so brutally cut down—errors of insufficient vigilance, of refusal to think the unthinkable, of immobility in the headlights of an onrushing catastrophe—these he will not make. His dreams keep him in condition for the next struggle, or the next great escape.

When he had deep body work done, the first part of the session, on the front, elicited behind his closed eyes gargoylesque imagery of Nazis and death. This prepared the way for work on his back, which evoked unaccustomed visions of angels and, when the back of his neck was touched, a flood of pure light, as if this guardian of a "stiff-necked" people had earned his rest and revelation. It was, he told me, the most beatific vision he had ever had.

In the electricity of our sacred visions, the voltage of the sacred continues to do its work. Of course, the earth does not literally open up to swallow those who trespass upon the sacred. But in another sense it may. The sun continued to rise peacefully over Auschwitz, but the sun set rather precipitously on the Thousand-Year Reich, and for reasons organically connected with the Nazis' fundamental ignorance of their proper place in the order of life and the limits that place entailed. The Nazi death machine was itself returned to dust.

Those who told stories of the shocking price paid by those who infringed upon the ark of the covenant did not live in a world ordered so differently from ours. They knew full well that often it is the wicked who prosper while the righteous endure hardship and injustice. From our perspective, the old stories of divine retribution might appear to be scare tactics to keep the gullible in line, the way some parents invent bogeymen to reinforce their injunctions. Indeed, as the biblical tales were told by a people often abused and oppressed by larger neighbors, the image of a cosmos that surrounded the sacred with high-power lines of moral order may seem mere wishful thinking.

Or perhaps the high-voltage cosmos of our ancient religious worldview captures in those stark images of the wrath of God (or goddess) a deeper wisdom than informs our conduct today. We depend upon Mother Earth for our very survival. We are part of Her, and She is part of us. Yet, like Actaeon, we cast a wholly mundane, crassly calculating eye upon Her, blind to her sacred character. In this careless gaze, are we not endangering ourselves just as did the hunter in the myth? As we poison the air we breathe, as our technology transforms the atmosphere that protects us from dangerous radiation from the heavens and our fires alter the climatic patterns that give us our daily bread, our tools are like the dogs that turned upon their master when he was revealed to them in his vulnerable form as a stag. Forgetting our place in the cosmos, we delude ourselves into seeing ourselves only as hunger, forgetting the reality of our dependence and vulnerability in the larger whole of the biosphere.

To treat the sacred without respecting its sacredness—this is the heart of what traditionally has been called sin. The earth yawning before us gives testimony that there is an order, not of human devising, that does indeed wreak consequences upon the sinner.

The plague of drug abuse and addiction is one of our deadly diseases. We gorge ourselves on substances that wiser peoples have used sacramentally. To invite visions for spiritual guidance, or states of "enthusiasm" (in Greek, "the God within"), other cultures have used plant substances to unlock sacred chambers of human consciousness. But the same wine used in Jewish Sabbath and in Christian Communion also rots the livers of countless of our contemporaries. The leaf the Indians used ritually is chain-smoked by millions today, and as a consequence the earth daily swallows a thousand of our countrymen.

The wage of sin, said the apostle, is death.

The gods of the Hindus might have taught Artemis that the appreciative look of a man upon the comely form of a woman might not be sacrilege but instead might partake of the holy. But a society mindless of the sacred nature of sexual energies gets epidemics of sexually transmitted diseases and teenage pregnancies. We bury more infants than we should in a country with as much material prosperity as ours.

Desire gets out of hand for those in a state of sin perhaps because the real object of desire is to connect with the sacred. (He thirsted for Spirit, said the poet Robert Bly about his alcoholic father, but reached for the wrong one.) It is our insatiable hunger for more and more things that feeds our seeing the sacred biosphere as mere resources to exploit to support our addiction. In our intoxication, we tear apart our own house.

A society that believes there's nothing sacred, far from being enlightened, is as imperiled as the illiterate intruder in the power station who proceeds past the sign where the apparently senseless markings appear.

ONE

A *Land Flowing with Infant Formula and NutraSweet*

CHAPTER 1

A Question of Purpose

THE MAGNET

In *The Illusion of Choice*, I set forth a simple thesis. I try to demonstrate that the market system is not the pure mechanism for channeling human choices that its ideological defenders make it out to be. It does facilitate human choice, but it also imposes its own "choices" on the market society. The system, with its exquisite sensitivity to some of our needs but big blind spots when it comes to others, has a logic of its own. Over time, a society in which market forces are unleashed will develop in predictable and regrettable ways that are the fruit not of human choice but of the unfolding of that systemic logic.

Has America lost its way? Perhaps the way we've taken is not really ours. Our situation is like that of some iron filings in the presence of a magnet, as described in Oscar Wilde's fable:

> Once upon a time there was a magnet, and in its close neighborhood lived some steel filings. One day two or three little filings felt a sudden desire to go and visit the magnet, and they began to talk of what a pleasant thing it would be to do. Other filings nearby overheard their conversation, and they, too, became infected with the same desire. Still others joined them, till at last all the filings began to discuss the matter, and more and more their vague desire grew into an impulse. "Why not go today?" said some of them; but others were of the opinion that it would be better to wait till tomorrow. Meanwhile,

15

without their having noticed it, they had been involuntarily moving nearer to the magnet, which lay there quite still, apparently taking no heed of them. And so they went on discussing, all the time insensibly drawing nearer to their neighbor; and the more they talked, the more they felt the impulse growing stronger, till the more impatient ones declared that they would go that day, whatever the rest did. Some were heard to say that it was their duty to visit the magnet, and that they ought to have gone long ago. And, while they talked, they moved always nearer and nearer, without realizing that they had moved. Then, at last, the impatient ones prevailed, and, with one irresistible impulse, the whole body cried out, "There is no use waiting. We will go today. We will go now. We will go at once." And then in one unanimous mass they swept along, and in another moment were clinging fast to the magnet on every side. Then the magnet smiled—for the steel filings had no doubt at all but that they were paying that visit of their own free will.[1]

This fable can serve as a metaphor for the path of development taken by the members of a market society, like ours, over the course of generations. We see ourselves as free agents, making choices, controlling our destiny. But embedded in a field of forces that, however invisible, channels our movement in ways we do not choose, we leap into the embrace of a system beyond our control.

The first step in liberation is to recognize the existence and power of the magnet. That was the purpose of *The Illusion of Choice*. The second step is to comprehend and experience how important are the costs of the course onto which the magnet has pulled us. That is the purpose of this work.[2]

POOR LITTLE RICH GIRL

American society is so prosperous—yet at the same time so impoverished. These two truths are organically related. I am not referring to the pockets of poverty in our midst, the islands of

Third World infant mortality rates and life expectancy. I am not one of those who believes that the wealth of the rich rests on the backs of the poor. The market does take advantage of cheap labor wherever it is to be found, but the subcultures trapped in poverty are a weight on the forward march of American prosperity, not a support for it. Wealth feeds far more on wealth than it does on poverty.

The impoverishment to which I refer is part and parcel of the "good life" as our market system has rendered it. There is, for instance, a fraying of the bonds that tie. Community is shattered under the impact of an atomistic economic process. Family relationships get short shrift as the care of children is subcontracted out to strangers so that what is regarded as the real business of life—participation in the productive economy—is not interrupted. Separate gardens of private opulence are embedded in a deteriorating public space. The building of temporary constructions of human prosperity, moreover, seems to be at the expense of the long-term integrity of the ecosystem.

And ultimately, there is a poverty of the spirit. One economist has written about our *Joyless Economy*.[3] Like the "poor little rich girl" of our national mythology, we find that being rich on the outside does not necessarily convert into feeling rich on the inside.[4] *Abundance for What?* asks the title of a book of our era. Even in an earlier era, that most astute observer of the American scene, Alexis de Tocqueville, discerned a problematic spiritual condition that seemed to take the blessing out of our blessings: "In America I saw the freest and most enlightened men placed in the happiest circumstances that the world affords: it seemed to me as if a cloud habitually hung upon their brow, and I thought them serious and almost sad, even in their pleasures."[5]

Certainly, an old and deeply ingrained part of our culture's psychological and spiritual heritage was reflected in those clouded brows. But with the gathering momentum of the market system, another—a systemic—dimension also becomes visible.

THE RUBE GOLDBERG CONTRAPTION

This problem with the market society exemplifies a larger dilemma of civilized peoples: What purposes are being served by the systems of our creation? In my book on the evolution of civilization, *The Parable of the Tribes*, I used the metaphor of the Rube Goldberg machine, those comic cartoon inventions that were funny because of the grotesque mismatch between means and ends. "If we were to persist in viewing the great edifice of civilization as a structure for the purpose of meeting human needs," I wrote, "civilization would seem to be a gigantic Rube Goldberg contraption" (p. 9). The lives of hunter-gatherers, it turns out, were not so nasty or brutish; and much of the course of civilization has brought great hardship and oppression to the mass of humanity.

The reason civilization has not better served human needs is that forces other than human needs—forces beyond human control—have played a predominant role in shaping the evolution of civilized societies. The problem arose from our species' taking the unprecedented step of extricating itself from the biologically evolved order of the biosphere. In that order—as in a libertarian polity—each creature was free to follow the law of its own nature. But that law had been inscribed by a process that assured that the laws of all the creatures added up to a viable whole. In the system created by the patient process of natural selection, it is indeed as if an "invisible hand" were operating to lead to a harmonious and optimal result.

But then, around ten thousand years ago, by virtue of our gift of creativity, we began to free ourselves from the limits of the niche in which our species had evolved. By freeing ourselves from the constraints of nature's regime, however, we unwittingly plunged ourselves into a dangerous anarchy. Civilized systems—designed by conceptions in the mind and not in the loins—were compelled to interact with each other outside any order that protected the harmony and viability of the whole.

The anarchy of the intersocietal system meant that a struggle for power—a war of all against all—became inevitable; this struggle for power, combined with the open-ended possibilities for cultural innovation, mandated that civilized societies would inevitably develop in the direction of power maximization.

With humane but weak societies swept aside by societies that were powerful, though also often antihuman, the evolving structure of civilized society was inevitably dictated by the demands of power. With the selection for the ways of power beyond the ability of humankind to stop, people became the servants rather than the masters of their systems. Under the reign of power, human creativity did not so much drive the engine of social evolution as become grist for its mill.

Among civilized societies, market societies appear relatively benign, and human needs certainly do figure strongly in directing the production of the economic system. Yet *The Illusion of Choice* shows how there are at work within market societies systemic forces analogous to those operating on human civilization as a whole. So strongly does the market's own power distort the social universe over the course of generations that the image of the Rube Goldberg contraption comes again to mind.

All this apparatus—reaching to destroy the tropical forests for cheap hamburgers, giving every town its commercial strip to make it more convenient for people to spend their money, belching millions of tons of poisons into the atmosphere so we can go from one unsightly place to another—to what end? The global market system grows mightier, but what does this "growth" amount to in human terms? Between people and their systems, which are the means and which the ends?

THAT'S LIFE

I have always been intrigued by the line, "A chicken is an egg's way of producing another egg." It raises interesting questions about what is the means and what is the end. The humor—the surprise—in the line about the chicken is in its attribution of intention to an egg. How is something that was itself just produced to be made into a Prime Mover?

Nowadays, we understand life to be the product of accident, not purpose. In the course of time, matter assembles itself in various ways. Whatever structures can maintain themselves get to stick around. Those that can replicate themselves can spread. Viable design arises by chance, and the viable inherit the earth. A human being, we are told, is a "selfish gene's" way of perpetuating itself.

For some people, the idea of this as an accidental universe fatally wounds the hope for meaning and purpose in human life. If there was no Purpose behind our creation, how can human life have purpose? But this logic does not hold water. By the same reasoning, one might argue that if there was no life on earth before the beginning of life, how can earth give rise to life? Just as life appears as an *emergent* property of a universe of nonliving matter and energy, so does purpose emerge with the development of the living system.

The dead have no purpose. But the living are crafted with an allegiance to life, a dedication to its continuation. When we are hungry, our bodies are filled with purpose. Our purpose maintains life, but it is not just our own lives we serve. The pleasure of mating makes us the means of life's continuation. We are led, as if by the fondling of an invisible hand, to perpetuate our kind.

Altruism, too, appears as part of our natural purpose. The many ways that parents sacrifice for their children in day-to-day life is an example. In many species, the mother will voluntarily endanger herself to draw danger from her offspring. Natural selection may incline us to act altruistically on behalf of those with whom we share our genetic heritage. As the noted biologist J. B. S. Haldane quipped, "I would willingly lay down my life for more than two brothers, four nephews or eight cousins."[6]

A profound and ancient voice within us makes us willing and happy soldiers in the struggle of life to develop its miraculous empire in the harsh terrain of this overwhelmingly dead universe. A high purpose, indeed. That such a purpose should be inscribed upon our hearts as we evolved in an accidental universe is no accident.

THE FAT AND THE LEAN

With the rise of civilized systems, the evolution of life inaugurated a new and dangerous experiment. Dangerous because the duality of evolutionary processes—the biological joined by the metabiological—introduced the possibility of perversions and conflicts into the human system.

Some years ago, Robert W. Tucker wrote an article entitled "Swollen State, Spent Society." Subtitled "Stalin's Legacy to Brezhnev's Russia," it was about the pathologies of the Soviet system of power. The tyranny of the Soviet state had enabled it to become impressively capable of protecting what was, from the point of view of the human beings living under its aegis, a system not worth keeping. The central fallacy of totalitarianism, it might be said, is in making the people into servants of the state rather than utilizing the state as the instrument of human well-being. (In recent years, as the restructuring of Soviet society in a more life-serving form groped forward, the Russians uncovered the bones of many of the millions of the dead, Stalin's victims, that signal the sickness of this inverted system of power.)

We Americans tend to think ourselves free from exploitation by such perverted power systems. In our in-many-ways free society, the ideology of human sacrifice for the state has little currency. "The pursuit of happiness" is enshrined as one of our sacred national purposes. (Some would argue, indeed, that the cult of fulfillment has created tyrannies of its own.) And yet with us and our system too, there arises the question of which is the master and which the servant.

French economists of the nineteenth century—with an allegiance to the market's expanding empire, to the system's concept of progress—feared that "without the goads of material desires and envies, the natural laziness of mankind would triumph and civilization would slide back 'into the intellectual somnolence and material privations of primitive ages.' "[7] The human being is, therefore, to be led into a small-minded place so that his desperate strivings will fatten the larger system. A kind of human regression is promoted in the name of civilization's progress.

THE GOOD LIFE

The legitimate purpose of a social system, I would argue, is to facilitate its people's living *the good life*. In our society, some ambiguity has come to surround the ancient notion of "the good life." A phrase that used to center on virtue now focuses more on indulgent pleasure: from the image of the upright man walking the straight path, to the man reclining by the swimming pool drinking a rum punch through a crooked straw. The idea of the good life as one that adheres to principles that contribute to the greater good has been displaced, to some extent, by the idea of the life that feels good.

A century ago, the expectation was that increased wealth and leisure would lead to virtue and enlightenment. The human spirit was to be uplifted. As American abundance grew, these hopes were disappointed. The leisure that prospered in the burgeoning market—"saloons, amusement parks, vaudeville, sports"—"overturned the expectations" of some of the philosophers of abundance.[8]

What's the problem? The debate over that question usually involves an exchange of fire between two positions. According to one position, the problem is the unevolved state of the mass of humanity. People are disappointing. They don't want what is "really good." To some of the market's ideologues, by contrast, there is no problem. People turn to the market to get what they want, and despite the lamentations of some "high-minded" snobs about the philistine tastes of the consuming masses, whatever gratifies people is by definition good.[9] (What does it matter whether people buy tickets for Schwarznegger's *Terminator* or for Shakespeare's *Tempest*—as long as they are entertained?)

Both those positions share the assumption that people are getting what they want. Both assume liberty, and whereas one side thinks the liberty is abused, the other finds no basis for making negative judgments about people's pleasures, freely pursued. The market lets people decide what is good. And, according to this view, any complaints about the choices they make are, ultimately, complaints about human nature.

A third position arises from a recognition of the market's power. In the face of that power, people are not fundamentally free. The market's power includes the power to *seduce*. If the expansion of the system's empire requires the rechanneling of human needs, the system has the power to engineer the necessary restructuring of the human psyche. People can be formed as means to the ends of the surrounding system.

From Bernard Mandeville's famous *Fable of the Bees*, generations before Adam Smith, the notion had been broadcast that the good of the social whole depended on the depravity of its individual human parts. In Mandeville's Utopia, "every part was full of vice, / Yet the whole mass a paradise."[10]

Mandeville's teaching, like Machiavelli's intellectual buttressing of the expansion of a different kind of power more than a century earlier, created a scandal. At its first hearing, Mandeville's vision seemed to the religious and ethical leaders of his era a diabolical one. Even into the nineteenth century, the moral dimension of the struggle persisted. The French economists of the era wondered, as Rosalind Williams expresses it in her work *Dream Worlds: Mass Consumption in Late Nineteenth-Century France*, "How could the modern economic imperative to multiply needs be reconciled with the moral tradition inherited from Christian and non-Christian antiquity, which counseled self-discipline and restraint of desire?"[11]

Like Machiavelli's ideas, the ethic of superfluity and indulgence gained currency with the passage of time. That which had been opposed as the Devil's own heresy eventually became established as the orthodoxy of the growing power system. The magnet pulls, and the filings are drawn into its embrace.

Now there is no real contest. Go now, pay later. Ceaselessly the voice of the market—expressing itself in the barrage of commercial messages—teaches us to indulge our whims, to yearn for all that we do not have. Over time, we as a people learn to understand the "good life" in terms radically different from the teachings of the wisest people of our cultural tradition.

In the Image of Our Creator

What about those wants that are being satisfied? What about all that satisfaction, about whose sources the market's ideologues say judgment is impossible? Again, the question is, Whose purposes are running the show?

The market ideology tells us that the market is the servant of its consumers. They are sovereign: anyone with the coin to pay will find the market willing to do his bidding. But the market is not so passive. Like the child king, the "sovereign" consumer of the market society is surrounded by a powerful regency that is able and willing to manipulate him.

One of the great achievements of advertising, and one of that industry's great stories, is told by Roland Marchand in *Advertising the American Dream*. It concerns the virtual creation of halitosis as a problem. The advertisers of Listerine, a product languishing in obscurity, created a new anxiety—Do I have bad breath?—that within a few years made Listerine a highly lucrative product.

The consumer is a product's way of making another product.

The famous advertising executive Ernest Dichter described the task of American advertising this way: "We must use the modern techniques of motivational thinking and social science to make people constructively discontented."[12] Blessed are the discontented, for they feed the growth of the system. "If you are relatively happy with your life, if you enjoy spending time with your children, playing with them and talking with them; if you like nature . . . if you just like talking to people . . . if you enjoy living simply, if you sense no need to compete with your friends or neighbors—*what good are you economically?*"[13]

The purposes of human beings and those of their systems overlap, but they are hardly identical.

Here, the market system is simply playing a variation on an old and tragic theme. As a cultural animal, the human creature is born to have a degree of malleability. How else could we fit into diverse cultural environments? But our malleability is not that of clay, which has no inherent tendencies of its own. It's more like spring steel, easily bent but straining to return to its own true form. Like the bound foot of a Chinese woman, it may be molded to the form demanded by the society, but only at the cost of agony. Since the emergence of the new evolutionary dynamic with the rise of civilization, human beings have been twisted and bent to fit into their evolving power systems.

Our economic system is voracious, taking the entire planet into its maw. It is insatiable. The market has no concept of enough. With its power, the market recreates us in its own image. We become the Economic Man of the system's ideology, infinite in wants, craving more as though the millionth mouthful satisfied our hunger as much—or as little—as the first.

The market economy is by its nature restless, Faustian in its incapacity to sit still, to accept the present moment in its fullness. The market prefers those with a burr under their saddle. It is not, therefore, the content who inherit the earth. As empirical study has revealed, a society's economic growth (that God of the modern world) is directly correlated with the level of anxiety in its members.[14]

(Illustrating the nature of the emergent institution of advertising in the 1920s, Marchand presents an ad from Eaton to sell stationery. "Would you criticize a Friend behind her back?" asks the headline. In the text, the "advertiser-as-adviser," as Marchand terms the pose, asks, "Does your writing paper talk about you behind your back?" Fanning the embers of people's social anxieties, the untrustworthy adviser promotes the passion to consume.[15])

Human satisfaction is not the evolving system's true purpose. The progress that is our most important product—in the slogan Ronald Reagan once mouthed as General Electric's spokesman years ago—is not, ultimately, progress in the fulfillment of our own God-given design.

SACRIFICE

In a famous passage, John Adams said, "I must study politics and war, that my sons may have liberty to study mathematics and philosophy . . . commerce and agriculture, in order to give their children a right to study painting, poetry, music."[16] Here is another expression of the hope that progress would allow an elevation of our pursuits. It is the hope that in a world of peace and prosperity, the human spirit, freed of the weight of life's baser struggles, will ascend.

The line is quoted in the 1976 movie *The Missouri Breaks*. After a relentless crescendo of viciousness and violence, this film by Sam Peckinpah gives us a momentary respite. It is a felicitous scene of peaceful family life, as one of the characters, a fugitive from vengeance, is welcomed as a guest by a hardworking married couple and their children. The line from John Adams is quoted by the host, who is expressing his hopes for the good life his hard work will make possible for his children and grandchildren.

From one perspective, this wish of Adams, reiterated by the struggling farmer on the American frontier, already suggests the human spirit at a high plane. The speaker shows that he understands the purpose of his life in terms of his service to those coming after him. He is willing to sacrifice for his children and their children.

After the family meal, the man bids his wife to get blankets for their guest and to show him out to the small building where he will be sleeping. A moment later, we see the guest, at the wife's explicit invitation, humping his hostess against the wall of the building. (It is while he is engaged in this act that vengeance catches up with him; a gunshot thunders and blows him apart as the woman screams in horror. At that instant, the film cuts away, showing us nothing more of this hospitable family.)

The shocking scene against the wall shows the previous welcome scene to have been just a set-up. The network of family love and loyalty was displayed to us only so that it could be unmasked as a sham. As for the man who quoted Adams's noble thought, he is shown to be a fool. He who would serve others is being betrayed by those he trusts. In his folly, the film is telling us, the yeoman farmer fails to recognize the true nature of life: a war of all against all, in which each pursues his own happiness, loyal only to his or her own lusts and appetites. In this Peckinpah vision of the American frontier, each person is willing to sacrifice anything that gets in the way of his or her satisfaction and anyone who represents an affront to narcissistic pride.

WHAT HAS POSTERITY EVER DONE FOR ME?

Has America lost its way? The question seems to be rising to the surface of our national consciousness.

An enormous national debt amassed from a decade of private greed and public hypocrisy has created a debilitating budgetary crisis. The American public is apparently enraged by the incapacity of its leaders to govern. But should not our finger-pointing be directed at the mirror rather than at the people we send to Washington?

I have never much liked that saying "People get the government they deserve." Who could ever have deserved a Stalin or a Pol Pot? All too often in history, whole generations have been merely innocent sacrificial victims on the altar of their leaders' crazy ambitions. But is not the present budgetary paralysis a result of our unwillingness as a nation, over an entire decade, to make necessary sacrifices? Those leaders who have told us we could have a free lunch have been rewarded by the voters. When Ronald Reagan told Congress, "Go ahead! Make my day!" the public reacted as if his defiance of the need to pay for what we were getting was vintage machismo, like that of a Clint Eastwood hero. When George Bush launched his campaign with "Read my lips," his readiness to stand up to Congress against taxes helped knock the "wimp factor" out of his public image.

If we, like the ancient Greeks, have killed the messenger who brings the bad news—remember Walter Mondale on the need for taxes during the fat times of 1984?—how can we be surprised if the government is paralyzed? Each side tries to make the other break the bad news to us, the news that sacrifice is now required.

The United States has sent several hundred thousand of its young men and women to the sands of Arabia to confront Iraqi aggressors. I get a call from an acquaintance fairly high up in the policy-making circles of the American administration. He asks me, What would the American public buy as a reason for going to war to force Iraq out of Kuwait? I respond in terms of the historic opportunity to define the post–cold war era as one that establishes a more just and secure world order based on a global system of collective security, a major step forward in solving the most fundamental problem of civilization over the millennia. My acquaintance is sympathetic to my point of view, but his bosses don't think such ideals will play well in Peoria. They think, he says, that the "man in the street" is more responsive to talk of the need to keep so much of the oil we require from being effectively controlled by one malign power, the need to protect American jobs. American aren't ready, in this view, to sacrifice for higher ideals.

Is that what we Americans are about: wanting reliable, cheap gas to take us to our free lunch?

Why worry about saddling our grandchildren with debts? "What has posterity ever done for me?" Why should the rich sacrifice to take care of society as a whole? Why should the world's most powerful country—the one remaining superpower—worry about the persistence of an intersocietal system ruled by brute force? Why should the strong sacrifice to protect the weak?

I would like to believe that our leaders seriously misread the willingness of the American people to do what should be done even at the cost of our own immediate gratification and comfort. But I'm not sanguine. The record suggests that if our elected officials are expert in one thing, it is in getting reelected. Who am I to second-guess such certified experts in reading the American electorate?

Over time, "Cast your bread upon the waters" became "You get what you pay for," which subsequently devolved into "Buy now, pay later." Now it's "Buy now, let someone else pay."

Where did this *"Après nous, le déluge"* come from? Perhaps it is, in part, from the flood of commercial messages to which we have been subjected over the course of this century. Daily, it is said, the average American is exposed to three thousand commercial messages. Commercials may be more powerful in teaching our children what life is about than parents, schools, or churches. And the constant underlying teaching of this mighty American institution is "Indulge yourself. You can have it all, and you can have it now."

The richest people in the history of the world, living off their capital, economic and moral. Did our ancestors fight wars and set up a free political system so that their descendants could follow the maxim "Party till you puke!"?

BY DESIGN

Back in the days of the "counterculture" in America, twenty years ago, another bumper-sticker dictum expressed an approach to life: "If it feels good, do it!" I was among those who saw in this approach the promise of liberation. The middle-class society of America, with its repressive rules and conformism, with its fundamental mistrust of the body and of the spontaneous and creative spirit, seemed a prison from which we needed to free ourselves.

If it feels good, the body is sending a message worth heeding. Billions of years have crafted us into instruments of mind-boggling complexity and beauty, imbued with a natural wisdom. Who is society to quarrel with the wisdom of the ages?

It is easy to see how the ethic of "If it feels good, do it!" could be channeled back into the very mainstream from which it tried to diverge. The market system that harnessed the Puritan stream of our cultural heritage to drive the system of production could use the hedonistic strain of the counterculture to feed the engines of consumption. The idea of the natural wisdom of the body could be reduced to the mere pursuit of pleasure. The hippies of the 1960s and 1970s were safely absorbed into the system as the yuppies of the 1980s. If it'll make you feel good, buy it.

The pursuit of pleasure does not seem to leave everyone feeling good, however. Having had their fill of pleasure, many feel empty.

A friend of mine responded to my Rube Goldberg image: "You talk about how the elaborate structures of civilization give a rather paltry payoff in terms of human satisfaction," he said. "But for me, the Rube Goldberg problem shows up at a different level. Our bodies, too, are constructions of great elaboration. Any single human body, in fact, is probably a more complicated machine than the whole apparatus of civilization. But when I look at the payoff of this incredible body of mine—in terms of the level of the pleasure I experience—it seems like another one of your depressing Rube Goldberg jokes. Trillions of cells, each a masterpiece on its own, organized into this marvelous whole, all laboring to yield what seems to me my pathetic experience.

"Maybe the fault lies not in our systems," he suggested to me, "but in ourselves. Maybe it is in the nature of the beast that, ultimately, human life is rather empty."

This sobering thought may not be easy to dismiss. The record of history does not suggest that it is our lot for our cup to run over. The message from the body is perhaps more often pain and emptiness than joy and fulfillment. But perhaps it is those who learn too many of their lessons about the human potential from history who are doomed to repeat its depressing pattern. History has put into the human consciousness a great many voices, not all of them friendly. It becomes difficult to know to which to attend, even to know what feels good.

INSIDE OUT

The idea that the legitimate purpose of society is to help its members lead the good life suggests that the proper direction of causality is from the inside out, from human needs to the design of society. A benign world, an ideal world, would make the sacred needs of the human being the foundation of civilization. The various civilized societies would represent ways of facilitating the flowering of the human spirit. And the international system would be designed to protect and nurture such humane societies.

But there has been a destructive reversal of this causal flow. The anarchy of the system of interacting societies has imposed inescapable demands on every civilized society. Every society is compelled, for its very survival, to structure itself for power.

These societies, in turn, compel their members to adapt to social demands that are in many ways antagonistic to their inborn natures.

Socialization into societies structured by the demands of power instills into the human psyche an alien voice. Freud had a wonderful image for the superego of the civilized human beings he studied in his practice in Victorian Vienna. Civilization masters the individual, Freud wrote, by setting up "an agency within him . . . like a garrison in a conquered city."[17]

A society that tells people that what they should be is in fundamental ways different from what they are by nature produces what Nietzsche termed the "sick animal." Energies within us, harnessed by a superego antagonistic to human nature, are turned against the natural impulses of the id. Like vectors canceling each other out, the warring parties of the psyche leave the experiential payoff of human life a diminished, paltry thing.

The market system arose in history as one such power system. The productive power of the market societies compelled other societies to match them and thus, often, to emulate them. And within these societies, the system has exerted considerable force in the molding of the human material developing within them.

The consumer-driven market society of the contemporary world instills its own voice—its own cacophony of voices—within us. The flood of commercial messages tell us where happiness is to be found. Buy it from us. Smoke these, and you'll be as exuberantly joyful as this beautiful young woman skipping hand-in-hand with her lover. The voices echo inside our minds, the voices of our cultural teacher: this product makes one sexy; this one makes one strong and manly; this one brings good fellowship.

Lead us into temptation, for thine is the kingdom.

Is there within us a natural voice that could give us wise guidance? Who could hear it over the seductive chatter of three thousand commercial messages a day rattling in our brains? What if a native wisdom could tell us how we should live our lives? The foreign commander of that Freudian garrison has usurped the role of telling us what *shoulds* come from the Almighty.

So long as power flows from the outside in, human life is turned inside out. The systems surrounding us encage the nature within us. Because of the blows to the human vessel, our cup does not run over, it leaketh out, making us grateful to the systems that will sell us more to pour in.

Human beings become the means, as the systems of power pursue their own purposes.

CHAPTER 2

Everything Money Can Buy

Almighty Dollar

My father was an economist, and I respected the clarity and rationality he brought to whatever question came before him. I grew up consciously taking him as a positive model, and I do not now repudiate that identification. I do not regard the famous putdown of his profession as applying to him—that an economist is someone who knows the price of everything and the value of nothing.

There is a long-standing conflict between "mystical" America and "practical" America over the Almighty Dollar. Here in *Fool's Gold*, I am lending my voice to that chorus of criticism of our economic machine and of the ways of thinking that support its heedless and excessive ways. But, as my father's son, I will not join in some parts of that song.

Consider, for example, the recurrent protest about using money as a universal standard for measuring the whole spectrum of values. "You can't put a price on this," people will often say, seeking to protect some important value or other from being consumed in the voracious maw of the market. "No amount of money," someone will say, "can offset the damage . . . " Philip Slater, for example, expounds a critique of the use of money as a universal standard in his book *Wealth Addiction:*

There's an old saying about the folly of trying to compare apples and oranges, but this is precisely what money is for: if apples are 10 cents each and oranges are 20 cents each, then an orange is twice as good as an apple. This doesn't tell us much about the difference between *experiencing* an orange and an apple but it is extremely convenient in the marketplace.

The idea is that comparing different things on one scale—"this sunset is worth three sets of tennis, one episode of 'Starsky and Hutch,' and a banana split," is how Slater lampoons it—is foolish and evil.[1] I don't buy it.

Slater's somewhat sneering remark that a standard of comparison is "convenient in the marketplace" can be restated another way. One could say, "It helps us in making choices." Choices are inescapable. The economists are right that scarcity is a fact of life; that is to say, we can't have—or do—everything. That is to say, we have to choose among alternatives that involve trade-offs. If, after my basketball game, either an apple or an orange would suit me equally, the fact that the orange costs twice as much will help me make my choice wisely.

In the absence of some standard of measure, some way of weighing apples against oranges, our choices are bound to be foolish. The congressman stands in the well of the House Chamber, and makes his argument for spending $26 billion for a military aircraft called the Osprey. "If we save the life," he declares, "of *one* Marine or *one* Special Force, it's worth it to have this technology."[2]

Really? $26 billion to save a single life? One can arrive at such preposterous conclusions if one holds to the idea that "the value of a human life cannot be measured in dollars." But we are constantly—and unavoidably—making choices between dollars and lives. And we forgo spending when considerably less than $26 billion would save a life. Each one of us could spend all our disposable income making our homes and cars safer. (In an example adduced by Robert Frank, we could decrease the likelihood of our dying in an automobile accident by replacing our brakes many times each year. But we don't, presumably "because the costs would so outweigh the expected benefits."[3])

There are a great many policies that we, as a society, could implement that would save lives. (Doubtless many of them we should.) But we don't because of the expense. The $26 billion for the Osprey could, if properly spent, save the lives of thousands of American infants and probably millions of lives in poor countries around the world.

We do not act as if the worth of every human life were beyond measurement in dollars. Partly, this is because we don't care much about some lives, like those of people dying of tropical diseases or malnutrition in Third World countries. It may also be partly because we are foolish in some of our decisions. But in large measure it is because we would be completely disabled from making rational decisions about our personal lives or our society if we treated each life—our own or anyone else's—as an absolute value.

An absolute value—one that cannot be weighed against competing values—would afflict us with paralysis. One absolute value in our universe would devour all our resources up to the point that there was nothing more we could do in its service. In a world, like ours, where different values inevitably compete for our attention, our moral system cannot contain two or more absolute values. If protecting the environment in Africa means more people starving to death, and both the wholeness of the biosphere and the sanctity of every human life represent absolute values, we can have no basis for deciding on one policy over another.

Any time we make decisions—about what to do with our time or any other of our resources—we are *implicitly* putting all the diversity of our values on a single standard so that we can weigh and balance them against each other. Given a single standard, does it matter if we make it *explicit?* Does it change anything if we *quantify* the different weights we assign? Is there any problem with making *dollars* the units for measuring the competing values?

EQUIVALENCE

At a major intersection a couple of miles from my house, in a parking lot, an enterprising little capitalist occasionally sets up shop. From the back of a truck, he unloads an assortment of framed posters for sale at a mere five dollars. Because framing, by itself, generally costs a lot more than that, I regard the deal this curbside merchant offers as an extremely good one.

One day, instead of driving past the dozens of posters on display, I stopped to shop. A friend of mine had told me of his daughter's passion for tigers and had asked me to keep a lookout for any good pictures of the creatures. A fetching picture of a mother and her cub was not hard to find, and I bought it.

I remember less about the picture of the tigers, however, than about the experience of walking along the display. There were pictures to appeal to a diversity of tastes. There was a series of young, nubile women, their breasts straining against a minimum of fabric to reveal themselves. Immediately next to these were several portraits of Jesus, in various poses of beatitude, with streams of light to remind us of his connection with heaven.

What struck me was that, in the context of this display in the marketplace, these pictures were simply different versions of the same thing. Whether appealing to our lust or to our piety, they were all just posters on paper framed in metal: price, five dollars. Savior and sex object are rendered as equivalent commodities. Like apples and oranges in a fruit market.

The exhibition of how our market system reduces everything to commodity status on the same level put me in mind of the economy of the aborigine people on an island near New Guinea. On this island, Rossel, "there are two kinds of money for two kinds of objects: *nko* money for ordinary transactions and *ndap* money (which is handled only by men, and then in a crouching, reverential attitude), which alone can be used to acquire prestige wealth: wives, concubines and pigs."[4]

We can surmise that the men of Rossel would be offended at the thought that special objects might be bought with ordinary money. (Many in our society, I would expect, would find offensive the way the roadside display coupled semipornographic pictures with icons from their religious tradition.) The different systems of money serve the purpose of expressing an important division in their experience between the realms of the ordinary and the extraordinary. "To conceive that wives, concubines and pigs, each with their characteristic delectability, may be worth only so many coconuts and therefore purchasable for enough *nko*, means that we must sweep away the differentness of things, leaving only the pale essence of 'value.'"[5]

Yet, I think it is safe to presume that there is *some* kind of trade-off between ordinary objects and those with special meaning. The men of Rossel, in spending some of their time attending to coconuts and other staples, presumably are forced thereby to limit their pursuit of goods in the other category. Though the two languages of currency bespeak a difference, the languages presumably admit bridging, by some process of translation.

Although it seems offensive to translate the sacred into terms of the mundane, the consequences of failing to do so are also offensive. If human life, for example, is sacred, then it is offensive to adopt social policies that result in needless, avoidable deaths. It is offensive to choose one policy when another that is equally within our means would save more lives. Yet that is what we do when we spend hundreds of thousands of dollars to save a single life with heroic medical procedures such as organ transplants, while dozens of other lives might have been saved if those same resources were devoted, say, to prenatal care or to other forms of preventive medicine.

Obviously we have difficulty treating hypothetical lives, calculated on the basis of probabilities, as though they were as real, as if they were as much our responsibility, as a particular life that is right before our eyes. But the state of Oregon has begun administering a state health service policy that favors making allocations according to what would save the most lives.

Some people, focusing on the particular little boy who dies for want of an exorbitant liver transplant, are outraged by Oregon's approach. How can lives be weighed in terms of dollars and cents? Who are we to play God?

It is inescapable, however, that our actions—and inactions—will govern life and death in our community. Either way, in that respect, we play God. The issue is not the nature of our role, but the power of our imagination to recognize the full ramifications of our acts of commission and omission. The issue is not reducing lives to dollars but using dollars to comprehend the inescapable fact that some lives *are* being weighed against others. The baby who dies because we neglected to attend to its plight is also our responsibility. We played God, but carelessly.

Yet surely not all things ought to be treated alike. Human lives should not be treated as just so many pounds of gravel. A grove of sequoia cannot rightfully be translated into so many radial tires.

Is there an inconsistency here? Can the need I asserted earlier for a universal standard of value be reconciled with an acceptance of the notion that there are realms of the sacred and the profane, and that the two realms ought not be treated wholly the same?

Perhaps the key distinction is between *measurement*, on the one hand, and *exchange*, on the other. To recognize, as Oregon does, that saving lives costs money, and thus that scarce money (resources) must be allocated, is in a fundamental way different from saying that human lives are mere commodities to be bought and sold like any other.

There are some things we don't allow to be sold (though the realm of such things may be in danger of shrinking under the onslaught of market-think): babies, for example; love, for another. Anyone who exchanges sex for money we regard as having been party to an immoral exchange. To treat such things as commodities, most of us feel, would be to betray their sacred nature.

Even sacred things we would not sell we must weigh against other values. Would I be willing to go to war or, perhaps more to the point, to send my son to war despite the possibility that death would be the result? I love my son deeply, and even the thought of his death is too painful for me to face very directly. Yet under some circumstances I would be willing to send him off to war, perhaps even to his death (just as there are some things, including my children, for which I would give my own life). It would have to be in defense of something quite sacred. Like the Rossel islanders, I would never exchange him for anything of merely mundane value.

We do not think it monstrous if a father is willing to risk his son's life in defense of sacred values—the lives of the community, the homeland, liberty, and so on. But what would we think of a father who would let his son be killed merely to make the father rich? Might I endorse my son's going off to fight in a war that could protect the tropical forests of this planet? I might. I imagine that there exists a (huge) sum of money with which every acre of tropical forest could be bought and kept secure. Is there any amount of money—for purely mundane purposes—for which I would risk my son? Not on your life!

TRANSFORMED BY POWER

One of the thrilling moments of the history of our time was the fall of the Berlin Wall in 1989. It is doubtful whether, two centuries hence, the event will still be celebrated as is the storming of the walls of the Bastille in Paris exactly two centuries before.

But in some ways the overcoming of the second wall was the more wonderful event in the annals of the triumph over oppressive power, accomplished as it was without bloodshed and followed, thus far, by no reign of terror.

But it was almost humorous how the triumph of liberal capitalism over communism led immediately to commerce in Berlin Wall relics. A market sprang up immediately dealing in chunks of the fallen wall. I dread to think of the day the Wailing Wall of the Old Temple in Jerusalem might be merchandised piece by piece.

The problem with power systems is that they translate everything into their own terms. Look what happened to Christianity when the swirling forces of the intersocietal struggle for power wrought their will on the new religion. The cross that symbolized the teaching "Love thine enemies" would, after a few centuries, lead armies into battle. By the time of the Crusades, a religious military order, the Hospitalers, fighting for the religion of "Resist not evil" could intone in their rites: "Take this sword; its brightness stands for faith, its point for hope, its guard for charity. Use it well."[6]

The market system, which makes a portrait of the man who said, "Ye cannot serve God and Mammon,"[7] just another roadside attraction, exerts its own kind of power. As *The Parable of the Tribes* helps explain how Constantine could beat the cross into the sword, so does another dynamic explain the fate of Christmas in a market society. Of all the components of the myth of the birth of the son of God, the market seized the part where the wise men give gifts to the child. The giving of gifts swallows all the rest. In Menotti's opera *Amahl and the Night Visitors*, one of the kings acknowledges that the child they seek has no need of their gold. But such is the nature of the market as a power system that it has need of nothing else.

AN IDEA OF LIMITED UTILITY

It was my Frisbee that first led me into the dark chasm, the void of unreality, that underlies much of our conventional economic thought. Back in those days—the late 1960s—it cost less than two dollars to get a Frisbee of the weight I prefer. (Not one of those massive "Championship" models that fly with all the lyricism of a football, but one that, at over one hundred grams, has enough heft to maintain its poise in the face of a puff of wind but is still light enough to dance as it flies.) This tiny expenditure could give me hundreds of hours of joyful activity. (Actually, I also needed a friend to throw it with and a field on which to conduct our three-dimensional ballet. But neither of these is available in the market-place.)

So little money, so much pleasure. The ratio between the two was of a different order of magnitude with the Frisbee than with any of the other things I bought with my dollars. This got me thinking about the economic concept of "utility."

Economic Man is engaged in a game in which the goal is the maximization of "utility." "As a customer," writes Paul Samuelson, "you will buy a good because you feel it gives you satisfaction, or 'utility.'"[8] (Utility is a concept that provides a single universal measure encompassing all the positive feelings we derive from any of the choices we make.) "'Utility' is simply a subjective measure of the usefulness, or want satisfaction, that results from consumption."[9]

To the convenience of collapsing all our goods onto a single scale is added another great convenience: the assumption that the expenditure of money can afford a rough gauge of the utility attained. Summarizing the views of Jeremy Bentham, the eighteenth- and nineteenth-century founder of the utilitarian philosophy, C. B. MacPherson writes: "He held that wealth—the possession of material goods—was so essential to the attainment of all other pleasures that it could be taken as the measure of pleasure or utility as such."[10] (I recall a line from *Mad* magazine in the 1950s, "There are things in life more important than money, but they won't go out with you if you haven't got any.") In Bentham's own words, "Each portion of wealth has a corresponding portion of happiness."[11]

Bentham challenged those who are not satisfied with the adequacy of "money [as] the instrument of measuring the quantity of pain and pleasure" to "find out some other that shall be more accurate, or bid adieu to politics and morals."[12] I'll be damned if I'll bid adieu to politics and morals, but I have no superior instrument to propose. But I'd prefer to look for the coin over where I dropped it, however dark the spot, rather than under the lamppost just because the light is better.

Americans don't much like playing games that have no way of keeping score, however. And in our positivist age, what is measurable is readily presumed real, and whatever cannot be measured is as readily treated as though it did not exist. Thus the economics I was taught as an undergraduate at Harvard pretty well absorbed, without the light of any explicit philosophic discussion, the Benthamite assumptions. And our political system seems to operate on the similar foundational premise that the growth of GNP equates to a corresponding increase in our national welfare.

The Frisbee led me to draw upon a couple of venerable instruments, not always venerated in our scientific age, to reexamine these assumptions. Those instruments were common sense and the capacity to reason.

A DOLLAR SPENT

"A penny saved is a penny earned," as Poor Richard says. What the economists say—giving voice to the logic of the market system—is, "A dollar spent is a dollar enjoyed."

But what about the dollar (plus) I spent on my Frisbee? That dollar was enjoyed more than the five dollars I spent, having a rather pleasant time, eating at the King Tsin Chinese restaurant on Solano Avenue.

According to economic theory, one will keep spending on good number one as long as the "marginal utility" of that good—the utility of the last unit consumed—exceeds the (expected) utility of a unit of an alternative good number two. So, if Frisbees give me so much pleasure, why did I spend on the Chinese meal rather than buy two or three more Frisbees with the same money?

The reason was simple. Having one Frisbee was enormously better for me than having no Frisbee. But having two (or more) Frisbees represented no meaningful improvement over having one. One is essential, but one is enough. Economists have a name for that also. It is "diminishing marginal utility," meaning that as one consumes more and more of something, one tends to derive less and less utility from it. The old jingle from the cigarette ad— "Smoking more now and enjoying it less?"—captures the idea nicely.

But though economists are prepared to talk about the diminishing marginal utility of consuming a particular good, mainstream economics is not, as other critics have noted, ready to confront the possibility of the diminishing marginal utility of consumption per se. What if a person would be happy with a jug of bread, a loaf of wine, and some Thou? No need for a vast economic apparatus to keep such people happy. A little wealth is needed, but not much. The utility of that first little bit is great, whereas that of a great deal more wealth might well be little. If people are by nature like that, their interests and those of a market economy predicated on growth without limit are far from the same.

At this point, it is important to recognize that the essential problem here is not in the domain of the intellect but in the domain of power. Bad theory is not the heart of the problem, for the bad theory should be understood as propaganda for a powerful economic system that can elevate and institutionalize the ideas that serve it.

Economic theory has given us Economic Man. Far from being satisfied with bread, wine, and Thou—or with a Frisbee and a different, more athletic Thou—Economic Man is beset by infinite wants. With infinity, one is never closer to the end no matter how far one counts. Therefore, the intensity of Economic Man's wanting never slackens. Undiminished intensity of wanting means no diminishing marginal utility in his spending. Each dollar spent on the movie star's fourth Rolls Royce is presumed to enhance his welfare as much as the earlier dollar spent on bread and wine. (Conventional economic theory also disallows our making "interpersonal comparisons of utility," on the basis of which we might claim that the dollar would be better spent getting necessities for a poor person than getting the fourth Rolls Royce for a rich one.)

Such an implausible perspective helps rationalize and justify great inequalities of wealth, and thus is useful in the service of the wealthy class. But even more, it helps to buttress the system that produces that wealth, and that itself embodies undiminished marginal voraciousness.

I RESENT THAT

Ludwig von Mises thinks he has my number. Von Mises is one of the foremost twentieth-century philosophers of the market ideology, and he would classify me as a member of a rather despicable genus: those intellectuals who obscure, beneath the cloak of a philosophy critical of capitalism, "The Resentment of Frustrated Ambition."

Members of this genus resent capitalism, von Mises explains in *The Anti-Capitalist Mentality*, because of the system's implacable fairness in rewarding people according to the value of their contribution to their fellow human beings. In the market system, those who satisfy the wants of a smaller number of people will be rewarded with less wealth than those who satisfy the wants of more people. If you want to delve into "writing poetry or philosophy," von Mises grants, "you are free to do so. Then, of course, you will not make as much money as those who serve the majority."[13]

If I am a writer, therefore—one who brings to the market the craft of the "wordsmith"—I am at liberty to apply my skills to works like these rather than to writing jingles for Coca-Cola. But I have no one to blame but myself if I must perennially struggle to put food on the table while someone who took the road I eschewed can easily put a big spread on a finer table. Coke gives pleasure all over the world to untold multitudes (fifty million times a day—at home, at work, or on the way—Coke gives the pause that refreshes), while my works over an entire lifetime reach only a comparative handful.

The problem, says von Mises, is that some people cannot abide acknowledging that the system "treats everybody according to his contribution to the well-being of his fellow men." The more sophisticated of those who are seeking a scapegoat, he argues, "sublimate their hatred into a philosophy, the philosophy of anti-capitalism, in order to render inaudible the inner voice that tells them that their failure is entirely their own fault."[14]

Does the shoe fit? First, do I hate the market? No, I don't hate it. It think it is, in many ways, quite marvelous. If we lived in a nonmarket society, it seems quite likely we would be beset by other problems—possibly more dire than ours—to which market mechanisms might provide part of the solution. But living, as we do, in a society where the forces of the market have run rampant, inadequately checked by the collective decisions we arrive at through our political system, our challenge is less to sing the market's praises than to correct its faults. Because I regard the accumulation, over time, of the uncorrected market's detrimental effects as most pernicious, I might as well plead to this part of von Mises's indictment.

Next, do I resent the market's treatment of me, its message—expressed in scant dollars—that my contribution is of little worth? Frankly, there *is* something about my economic position in the world I resent. I do resent, at times, how difficult is my struggle to survive while doing the work I think I'm supposed to do. My best friend from high school makes twice as much money in a year as I can get from the market in a decade. He gives legal counsel and representation, in a particular branch of the law, to corporations. I'm sure he is very good. Back in the days when we were both applying our minds to the same tasks, his work was not superior to mine. If we postulate that we are each, in our own way, producing work of comparable inherent *quality*, the question arises why we are rewarded so unequally. Von Mises would say that our respective efforts command such different prices because our products are of correspondingly different *value*, with value understood as meaning "contribution to the well-being of our fellow men."

The "message" I get from the market about how much I'm contributing to my fellow human beings does not much bother me, as I am not plagued by an inner voice speaking to me about my "failure." And I don't resent my not being as rich as my friend. I really don't need such wealth. Indeed, I don't even resent the relative simplicity of our lives: living high on the hog isn't within our means, but in fact our lifestyle (for the most part) suits us fine. We genuinely enjoy what we can make with such foods as cabbage and potatoes and onions and rice and millet. (I joked recently that after generations of my ancestors' living as peasants I have, after a brief blip into middle-class life with my parents, reverted to form. Of course, my ancestors didn't have a word processor on which to write about their cabbage soup.)

More than our privation, I do resent our chronic insecurity, and accordingly I do have some *personal* resentment toward the system that does not take better care of us.

But what I really resent is von Mises's facile dismissal of criticism of the market's reward system, which is to say, of the market's system of values. It would comfort me profoundly to believe that I lived in a world where people are rewarded according to the true value of their contribution to human well-being. That would be good news regardless of where I fit into such a world. Conversely, whether I were rich or poor, the understanding that my world is badly skewed in its system of values would be painful. Regrettably, the facile belief of the market ideologue does not stand up in the light of the Frisbee phenomenon.

SELLING WELL-BEING

Which do you suppose is the bigger financial powerhouse, Wham-O, Inc., the manufacturer of the Frisbee, or Philip Morris, purveyors of cigarettes? Which entrepreneur will the market reward better? The one who sells a device that will give many hours of joy over a few years before, for a pittance, it needs to be replaced? Or the one who sells an addictive substance that must literally be "consumed" to be used, and that itself consumes the lives of its devotees? The lover of the cigarette, of course, is always going back to the store for more, casting his or her "votes," as von Mises calls consumer dollars, for those great benefactors of humanity, the tobacco moguls. When I looked into the stock of Wham-O, a few years back, it was teetering on the edge of oblivion.

Imagine a person who discovers something that will contribute enormously to human well-being. Will he or she necessarily be rewarded with riches?

One somewhat fanciful example would be the discovery of some magical incantation that can bring a lifetime of happiness.

One could imagine this formula traveling around the world by word of mouth and greatly improving the human lot without, however, enriching its discoverer. Indeed, this example bears some relationship to the discovery of religious truth, and historical examples such as Buddha or Jesus or the Baal Shem Tov do not suggest that wealth is the reward for contributions of this nature.

A more concrete and, in modern terms, practical case in point is the recent discovery that the thousands of babies who die every day in the world of dehydration from diarrhea could be saved easily by the administration of a simple formula of water, sugar, and salt. Even separately packaged envelopes of this formula—just add water, and stir—for those incapable of measuring and mixing can be provided for just pennies. The materials are simple and readily at hand. No patents are involved.

The discoverer of this remarkably effective remedy may eventually save as many lives as the purveyors of tobacco help to kill, but there is nothing in the structure of the transactions of this life-saving work that will enrich anyone. The discovery a couple of centuries ago that citrus fruit eaten during long ocean voyages could prevent scurvy is another illustration of this.

But the real issue does not concern the enrichment of such benefactors of humankind. The evidence does not suggest that the likes of Buddha or Albert Schweitzer care whether they get rich in proportion to the value of their contribution. More fundamental is the bigger question of the dollar as the language of value.

Certainly, dollars are the language of the market. The system speaks exclusively in these terms, so the market's hegemony as an arbiter of our lives is aided by those beliefs that equate the needs of the system with the needs of humankind. Von Mises's claim about the market's reward of human benefaction is one such belief. Bentham's assertion that money expended is a reasonable measure of happiness is another. In each case, the market's terms of discourse are taken as the given, and the values of human well-being are translated into the system's matrix. Nothing is lost in the translation, say the system's defenders.

What is at stake is a good deal more than esoteric beliefs in the realm of philosophy, that domain whose practitioners "satisfy the wants" of a rather tiny minority of humankind (unlike those who compose the jingles for Coke). What is at stake is the whole issue of how people live. How do people seek satisfaction, and where is happiness truly to be found?

BUYING HAPPINESS

Bashing the philistines has long been a kind of intellectual fashion. Bourgeois life—with its perpetual money chase, with its pursuit of two cars in every garage—has been disparaged almost as long as there has been a bourgeoisie. Materialistic values—the belief that happiness is to be achieved through *things* and their accumulation—are challenged, not surprisingly, by many whose currency in trade consists of words and *ideas*.

But the market's world of "everything money can buy" cannot be reduced to such simplistic materialism. The full spectrum of what money can buy is not so purely "material," and its pursuit cannot be so easily dismissed as shallow, unenlightened, and misguided.

As I sit writing this, my fourteen-year-old son, Aaron, is in the next room in the hands of a master body-worker to whom I have brought him. This work will—or so I believe—help my boy release some of the childhood traumas still "stored" in his body (such as the one from the time he fell on the stairs and broke his jaw), and help him grow into a stronger and more balanced posture in the world, and integrate more fully his physical and emotional being. I feel I've benefited from this course of work on my own body, and I can provide it for my child if I can pay the (not insignificant) fee.

Also out there in the marketplace of our "materialistic" society—along with all the Bart Simpson sweatshirts, decorator lamps, and sports cars—are dance lessons and Bibles, psychotherapy and visits to one's family in another part of the country. "Everything money can buy" includes a great deal that is nonmaterial in nature. Many of those dimensions of life that are often contrasted with materialism—the refined, the spiritual, the artistic, the intellectual, the human—are often accessed or facilitated or strengthened through goods or services that are sold in the marketplace. It is a caricature of the values represented by the market, therefore, to reduce them to Jim and Tammy Bakker's gold-handled bathroom fixtures.

But still, there is a problem. Though the market gives access to goods of highly diverse kinds, the market nonetheless presents an extremely skewed image of the good. Not everything of value can be bought and sold. Not everything that can be bought and sold is equally readily marketed. And it is the inherent thrust of the market to magnify the importance of what can readily be marketed over what cannot. Over the course of time, therefore, in the grip of market forces the shape of human life comes to be distorted.

We are engaged, presumably, in the pursuit of happiness. The market places before us what it represents as the means to attain it. But, as Michael Schudson writes in his book *Advertising, the Uneasy Persuasion*, the "marketers do not actually seek to discover what consumers 'want' but what consumers want *from among commercially viable choices.*"[15] Just look at the ads to which we are exposed. The real energy of the ads is not in the products themselves but comes from elsewhere. The watch is nice, but the excitement of these young women getting ready for a night on the town is what really gives the Citizen Watch ads their verve and appeal. When I was a boy, the Marlboro ads were a part of my arcana of mythology. The assured manliness of the Marlboro man

on the horse tapped into my image of the heroic, and the closeness of the whole scene to the elemental forces of nature touched
a part of me that was groping for the sacred. I recall how, during
the long Minnesota winters of my adolescence, while the earth lay
dead and hard and devoid of fragrance beneath our feet, the verdant pictures in the Salem cigarette ads in magazines were objects of deep and aching yearning.

What do we really want? To be loved? To be part of a friendly
community? To be attractive? These cannot be bought. But these
fundamental values can be used to sell the commodities the market has to offer. Are you nostalgic for an America where life was
down-to-earth and family values were strong? Drink Country-
Time Lemonade. Do you want to partake of the sexual vibrancy of
youth? Drink Coca-Cola. It's the real thing.

Day after day, the market teaches us that the way to achieve
values that money cannot buy is to purchase what the system *can*
sell. We are, by nature, inclined to the pursuit of happiness. But
then, by the most powerful forces in the world around us, we are
turned to the maximization of material wealth.

Feedback Loops

If dollars don't change hands, the event is invisible to the market
and thus devoid of significance or even reality. Sure, a Bible can be
purchased in the market. But a Bible is rather like a Frisbee. I've
known people for whom the Bible is a permanent companion, and
one can see on the pages of the book various evidences of reading and rereading—passages highlighted with different colors of
ink, smudges and fingerprints, a waviness to the pages. One Bible,
or maybe a couple, lasts them for years, perhaps a lifetime. Who
needs more? Even if everyone in the country were a devout fun-
damentalist, the traffic in the Bible would never be terribly important commercially.

Diet books are a major industry in publishing. It is precisely because these diets don't, for the most part, really work that so many

resources are channeled into this commerce. The market specializes not in satisfaction, not in well-being, but in desire. Each diet that fails perpetuates the desire for help. That makes dieting books *important* to the book industry.

To the market, the sale of a Bible that is lovingly used every day is no more important an event than the purchase of an equally priced book that is quickly discarded, or that sits on the shelf forever unopened. The profound transaction that takes place between the believer and the Bible involves no exchange of money, so it is the same as if it never happened.

Others have remarked upon the transformation of *holidays* in the course of the past century, as the market has extended its dominion over our lives. Originally, they were "holy days," with meanings that were commemorated in community ritual and celebration. Already by the time the Lynds wrote *Middletown* (about Muncie, Indiana, in the 1930s), the lineaments of the change were apparent: holidays had been reduced to occasions when, instead of going off to work, people engaged in private enjoyments and consumption. Come to our giant Labor Day sale! Spend Memorial Day at our resort. The market is about individual social atoms coming together for mutually beneficial exchange. So, it favors not the communal gathering of citizens in the town square, with the town band and civic leaders holding forth, but the scattering of consumers to their separate pursuits.

From one perspective, advertising (like money) is a neutral institution. Like a blank sheet of paper, it is an open space that can be filled with messages for good or ill. One can advertise against littering as well as for Big Gulps in styrofoam cups. The market for TV ad-time is open to anyone who can pay. But this perspective disregards the facts of power issuing from the structure of the economic system.

Our communal need for a clean environment just cannot translate as readily into the capability to advertise as can the private needs expressed in terms of buyer's satisfactions and seller's profits. Those who advertise to persuade us to part with our two-year-old car for a new Buick are directly empowered by their success to buy more air-time to persuade more people to do likewise. But even if those who advertise to exhort us not to litter succeed wonderfully, the success of these public-spirited advertisers does not enrich them. The structure of the system thus creates a fundamental difference between the power of private and public needs.

With the selling of Buicks, there is a feedback loop that perpetuates success, as every successful act of persuasion puts more resources into the hands of the persuaders. It is very different with the effort to clean the environment: because the anti-littering campaign operates at variance to the system's lines of force, the advertising campaign must continually reconstitute itself. No matter how persuasive the advertising campaign, putting new ads on the air requires a separate campaign of passing the hat. The inevitable consequence of this fundamental difference is that over time one kind of good grows more powerful in its position in human and social life while the other becomes increasingly residual.

What is fed by the flow of dollars grows fat. What lies outside the network of commercial transaction wastes away.

Recall the lines, quoted earlier, "If you just like talking to people . . . if you enjoy living simply, *what good are you economically?*" The systematic distortion in the market's sense of what is "good" continually threatens to undermine the truly sacred transactions of our lives. Recall my earlier remark about my infant son and his mother: "His ancestors have been sucking on her ancestors for 50 million years." But from the perspective of the market, of what use is this transaction? Its value is invisible. It is worse than nothing—it's a missed opportunity. Here, where something of real value—that is, for which money is paid—could be exchanged, this mammal is taking care of it all herself. The system thus uses its power to displace that which has, in its terms, no value, with that whose value computes in its system.

"Breast-feeding was denigrated," in ads directed at Third World women, "as dated, inferior, unchic." "'Give your baby the benefit of modern research,' urged a Pakistani ad. Pictures in advertisements showed beautiful babies in the arms of upper class women," writes Eric Clark in *The Want Makers*. "Formulas were presented as scientific and upmarket."[16]

The scandal that arose in the 1980s revealed how disastrous were the consequences of such efforts to change the structure of the mother-infant transaction. In many poor countries, babies were deprived, as their mother's milk dried up, of a reliable source of nutrition, and of vital immunities, and were compelled to depend instead on infant formula, whose supply depended on its parents' finances, and which needed to be mixed with water that itself often carried disease. Many thousands of babies died, while those who were making this great and measurable contribution to the well-being of their fellow human beings were rewarded with greater profits.

LOSING OURSELVES

The relationship between the system's values and our own human values is highly complex. There are elements in our own cultural tradition in the West, and in America in particular, that make us especially liable to the appeal of the market's "materialistic" bias.[17] And our human values are continually straining to recover the truly nourishing goods that the market tends to take away. But there remains an important dimension in which the market, by virtue of its power, restructures our language and our understanding, our very relationship to our being.

Even when we undertake to redress the market's excesses and distortions, the market's prejudice in favor of what money can buy infiltrates our discourse. Should Californians impose strict environmental regulations to protect the air they breathe and the food they eat (the famous Big Green initiative of 1990)? The arguments for the proposition are principally concerned with human health. The arguments are often couched in terms of the market: pollution costs us x dollars in days of work lost plus y dollars in health care costs. As if the value of preventing illness were to be measured by the cost of its treatment. As if the sacred realm of human experience had vanished. As if the stuff on the outside of us—the external framework of measuring values in terms of accumulated wealth—were the ultimate point of reference.

It is the external transaction, not the internal experiential and spiritual condition, that is treated as real in the system. Thus we measure our "standard of living" in terms of an external measure, GNP, with hardly a glance at the Benthamite assumption about how the external financial measure translates into human well-being.

A system for which the purchase of two books that sit unread is twice as good as the purchase of one book lovingly studied for years will naturally wish to teach us that *being* is unimportant, that *having* is all. Losing ourselves, we represent the values we have lost using the language our most powerful system promotes.

In a study of advertising in America in recent decades, Belk and Pollay found an overall trend of change in the nature of advertising's appeal. Over time, the ads placed less emphasis on values of *instrumental materialism* (Buy this so you can *do* that!) and more and more emphasis on values of *terminal materialism* (Buy this so you can *have* it!)

The market indeed is open to many values, but it is the accumulation of things that it most readily provides. Over time, consequently, it is more likely a closet of clothes rather than a course of psychological or spiritual healing that we will be taught to invest our funds in. Experience—the flow of life—coagulates into dead stuff.

We are led outside of ourselves, alienated from the realm of genuine experience in which we inescapably live into a dead museum of things that stand as concrete symbols of those inner states we forget how to embody ourselves.

INDIAN GIVER

When I was a kid there was an expression you don't hear much any more: Indian giver. It meant someone who gave a gift and then expected to get it back. It was a pejorative term, and I suppose the expression has fallen into disfavor because people think it is an ethnic slur against the Native American. But from reading Lewis Hyde's book, *The Gift*, I have come to understand that it is not the name itself—Indian giver—that shows our ethnocentrism. It is our thinking that there is something wrong with being an Indian giver.

The root of the matter is that the Indians had a different sense of ownership. And different does not necessarily mean worse—especially in this case. Among the Indians, a treasured object would be the "Gift"—something that would move among the tribe's members, never *belonging* to anyone. So an Indian might pass the Gift to an Englishman who, with his sense of property, would think, "Great! We can keep this in the British Museum." The Englishman is interested in accumulation, and so he is annoyed when an Indian, seeing the Gift in the white man's house, keeps it moving by taking it with him.

In the Indian giver and his counterpart—what Hyde calls the White Man Keeper—we see two ways of relating to the goods of life: as things that flow on through, or as things that are stored and possessed.

We all know how the contest between these two approaches to life turned out. Those who were concerned with acquisition acquired the homelands of those who were not. The continent is now possessed by those with a penchant for possession.

But to say that the way of possession has triumphed is not to say that *we* are the winners. Not if we ourselves are possessed by the spirit of possession. We live in the richest country in the history of the world, but it seems we're always hungry for more—as if our things were themselves so much stored-up happiness. As if money, embodying all the gratification we have delayed, or been incapacitated from experiencing, were a promissory note that promised a future of fulfillment. Like magic.

I remember seeing on television a few years back a feature on some Hollywood mogul with 250 telephones lining his Beverly Hills estate, as if by magic his owning those phones assured that he would forever be connected with the world. And then there's Imelda Marcos's amazing collection of three thousand pairs of shoes—as if she thought that, by magic, she herself would last until all those shoes were worn out.

But life is not like that. As the saying goes, "You can't take it with you." Anyone who insists on fighting that fact of life is sure to end up a loser.

Life is a gift that is not ours to keep. All we can do is pass that gift along in our tribe, which alone endures.

The Lord giveth and the Lord taketh away. There's the archetypal Indian giver.

TERMINAL MATERIALISM

I see nothing wrong with cherishing material objects. It is a question of whether the investment of libidinal energy is in the service of life or death.

What possessions are most valued by people? What objects would people choose to rescue from their burning home? In their study of *The Meaning of Things*, Csikszentmihalyi and Rochberg-Halton report that those possessions people treasure most are those that stand as emblems of their most important human connections: this bowl, because it has been in my family for generations; this quilt, because my mother made it; this pin, because it was a gift from my best friend; these photo albums. "We found that things are cherished not because of the material comfort they provide but for the information they convey about the owner and his or her ties to others."[18]

We are creatures who, by nature, live by our interconnectedness with a larger human whole. But we are compelled to live within a system premised on our disposition to function as social atoms. Gradually, the accumulation of things can displace the connections among people.

The materialism that our production-maximizing system works to foster is terminal in more ways than one.

It is life's way for the creatures that are the components of the biosphere continually to cycle and recycle the goods on which life depends. The gift keeps moving. Treasure is not stored forever, except in the flowing system as a whole.

"Diamonds are forever," the ad says. But it is really the love the merchants want you to express with the stones that perpetuates the flow of the human community. Say it with diamonds, the sellers say, for the market has a limited language.

It is not economists who know the price of everything and the value of nothing so much as it is the market system itself. The very founder of the market ideology, Adam Smith, was aware of a distinction to which the market economy is blind, the distinction between *use value* and *exchange value:* "Nothing is more useful than water; but it will purchase scarce anything; scarce anything can be had in exchange for it. A diamond, on the contrary, has scarce any value in use: but a very great quantity of other goods may frequently be had in exchange for it."[19]

There is nothing wrong, I have argued, with putting a dollar value on all the competing values one must weigh. The problem arises from the inevitable tendency to measure those dollar values in terms of market prices. To the market, the diamond is a treasure, while the water that sustains life is practically worthless. Following this information about value, treasure-hunters in the jungles of South America are pouring deadly mercury into living rivers and streams in their efforts to extract inert metals from the body of the earth.

Gratified—that is part of what I feel when friends of mine, to whom I am always glad to give tactical and strategic counsel, tell me, "Boy! You'da made a helluva lawyer. You'da made a fortune." Sometimes, I hear a little bit of "You should'a been a lawyer," and that gratifies me less. I hear embedded in that implied chastisement a variant on that old line, "If you're so smart, why ain't you rich?" But that may just be my thin skin. If I am picking up the implication that perhaps I should have done otherwise with my life, it probably reflects my friend's sense that a talent may have been wasted. I've sometimes felt that way myself when I've come across someone with a fine singing voice who has never performed in public.

What I sometimes say is that whatever talents I may have for being an attorney are already fully utilized. I'm already working as an advocate, presenting cases, arguing points, working to sway those who stand in judgment. It is the nature of the interests I represent (my species, and my planet) that obscures the similarity of the work. And it is the lack of correspondence between the structure of my relationship between me and my "clients" and the structure of market transactions that accounts for my failure in financial terms. If you represent one part of the system contending against another part, the fees are good. If you wish to work as advocate of the whole, there is no one to hire you and no one to pay you.

We are, of course, separate beings assembled together into a variety of organizations, and all these discrete entities possess legitimate interests that often conflict. It is likewise legitimate for us to work in pursuit of those interests. But life is also, and most fundamentally, about interconnectedness. That I have no one to bill for my "legal fees" is but an extremely trivial clue about a rather profound distortion in the functioning of our atomistic economic system. (It is like the way the sale of Buicks is a successful Buick ad's way of creating more Buick ads, while a successful ad against littering is fortified by no such feedback loops.)

When the connections are broken, death conquers. Each moment, our lives depend on our ongoing exchange with the atmosphere around us, no less vital for being invisible. Every day, the workings of the global market economy are straining further the precious film of life that surrounds our planet, poisoning the air and the water and the earth. Yet we mark the progress of our "development," the growth of our "wealth." As the sense of citizenship and the level of our public morality decline, we boast as social atoms about our rising "standard of living."

The price of everything and the value of nothing.

In our idiom, to say of someone "He has the Midas touch" is a term of praise. It would only be said of a "successful man," one of whom it can be said that "everything he touches turns to gold." But Midas's touch, granted at his wish, proved to be a curse. At his touch, his daughter—through whom his blood would flow into the next generation—became a lifeless golden statue. The very food King Midas needed for his sustenance turned to metal in his mouth before it could nourish him. It is interesting that our language suggests we remain in that state of ignorance that led Midas to make his fatal wish.

But we also know the danger. There is a recurrent image in the movies. The man is in the desert with bags of gold but no water. He dies a wealthy man. He is a recurrent image because we recognize in him a warning to us, a warning of the potentially terminal nature of our materialism.

TWO

Moral Fabric

CHAPTER 3

Limited Liability:
The Ethos of the Contract Society

STATE OF NATURE

"In the beginning . . . " Some important stories begin that way. At a crucial point in the development of Anglo-Saxon thought, the story continues, "Human beings led solitary lives." What was the importance, to each human being, of other people? In the version of human origins put forward by Thomas Hobbes, the role of other people was as natural enemies. Any man could kill any other man, and so in this state of nature people lived in terror of one another. To escape this war of all against all, people came together, in this Hobbesian story, and set a tyrant above them to hold them all in awe.

The line of thought leading to the liberal society of America started from similar premises about the state of nature, but it built from these premises to a different solution. Creating an absolute ruler to escape from the perils of one's neighbors, according to John Locke, would be like taking care "to avoid what mischiefs may be done them by polecats or foxes" while thinking it safety "to be devoured by lions."[1] Instead, thought Locke, people would form a social contract of a more benign sort. They would institute a social order that would end the anarchy of the state of nature—preventing people from preying on each other like foxes and polecats—but otherwise preserve the natural liberty of the human being. Thus we in America today find intact our rights as proprietors of our lives and property, and we enjoy the liberty to pursue happiness as we see fit.

This creation story has without doubt been valuable in important ways. By positing the solitary self as the natural unit of existence, it has sanctified the realm of individual liberty and made human fulfillment the fundamental end of social arrangements. In view of all the collectivist nightmares and other tyrannies in history—the swollen states and lean societies, the splendid palaces and yoked multitudes—the enthronement of the solitary, sovereign individual self seems a boon indeed.

Our creation myth—depicting solitary individuals coming together to form a social contract—helped us to avoid the hell of a totalitarian state. But where it has led us does not seem to be an earthly paradise. The flowering of the human self in this supposedly benign environment appears rather stunted. We are free from constraint, but free to do what? "When the going gets tough, the tough go shopping." We eat the fruit of the tree of this "possessive individualism" and find that we do not become as gods, savoring our ambrosia, but somewhat bloated on our sugary diet yet persistently plagued by unsated hungers. Pursuing happiness but strangely discontented. And the social costs to this individual pursuit of satisfaction, though not as grisly in their manifestations as a gulag, do mount up. Our social order threatens to break up along the fault lines of competing appetites and narcissisms.

Perhaps there is need of a new creation myth.

THE SELFISH AND THE UNSELFISH

I recall the time when I first confronted in a philosophic way the question of selfishness. As a kid growing up, I heard often enough that being selfish is bad. I was supposed to share my toys and not insist on more than my fair portion of a candy bar. I was supposed to help out with the jobs that needed doing around the house, many of which I found to be anything but fun. But, I was told, "You can't just go through life doing only those things you *want* to do."

Internalizing what sometimes seemed at least my share of conscience, I came to take some pleasure in doing unselfish and helpful things. I did my chores with gusto, enjoying making the bathroom fixtures gleam and buffed floors glow. Occasionally I would write letters to lonely relatives. It got so that I really *wanted* to do such things.

At some point in my adolescence, this led me to confront a seeming paradox. In life, I was told, I would have to do things I didn't want to do. But it seemed to me inescapable that anything I chose to do I must, in some fundamental sense, have decided I wanted to do. If it gave me pleasure to keep the whole cake for myself, that was presumably my selfishness. But what if it gave me pleasure to make a cake for other people to enjoy? Could that be called unselfish if I did it knowing it would make me happy?

All behavior, it seemed to me, was the result of motivation, and all motivation was derived from the sets of things the actor does and does not want. This would seem to be just as true of the philanthropist giving what is his to someone to whom he does not owe it as of the thief who takes what is not his because he wants it. Any course of action entails anticipated costs and benefits to the actor. People weigh the alternatives and choose the one they think feels best to them. Givers of charity—given their own psychological calculus, including guilt, on the one hand, and moral satisfaction, on the other—expect to feel better if they give the money to some worthy cause or needy person than if they keep it.

Nowhere in my own life have I been more giving, less "selfish," than as a father to my three children. And I feel a lot better than if I had put "my needs" first. So, obviously and paradoxically, I must have been taking care of my needs quite well. (Perhaps my need to be a good father and/or my need to see my children well taken care of.)

So, what is unselfishness? My adolescent reflections led me to conclude that, in some fundamental way, all voluntary human behavior is necessarily selfish.

BEYOND TAUTOLOGY

I have since come to understand that there is a danger in collapsing distinctions. Much of value can get lost in the rubble.

One example I discovered is the distinction between the "natural" and the "unnatural." Everything is natural, many people have told me. Are not human beings products of nature, thus is not whatever comes from us natural? Of course, it all depends on definitions. Words can mean what we say they mean. *Natural* can be defined so that everything in the universe is natural and nothing "unnatural" could ever exist. (The word *unnatural* should then be dropped from our vocabulary.) Yet there are distinctions to be made between a dam made by a beaver and the Hoover Dam, between an anthill and New York City. The difference concerns the relationship between biological evolution, along with the genetic blueprints it crafts, and the structures a creature develops. The anthill has a relationship with the biologically evolved nature of the ant that New York City does not have with the genetic endowment of its inhabitants. This difference corresponds to disparate effects as well. The dams of beavers, for example, do not undermine the health of their ecosystem, whereas those of human beings often do. The ants are in harmony with the demands of living in an anthill in a way that the residents of New York City are not at home in their environment.[2]

So also with selfishness and unselfishness. There may be, as I once concluded, a sense in which all our behavior is selfish. But surely it is useful to make some distinctions between the behavior of people who care about other people and those who do not. Any collapse of distinctions that leaves us unable to differentiate between the thief and the philanthropist has done us no service. It is particularly important that we who live in a liberal market society maintain a clear view of these distinctions. Every society must cope with the problem of selfishness. But the market system is singular in being premised on the assumption and acceptance of selfishness in human behavior.

In the predominant ideology of our system, it is called "self-interest." "The first principle of economics," writes Francis Edgeworth, "is that every agent is activated only by self-interest."[3] If this notion functions as a cornerstone of our world, it is important that we understand it. Is this "first principle" a substantive assertion about human nature—implying something like "People do not really care about each other, but only about themselves"? Or is it a tautology, saying nothing about people but only defining its central term—meaning something like "Whatever it is that motivates a person's action is what we mean by self-interest"?

As a statement about human nature, it is a rather powerful assertion, and a frightening one too—frightening either in what it says about what we are or in how economic thought has distorted what we are. As a tautology, the statement seems rather strange, and interesting only in raising the question of what is accomplished by defining things so.

One prominent ideological defender of the market system, Milton Friedman, attempts to cleanse the system of the taint of selfishness—without, however, changing the ideology's foundation on self-interest—by using the tautological interpretation. It is "a great mistake," Friedman declares, to interpret the market's "economic man" as a selfish calculator. "Self-interest is not myopic selfishness," Friedman writes. "It is whatever it is that interests the participants, whatever they value, whatever goals they pursue.

The scientist seeking to advance the frontiers of his discipline, the missionary seeking to convert infidels to the true faith, the philanthropist seeking to bring comfort to the needy—all are pursuing their interests, as they see them, as they judge them by their own values."[4]

Is this, indeed, the kind of "self-interest" the market has worked to enshrine as the fount of human motivations? Is the market really so neutral about the moral nature of society that it simply allows people to work to advance their own values, whatever they may happen to be? I think not.

The market ideology has not always dealt in this tautological evisceration of the concept of self-interest. At its inception, the market ideology did not flinch from the substantive assertions about human nature, and human society, embodied in the idea that the interactions among people are ruled by the pursuit of self-interest.

In a famous passage in *The Wealth of Nations*, Adam Smith writes: "It is not from the benevolence of the butcher, the brewer, or the baker, that we expect our dinner, but from their regard to their own interest. We address ourselves, not to their humanity, but to their self-love, and never talk to them of our own necessities but of their advantages."[5] There is no ambiguity here. The self-interest of the butcher, to which we are to appeal, is not just another form of what leads to the philanthropist's "seeking to bring comfort to the needy." What the philanthropist manifests is the "benevolence" to which "their own interest" is contrasted.

The premise of the market is that our economic life is to be driven not by a universal spectrum of our values but by a particular segment of value having to do with our regard for ourselves. The market society endorses the notion that the business of each of us is to look after our own interests and to leave others to look after theirs.

A VIRTUE OF NECESSITY, OR A NECESSITY FOR VICE

It is better to go with the grain of nature than against it. You get further traveling with the current than fighting your way upstream. So it is, some of the market's advocates say, that the market's realistic appraisal of the place of selfishness in human nature has contributed to the power and the virtue of liberal society.

No wonder the market system has proved so dynamic, choosing for its principal fuel the self-love of the individual. This fuel is a natural resource in inexhaustible supply. No wonder we have preserved our liberty, basing our political institutions on that same premise—that people cannot be trusted to use their power for any ends but their own. The worst nightmares of our times have been in those political systems that have indulged the fantasy that a select handful would keep reliable watch over the needs of the people. Based on realism, which is to say a healthy distrust of altruism, liberal society erected the system of checks and balances that has protected our liberty.

There is a great deal that is valid in these arguments. By not assuming the best, this philosophy has protected us from the worst. But in its embrace of some of the worst of our tendencies, this approach may also suffocate the best.

The liberal ideology represents itself as accepting people as they are. But the system may also work to mold us into its image of us: selfish social atoms with few bonds holding us together. A self-fulfilling philosophy. In the deepest visions of most cultural traditions, such an image omits much of what is sacred in the fabric of human life. Such molding fails to realize some of the most important potentialities of our human nature.

It is not entirely fashionable, in our age, to speak of "human nature." Where is it to be found? Which among all the cultural renderings of our humanity is to be taken as revealing our inborn nature? We are merely blank slates, some say, on which culture can freely write. It makes no sense, according to this view, to speak of human nature as if it contained anything of substance.

Elsewhere I have argued why this dismissal of a substantive human nature is wholly implausible when one considers the story of our species' evolution.[6] Moreover, the belief in the *tabula rasa* is not just wrong, it is also dangerous, removing as it does a vital standard against which the teachings of our cultures might be critically evaluated.

This anthropological kind of relativism, however, does serve the useful function of calling our attention to the undeniable power of culture. To be a cultural animal, the human being must of necessity be malleable. But our plasticity, as I said earlier, is not necessarily like that of shapeless clay but more like the growing foot of a traditional Chinese girl, flesh that can be bound and deformed.

We are born unfinished creatures, with an inborn nature but also, by nature, in need of culture's finishing touches. Our readiness for culture's formative influences creates the danger of deformation, should the cultural system develop in directions antagonistic to our needs. *The Parable of the Tribes* argues that the course of civilization's evolution has indeed been shaped largely by forces indifferent to us. The form our humanity assumes in the advanced and sophisticated cultures that dominate history, therefore, does not necessarily provide a lucid display of the natural inclinations of our inborn nature. Freud, looking around him at the distressed and neurotic personality structure of Victorian Europeans, propounded theories that illuminated far better the human condition of his times than the inherent nature of the beast.

So also with the selfish social atoms of the market society. What gives a person pleasure? The butcher and the baker, we are told, cannot be relied upon to find their satisfaction in benevolence; motivated by self-love, they seek their own advantage. We are divided into our separate, narcissistic spheres.

The market economy, through its voice in the advertising system, teaches us about the sources of our satisfaction. In its depictions, writes Michael Schudson, "the satisfactions portrayed are invariably private." "Even if they are familial or social," he reports from his study of "Advertising as Capitalist Realism," "they do not invoke public or collective values." The message beneath the message promotes an atomistic, self-centered way of life. The ads advance "a social order in which people are encouraged to think of themselves and their private worlds."[7]

Is this the *nature* of human life, or is it a particular and possibly distorted rendering of it? To what extent is this system realistic in telling us that a human being, such as the butcher, cannot be relied upon to seek his satisfaction in benevolence? Or to what extent is the system's ideology describing a reality the system itself has helped to create in teaching us that, motivated by self-love, we economic men and women naturally will seek our own advantage?

A study was done at Yale University "to see how far students behave like the rational egoists of the economist's theory."[8] Here is the set-up: There are two students, A and B, with a fixed amount of money available to be divided among them. Student A is charged with the task of proposing a way of apportioning the money. Student B can either accept or reject A's proposal. If B accepts, then the money is in fact divided according to the terms A proposed. If B rejects the proposal, neither student gets anything.

One of the findings is quite interesting. "Students of commerce and economics are much more likely than students of other subjects to try to get away with an unfair offer; conversely, they are much slower to walk away from palpably unfair offers. They seem to lack other students' passion for fairness."[9]

The author of a book that discusses this study interprets this finding in terms of a selection process, arguing that particular kinds of people are attracted to the study of different subjects.

Doubtless, the youth that go into any field—such as commerce and economics—are not a random cross-section of their age cohort. But I suspect that an important element of the explanation for the difference in behavior lies elsewhere. In this Yale study, I suggest, we may see a microcosm of the enculturating power of the market *Weltanschauung*. Socialized to see human interactions in terms of the profit-maximization of atomistic Economic Men, these students behaved according to the ideological image.

What course is most to my advantage? If I am A, how much can I get away with? If I am B, I should remember the rule that something is better than nothing. And what about fairness? That concerns relationship, and relationship is of little importance in a world where others are simply objects of greater or lesser use to each other. Fairness concerns morality, and morality counts for little in a world where all we should expect of ourselves, or of others, is that we all play to get ahead. The market thus creates a world in its own image, a nonviolent version of Hobbes's war of all against all.

WHERE THE GRAPES OF WRATH ARE STORED

Sometimes I miss my old anger.

I thought of this a few years ago when I read about the completion of part of the Central Arizona Project, which took billions of taxpayer dollars to divert Colorado River water for the benefit of city dwellers and farmers of the Arizona desert. Giveaway interest rates will provide the users precious water at a fraction of its cost, the article said, to help the farmers grow crops the government pays farmers not to grow.

This I read without surprise or anger—more a cynically bemused, "Ain't that the way it is." How this reaction revealed a change in me was brought home when, a few days later, I watched again that classic movie about the theft of water *Chinatown*. In it, a 1930s Los Angeles detective follows an apparent case of marital infidelity till it spills into murder and then finally plunges into an abysmal vision of the social order. A place where even the police bend to the will of a single ruthless man who can divert for his enrichment the lifeblood of the city—the scarce water around arid LA.

That film had captured well my feelings when it came out in 1974—a sense of palpable evil pulsing beneath the smooth surface of society. And rage.

Why, I wondered, have I changed? Of course, it was not only me. *Chinatown* came out the year the president of the United States was driven from office for trying to appropriate the laws of this country to serve his own ambition. It was an era of sanctimonious evil and smoldering national rage.

But there was more to it. My age, for instance. I was no longer in the heat of my twenties. As I neared forty, some "big chill" had cooled my anger. I had become less inclined to entertain the emotionally satisfying view of injustice as a function of personal depravity. Our pluralistic politics, in which everyone is expected to play to win, naturally produces a Central Arizona Project. In this land of opportunity and sanctified self-interest, whole classes of *decent* people can work to get others to pay to make their desert smell of orange blossoms.

But there was a gloss of moralism over this opportunism that still got to me. Some of these were the same folks who had promulgated myths of welfare queens in Cadillacs. And it was some of those who grow rich and strong off subsidized water who were offering us sanctimonious pieties about "getting the government off the back of the American people." I thought of that old dictum:

> The law detains both man and woman
> Who steal the goose from off the common
> But lets the greater felon loose
> Who steals the common from the goose.

That's where we get to when we reduce living together to simply playing to win. The more I thought about it, the more I realized I could still find where the grapes of wrath are stored.

THE BEGINNING

In the beginning, nature created human beings selfish and insatiable in their appetite for property. And the aggregation of men was void and without form; that is, there were just so many disconnected social atoms running about. This is an old creation myth that supports the development of a fragmented society of narcissistic individuals, productive of material abundance yet overcast with persistent discontent.

This is not, however, how the creation happened. Our ancestors were human for thousands, perhaps hundreds of thousands of years. But for many millions of years before we were human, we were social creatures. Long before we had language, we clung to one another for warmth and comfort. Long before we used tools, the heart of our adaptive strategy was the interdependence of a cohesive social group.

The anthropologists tell us that the human societies of the overwhelming majority of human history—the societies of hunting and gathering peoples—were not Hobbesian arenas of every person for him- or herself. Among the defining characteristics of these human societies, it is said, was the centrality of *sharing*. As human society evolved—up until the point where the face of our humanity began to be distorted by the anarchy among those societies that had broken out of our biologically evolved niche—the central drama was not the striving of each person against the others but the strengthening of the whole for the protection of all. In those societies we generally describe by the misguidedly pejorative term *primitive*, the person with high status is not the one who *has* the most but the one who *gives* the most to the others of the tribe. Hurrah for the one whose courage and skill brought back the beast for all to feed upon.

No doubt, it served the self-interest of the master hunter to be the benefactor of his little society, just as, in some inescapable sense, it serves Mother Teresa's self-interest to tend the poor of Calcutta. It hardly seems, however, an inherent factor of nature, foreordained by our Creator, that the members of society must speak to each other of the other's advantages and not of their own needs, appealing to their self-love rather than to their benevolence.

THE CONTRACT SOCIETY

This new creation story should not be misconstrued as providing a context for seeing the rise of the market society as the story of the fall of man. The civilized societies that developed over the millennia before Adam Smith's paean to the invisible hand were hardly, for the most part, ruled by benevolence. Given the predominance of predatory and tyrannical social orders in the human chronicle of the past five thousand years, the emergence of the liberal order of the market society can be seen in many ways as a genuine emancipation of the human spirit as well as of human energies.

If the market society does not represent the Fall, however, neither does it stand as the Promised Land. To us who live under the market's aegis, the challenge is not just to appreciate its blessings but to apprehend and liberate ourselves, as much as possible, from its particular curses.

The point of reexamining the story of our human beginnings, however, is to establish that the kinds of liberty and separateness fostered by the market do not reveal to us how we lived in Eden. The particular moral fabric of the market society—with its characteristic interweaving of blessings and curses, of protected liberties and institutionalized selfishness—is not a direct expression of nature. It is, rather, an artifact of a specific cultural development, built upon a unique history of institutions and philosophy.

In his book *The Political Theory of Possessive Individualism*, C. B. MacPherson describes the core concept underlying the market society. It is the concept of the individual, rendered with possessiveness as its essential core. "The individual [is understood] as essentially the proprietor of his own person or capacities," MacPherson writes. The radical separateness among such individuals derives from a further dimension of the individual's self-possession. The individual, owning his person and capacities, is understood as "owing nothing to society for them."[10]

It is as though the "self-made man" were man in his natural state. As though each human being, as proprietor, recreates the miracle of creation *ex nihilo*.

In this political philosophy, which MacPherson regards as foundational to the modern liberal democracies of market societies, and which he traces to both Hobbes and Locke, social bonds are slim and tenuous. In the perspective of this philosophy, he writes, "Society consists of relations of exchange between proprietors."[11]

What arises, in other words, is what I call "the contract society." This refers not just to that notion of a "social contract" that was conceived to serve as the creation myth for human society, the idea that society was formed by a contract entered into by wholly separate and autonomous individuals. Beyond that, the contract has come to epitomize the essence of human relationships, defining all the rights and responsibilities of people in relation to one another. In the contract society, I owe only what I agree to. And I enter only into those agreements that make sense in terms of my own interests. I don't owe others anything for *their* sake.[12]

The moral cost of the notion of the contract society is that it enshrines as right the egocentrism that most other moral systems have thought it important to hedge in with prohibitions and commandments. It gives license to forms of desire that earlier moral systems thought dangerous to the ties between people and even to the true fulfillment of the individual.

Of the theorists of the social contract, Wilmoore Kendall writes that they "divested the word 'right' of any moral connotations whatever." According to their theories, he says, I enter into society for strictly "selfish" reasons, without any sense of or commitment to "any duty toward my fellow man."[13]

The beauty of the market ideology is that, while enshrining selfishness, it did not need to disregard the idea of the public good. This is where the famous "invisible hand" enters in, transmuting by a kind of alchemy the base matter of selfishness into the golden achievement of the public good. Each individual, Adam Smith says, intending "only his own gain," "is led by an invisible hand to promote an end which was no part of his intentions."[14] Mechanism replaces morality. The design of the system, not the disposition of the human components, is to be the source of goodness.

As in economics, so in politics. The Madisonian mechanism of checks and balances would assure that "America did not need to have the virtuous *public* deemed necessary by classical theorists."[15] The design of the system was to create "a republic of laws and of institutions rather than a republic of virtue."[16]

Each part full of vice, the whole nonetheless a paradise. A paradise where the desert can smell of orange blossoms.

LIMITED LIABILITY

In the joke about the tyrannical regime, "Everything that is not mandatory is strictly prohibited." In the ethos of the contract society, whatever I am not expressly forbidden by our contract from doing, I have every right to do. "Where does it say that I can't?" as the figure of speech has it.

But is honoring one's contractual obligations a sufficient definition of human responsibility? Look at how the natural world around us is being laid waste. Hundreds of corporations spew their filth into the air and the water; they pillage the planet in the pursuit of wealth. How can whole classes of "decent people" contribute to this epochal crime of destruction with every sign of clear conscience?

The idea of the contract society offers a solution to this puzzle. The problem with nature, you see, is that it is not party to any contract. No contract, no responsibilities. "Where is it written that we can't destroy the earth?"

If it is not against the law, it is permitted. Milton Friedman makes a somewhat bizarre argument to establish that it is misguided for people to blame pollution on "business," that is, on "the enterprises that produce goods and services." "In fact," Friedman says, "the people responsible for pollution are consumers, not producers. They create, as it were, a demand for pollution."[17]

Don't blame me. I just work here.

It is true, of course, that we should take responsibility for our patterns of consumption and for the impact of those patterns on the wider world. But how reasonable is it to place the responsibility for pollution on the heads of consumers and to portray the industrial producers as but passive vending machines, as mechanical intermediaries between natural resources and human appetites, devoid of the burden of moral responsibility?

Given how the market economy is organized, the best way to control pollution is to have environmental laws passed. In the absence of laws to restrain all competitors in an industry, adopting environmentally responsible methods might put a single producer at a ruinous competitive disadvantage. Working to get such laws passed requires two things: knowledge and organization. In both respects, producers are immeasurably better situated than consumers.

Producers know infinitely more than consumers about what must be done to the world in order to make their products available for consumption. In addition, while consumers form an incoherent mass, producers are usually organized into industrial associations. When it comes to policy, Friedman's "business" is not really so passive. What Friedman's argument in defense of business neglects to notice is that the typical industrial lobby, far from being indifferent or helpless about the pollution its enterprises create, actively and strenuously works against the enactment of environmental controls.

Decent folks can work to perpetuate evils that serve their interests because, until a given course of action is forbidden, the moral universe of the contract society suggests that it is entirely allowed. (An old friend of the late Director of Central Intelligence William Casey described Casey as not seeing "an ethical dimension to business." "Is it illegal? If not, then you can do it. . . . You don't break the law. But bareknuckled competition? That's the American way. That's what *made* America."[18]) To argue that people—such as the owners and managers of corporations—have unwritten responsibilities requires us to concede that the circumscribed domain of contract does not encompass the whole realm of moral obligation. In the ethic of the contract society, I have a right to pursue whatever strategy will maximize my gain—belching sulfur or trading in ivory or storing toxins in flimsy drums—and I have no duty not to. My liberty is undiluted by generalized moral responsibility.

A recent film, *The Freshman*, carries the logic of the market in its relation to nature to a grotesque conclusion. The film, which is comic, depicts a club whose members pay royally to participate in the devouring of the flesh of a creature from an endangered species. The price is high because of the scarcity of supply. But whence comes the demand? The club members desire the meal not *in spite of* the destruction of creation it entails but precisely because of it. The fewer representatives of the species left on earth, the higher the price the members are willing to pay—up to hundreds of thousands of dollars for a single meal—for the privilege of being present at the destruction.

Importing and killing members of an endangered species is, of course, against the law, as the film itself makes quite clear. (We have made some progress since our great white hunters piled up mountains of buffalo skulls on the American prairie.) But this image captures nicely the ethic of the contract society as it applies to the consumer revolution: "the notion that any form of consumption is permitted," as Rosalind Williams puts it, "if a person can afford it."[19]

Obedience to the law can only be *part* of the moral fabric of a society. In the absence of a commitment to values that go beyond one's own "bottom line," even the laws themselves can become merely another part of the cost-benefit structure of the environment in which one is working to maximize one's gain. Smart corporate managers figure the likelihood of getting caught, multiply it by the likely penalty, and subtract this from the probable profit to be gained from breaking the law. If the result of these calculations is positive, breaking the law is good business.

Whoever said crime doesn't pay must not have had the bucks to hire the lobbyists to assure that a benign schedule of penalties got written into law.[20]

We see, on the program *60 Minutes*, how giant corporations routinely steal the inventions of individual patent-holders, knowing that there is no way the cost of their wrongdoing can ever catch up with the money to be made from ripping off a good innovation.

During an important playoff game in the National Football League, play is delayed while a player lies prostrate on the field. There is speculation in NBC Sports Central that the coach may have called for the injury to be feigned—a violation of the game's rules—to give the team, which has run out of time-outs, a needed interruption of play they could not get legitimately. The network commentator praises the apparent cleverness of the coach. The commentator evidently assumes that he and his listeners cohabit a moral universe in which you should play by the rules when it serves your purposes and break them when that serves your purposes better. So long as you are serving your own purposes.

The editors of *Good Money: The Newsletter for Socially Concerned Investors* published a story on corporate codes of ethics. They were struck by the finding, in a University of Pittsburgh study, "that corporations with codes of ethics are actually cited by federal agencies for infractions more often than those that do not have such standards for behavior."[21]

In trying to explain how this could be, the editors of *Good Money* cite another study from the University of Washington. This study examined the "ethical codes of conduct" of the two hundred or so Fortune 500 companies that have such codes to see with what issues these "ethical" strictures dealt. The findings of that study show that the "ethical" goals most often mentioned "all have something to do with the bottom line—with money and profit." These "ethics"—for example, calling for maintaining good relations with customers and suppliers as well as with the U.S. government, keeping honest records, avoiding conflicts of interest—all serve to help the corporation stay on the winning path. The least mentioned concerns, by contrast, "are all related to social concerns which would presumably cost the company money."[22] Where ethics concern the relation of the corporate social atom to the fabric of the larger social whole—for example, in matters of environmental affairs, product safety, civic and community affairs—the moral energy of the corporations wanes.

In the atomistic society, where the self is all there is to love, where there is no commitment in the heart to others or to the group as a whole or to its norms, life is Hobbes's war of all against all. It is not so bloody as the Hobbesian anarchy, because each can shrewdly calculate that he or she will get more if we exchange things other than blows. But in terms of morality, it is still a matter of playing to win.

In the contract society, it is generally good business to honor one's contracts. But if the path of honor diverges from the course of "good business," given the structure of the underlying moral philosophy, don't bet on honor.

Look out for number one. That is commandment number one, the first on a list of one. That is the direction in which the ethic of the contract society tends to move the moral understanding of the society's members. This egoism is not an embodiment of the natural human state. It is the artifact of a specific set of cultural beliefs and practices. Other kinds of society have generated their own forms of immorality and amorality too, of course. But to defend our system simply by pointing out the shortcomings of others—the fallacy of *Tu quo que* ("You do it too!")—is to abdicate our own responsibility.

The human being is born to be what the biologist C. H. Waddington called "the ethical animal," born ready to imbibe from our cultural environment a moral system to tell us how we should behave and what a human being should be. If we are taught that a person is supposed to maximize his or her own gain and to deal with others for the purposes of beneficial exchange, we will work—as much as the Hebrews striving for righteousness or the Romans seeking to embody virtue—to fulfill that cultural mandate.

JUST ANOTHER INSTITUTION

Perhaps it is a mistake to characterize the whole society as a "contract society" when it is only the economic system that defines itself in terms of exchange for mutual benefit. The editors of *Good Money* report a study showing that "individuals [from the corporate system] who stress self-respect, honesty and responsibility as top values and attributes in their personal lives don't typically act that way when they are at work."[23] The converse of this, obviously, is that people whose ethics in their economic roles are those of selfish social atoms do not necessarily act in the other parts of their lives as though they live in a Hobbesian moral universe.

Perhaps the morality of the economic realm of market society is more or less encapsulated from the rest of social life. Perhaps the economic system should be seen as but one more institution in a multidimensional social environment.

And, indeed, the reality of life in America is hardly summarized by the egoism, the selfishness, depicted in the foregoing portrait of the contract society. Not only are there examples of genuine social responsibility among corporations—corporations that do not simply take all they can get and give as little as they can get away with, striving to maximize only their own gain—but there are other institutional systems inspired by other realms of value.

George Bush's 1988 campaign theme of "a thousand points of light" was lampooned. Perhaps justly so, since it is not the essence of moral leadership for the one who seeks to lead our public life to promise us that others in the private realm will take responsibility for the unmet human needs in our society. Yet Bush was certainly correct that many Americans give voluntarily of themselves and their resources to help their fellows.

Voluntarism and charitable giving are both widespread in America. The economic system has its ethos, but we also have political, educational, and religious institutions, each with its own inherent set of values. Thus it is that in this "contract society" we have church groups putting on Thanksgiving dinners for the homeless; famous professional football players set up programs and spend their own time off the field to work with youth in the inner cities; volunteers are found in the waiting rooms of hospital intensive-care units, offering help and comfort to patients' families; political movements arise to preserve the redwoods for future generations; and so on.

Even so, the economy and its moral ethos are not so hermetically encapsulated. To see the market system as but one institution among many is to overlook the special qualities of the market as a power system. It is like the magnet of the fable, capable over time of pulling whatever else is in its environment into closer alignment with its field of forces.

In his study of the rise of the market society, *The Great Transformation*, Karl Polanyi describes how "the running of society [becomes] an adjunct to the market." To the extent that the market system can realize the goals of its *laissez-faire* advocates and liberate the system of exchange from control and regulation by other institutional spheres, working in the service of other systems of value, the market becomes not only free but able to reverse the direction of control. "Instead of economy being embedded in social relations [as was characteristic of all premarket societies]," Polanyi writes, "social relations are embedded in the economic system."[24]

The evolution of values in American society reveals the systematic pull of the powerful market system. When the Puritans arrived here, they had a deep appreciation of the idea that one cannot serve both God and Mammon. By the end of the nineteenth century, as Robert Bellah points out in *The Broken Covenant*, the power of the market had brought the values even of prominent religious leaders into line with the materialism of the market. "Godliness," said the Episcopal bishop of Massachusetts in 1901, "is in league with riches."[25]

In the early years of the American republic, the idea of success focused on the development of character. But, as John Cawelti demonstrates in his *Apostles of the Self-Made Man*, during the course of the nineteenth century, as the market system gained powerful momentum in America, the idea of success became less entwined with the inner person and focused more and more on mere outward and material success.

The capitulation of other realms of value to the terms of the market is not automatic. The defeat of alternative values is not a foregone conclusion, and is never total. But so long as the play of the market system is *insufficiently controlled* by other institutional systems—most especially by the political system, which alone can rival the market in a contest of pure power—the cultural landscape will be tilted the market's way. Whatever is loose will, as it were, roll downhill into the moral landscape of the contract society. Over time, unless and until the proper balance of power (and values) is restored, the moral culture as a whole will be transformed more and more into an image of the contract society.

EATING OF THE TREE

In the beginning, living creatures had no need of knowledge of good and evil. From the time that life began to assemble itself out of the primordial ooze until the rise of that quintessence of dust, the human being, the order of biological nature could keep all her children in their proper place. Whether by encoding instinct into a creature's genetic programming or by reliably providing the environment for the necessary learning, Mother Nature assured that the order to protect and preserve life would be maintained.

Then came the breakthrough into culture. Our species found the key to open the lock that confines life to biologically evolved patterns. We began to work our way into the freedom to live in ways undreamt of by Nature the architect when our genetic blueprint was laid down.

Yet the needs of life remained essentially unchanged—needs for harmony and cooperation among the members of the social group, needs for a viable and sustainable interchange between the animal society and its natural surroundings. With intricate order an essential characteristic of life, "anything goes" just does not work in a living system.

The combination of the new human freedom and the old need for order mandated that we become "ethical animals." To preserve the sacred ways of life in our newfound cultural world, it was necessary that we eat of the tree of the knowledge of good and evil.

A MATTER OF DISTASTE

It is no small flaw in a system if among its incidental by-products is a tendency to degrade the moral environment of the overall cultural order. The economic system that is understood as guided and regulated not so much by human morality but by the invisible hand has given us great abundance. Meanwhile, however, it has also corroded the channels along which the moral tradition of our heritage must flow from generation to generation.

The ideology of the contract society threatens, over time, to reduce that flow to a trickle. In *Habits of the Heart*, Robert Bellah and his co-workers report that it has become very difficult for many Americans to understand even their most deeply held ethical commitments in any language but that of "personal preference." The man who has turned away from a self-centered and materialistic life to a life of commitment to family values, Bellah tells us, can find no terms, no deeper point of reference, beyond "devotion to his self-interest" to describe either way of life.[26] The choice appears "arbitrary" and "inexplicable." The language that, in an earlier era, might have articulated "a larger sense of the purpose of life," a moral foundation, is no longer accessible.

The moral dimension that has become inaccessible to some has grown distasteful to others. We live, writes Verlyn Klinkenborg, in "an ironic age when moralists who love their morals are generally repugnant."[27] The descendants of those who first ate of the fruit of that tree in Eden now declare the taste of the fruit revolting.

The reasons for this distaste are doubtless complex, and this modern repugnance for a morality that takes itself seriously cannot be laid entirely at the door of the market system and the worldview it works to foster. After all, the Victorian age was an era simultaneously of *laissez-faire* capitalist ideology and of rampant moralism.

Nonetheless, the antecedents of this "irony" go back to the beginnings of the market ideology. In the very passage where he pens the famous image of the invisible hand, Adam Smith declares, "I have never known much good done by those who affected to trade for the public good."

Two centuries later, a president of the United States, an actor who could posture as a moralist when it served his purposes, who denigrated public efforts to care for the needy by promulgating the myth of "welfare queens" in Cadillacs, gave an echo of Adam Smith: "I have never looked for a business that's going to render a service to mankind. I figure that if it employs a lot of people and makes a lot of money, it is in fact rendering a service to mankind. Greed is involved in everything we do. I find no fault with that."[28] And Ronald Reagan proceeded to preside over an administration that was unsurpassed in American history in the number of its officials—entrusted with looking out for the public good—who were indicted for peddling their influence. I have never known much good done by those who trade the public good to serve their own greed.

The story of Edward Bok, related in Shi's *The Simple Life*, comes to mind. A century ago, Bok launched a highly successful business venture as publisher of *The Ladies' Home Journal*. After several decades, when the magazine and its publisher both were flourishing, Bok decided to leave business and begin a new career in philanthropy. To other wealthy and successful men, Bok advocated a similar change in activity and purpose: "Where a man's thought has been centered on himself, now he turns and thinks of others." He called attention to sources of satisfaction beyond possessions, saying that "the fundamental things which really matter are outside the pale of the banking-house."[29]

For providing this example and this counsel for the path of deliberate philanthropy, Shi says, Bok became the target of harsh criticism from "many in the business community." One attacked Bok for propounding "a dangerous and essentially anti-social doctrine," and suggested that Bok should be "morally court-martialed for deserting his post in the midst of the battle." The battle, of course, was in the competitive and productive arena of the market, where each is called upon to think only of his own enrichment, leaving the public good, in Adam Smith's phrase, "an end no part of his intention." Another critic, writing in the *Nation's Business*, ridiculed Bok for "attempting to Do Good." "Doing Good" he characterized as "patronizing the stupid and weak, giving the people something they don't want." Of Bok's idea that this Doing Good is a "worthwhile life," this representative of the business community wrote, "I contend that no 100 per cent American subscribes to such a doctrine."[30]

Attacking Bok's departure from the business of making himself rich by saying that "the 100 per cent American dies in harness" seems to make a duty of self-interest. The world whose ideology would leave the question of responsibility to the invisible hand seems determined to squeeze out all other moral frames of reference.

SEEKING THE SOURCE UPSTREAM

Many cultural currents swirl and eddy in American life. The moral fabric of our society is not altogether unraveled. If it were, our society would surely fall swiftly into chaos.

The market system is not an undiluted corrosive on our moral system. Honoring one's agreements—an ethic that the market promotes, though, as was said earlier, it gives insufficient moral underpinnings to it—is no morally trivial practice. Especially compared with some other systems that civilization has brought forward, the market can be seen as benign. Exchange, however self-interested, is a great improvement over armed robbery.

And the market is not the only aspect of our contemporary cultural system that may be working to undermine our grasp of the sacred role of moral and ethical values in the human experiment.

In his book *The Battle for Human Nature*, Barry Schwartz links three currents of our present ideological/intellectual worldview. One is that of market economics, the ideology we have been exploring here. The other two are behaviorist psychology and evolutionary biology. All of these, says Schwartz, utilize the language of science in a battle against "the language of morality in describing what it means to be a person."[31] It may be less illuminating to see these three currents of thought as independent tributaries to our cultural mainstream than as but different channels in the flow of a central ideational structure. This is certainly the thrust of Schwartz's delineation of their common patterns.

It may be, moreover, that this river of ideology that would displace morality from its customary—and sacred—place in human life has an identifiable and principal source in the landscape of our culture and its history: the dynamic of the market system. Ideas, after all, do not appear in a vacuum. Even more so, which particular ideas will rise to positions of cultural dominance is not determined in the realm of ideas alone, based on their intrinsic merits or appeal. Power wields its scepter over ideas as over other aspects of our lives. The market ideology—no less than the idea of the divine right of kings—can achieve hegemony if it serves the interests of power as it is distributed in a society. And the market—no less than the political systems of kingdoms—is a power system and as such can grant disproportionate power to those people, and to those ideas, that are most able to orient themselves according to the system's lines of force.

The possible role of the economic system as the source of the particular structure of "scientific" thought that Schwartz explores is suggested by a crucial passage in his argument. Significantly, when he seeks a critical metaphor to capture succinctly what evolutionary biology, behaviorism, and economic thought have in common, Schwartz says, "In essence, human beings [as portrayed in these theories] are economic beings." By this he means, "They are out to pursue self-interest, to satisfy wants, to maximize utility, or preference, or profit, or reinforcement, or reproductive fitness. They are greedy, insatiable in the pursuit of want satisfaction." The image of the self-serving Economic Man, in other words, is extended to incorporate all central dimensions of the human drama. It is a portrayal of our humanity that, as Schwartz says, "leaves out any consideration of morality."[32]

The battle for human nature, therefore, is one where more than "mere theory" is at stake. The real question is: Will anything stand in the way of our selfish pursuit of gain? That, at least, is the form the fundamental question takes as it is posed to us as individual thinkers and actors. This question appears before us, however, not just because we are human beings endowed by nature with a conflict between natural appetite and unnatural freedom from naturally imposed restraint. We are embedded in a system that is fueled by certain of our appetites and would be impeded in its expansion to the extent that we are willing to control those appetites in the name of moral values that we hold more important than our own unlimited gain. The underlying question, therefore, in the battle for human nature is: Will our deepest values and wisdom constrain the hegemony of the market's empire, or will the market succeed in driving out the moral forces with which it competes for the power to shape the human world?

In assessing this battle for hegemony in the terms of his analysis, Schwartz says, "It is a struggle that the language of morality seems to be losing."[33]

CHAPTER 4

Guiding Voices

Is there a necessary conflict between individual liberty and a well-ordered, humane society? Is human nature something that must be overcome to achieve a decent social order?

IF YOU KNOW WHAT'S GOOD FOR YOU

The market ideology offers a happy answer to that question: a benign order can be built upon craven human nature. The market is based on an idea of liberty independent of assumptions about individual virtue: vice for the parts, virtue from the mechanism governing the whole. The liberal market ideology, moreover, is suspicious of empowering any authority to make people be good. Better to live among foxes and polecats sating their appetites in a zoo designed by the invisible hand than to confront the lion of a political power (or even the suffocating python of a ponderous social morality). Let people be free to pursue their desires.

I resonate with the market's love of liberty. Jefferson was my father's hero, and I was raised to hate every tyranny over the mind of man. Let different moral opinions contend in the "marketplace" of ideas. The remedy for bad speech is not censorship but more speech.

When I came of age in the late 1960s, what seemed most problematic to me—as to many of my generation—was not the abuse of liberty but the abuse of power. But the way we in the counterculture understood liberty and power differed from the libertarianism of market ideologues. For it appeared to many of us that among the most dangerous abusers of power were the great corporate actors of the market system. Nonetheless, the "counterculture" and the market ideology did share some major philosophic convictions. "Do your own thing," is a notion that, in translation, is found in "liberal" thought from Adam Smith to Milton Friedman.

The love of "liberty" in our society tends to come in various stripes. Just as I am here decrying the detrimental effects of "liberty" in the economic realm, the established powers of mainstream society in America lamented much of what people of my generation and subculture were doing with our freedom in our personal lives. They didn't like the way we dressed and wore our hair, or our use of mind-altering drugs other than those habitually used by the older generation, or the rejection by many middle-class youths of mainstream notions of success and achievement.

The liberties we took exposed us not only to harsh criticism from the "establishment" but also to considerable harassment coupled with some repression.[1] Our idea of liberty and individualism seemed to be a threat to our "liberal" society. Those who wanted no one to interfere with their right to spew smoke into the atmosphere were prepared to jail young people who put the wrong kind of smoke into their own lungs. Different views of individual liberty were vying against each other.

The individualism toward which I was striving was based on the belief that somehow the organism could be trusted. The expression of liberty would not lead to vice. The body has a wisdom, and the recovery of access to that wisdom was an important project for personal and spiritual growth. Come to your senses. Lose your mind. In the unconscious dimensions of the mind, people in my "personal growth" subculture believed, one can find guidance, profound messages about truths denied or ignored by the small, conscious ego. Turn on, tune in. Listen to your Jungian dreams. Trust the natural; distrust social convention. This sense of the innate trustworthiness of the "natural man" provided the underpinnings of what can be called the human potential movement.

The market liberals have some beliefs that, though hardly identical and put in very different terms, are largely isomorphic with these tenets of my (what might be termed "Esalen") brand of liberalism. The market ideology says: No one is better able to decide what is good for a person than that person him- or herself. Let people express their needs and desires freely, therefore, in the market.

In the ideology of the market, however, the dimension of goodness—of morality and ethics—does not figure very prominently. Judgment is suspended: one want is as good as another. Satisfying wants is the proper business of society. Let us not worry whether people want snuff flicks or Bergman films. No one can judge whether the masses should use their leisure and their disposable income at amusement parks and burlesque halls rather than at the "elevated" cultural pursuits preferred for the masses by some high-minded snobs. In this suspension of moral concern, the liberalism of the market differs from that of the human potential movement.

The liberalism of the market ideologue also contrasts with the moralism of American cultural conservatives. These conservatives are willing to judge the way people live. As they see it, people left to their own devices cannot be trusted to know what is good for them, or to act in a way that is consistent with a healthy society. Goodness must be imposed against the natural grain.

It is not just groovy Californians sitting naked around their hot tubs in Marin County who evoke the criticism of the cultural conservatives. The attack on touchy-feely life-styles could be pre-dicted on entirely ideological grounds, for the Esalen liberals wield a moralism that in some of its very premises is antagonistic to the traditional morality of the conservatives. But to the conservative moralists, it is not just the indulgences in therapy and massage but, beyond that, the whole self-indulgent thrust of American consumerism that is a source of concern.

Though market ideologues are usually more concerned with the liberty of the profit-seeking producers, they also endorse the utility-seeking effort of the consumer. Conservative moralists, by contrast, are deeply suspicious of the selfishness and hedonism of the entire consumer society fostered by the market. Where the market liberal honors the economic individualism of the capitalist system, the conservative moralist is alarmed at the egocentricity of the individual and the concomitant corrosion of the integrity of the larger society. And whereas the market's advocates celebrate liberty, the defenders of traditional morality are apt to favor the imposition of the "good life" by social authority. Appetite must be constrained by inculcation of strong prohibitions through the socialization process and, where that fails, by the weight of authority standing outside and above the individual.

I believe both these positions are profoundly right—and also profoundly wrong. A better approach is possible to the search for the good life than is offered by either the market liberal or the moralistic conservative: it combines the liberty and respect for the individual from the one with the concern for virtue and the web of social relationships of the other. But that welcome synthesis cannot be achieved by human beings as either of those ideologies understands us.

The limitation, I would argue, lies not in human nature itself but in the understanding in these ideologies of what we are. The human being is, by nature, more than the marketeer sees and better than the conservative imagines.

Neither ideology thinks much of us. And the powerful cultural forces each represents treat us accordingly. One treats us as hungry beasts to be fed; the other, as wild animals to be kept in cages. That is why, however antagonistic their views appear to be, the two can so readily join forces to keep us content and contained in this zoo of a civilization we live in. That is why, when some radical ideas about what human life could and should be began to bubble up in the late 1960s and early 1970s, the bearers of those new ideas confronted a monolith of economic liberals and cultural conservatives antagonistic to the rise of this new kind of individualism.

The evolutionary thrust was blunted toward a new kind of cultural order to nourish this new individualism of the human potential movement. By the conservatives, it was continually the object of ridicule and attack. By the market system itself, it was largely co-opted, turned into a commodity like any other to be consumed by pleasure-seeking social atoms.

The clearest remnant of evidence that there may have been something powerful embodied in this movement is that so many moralists of the traditional order continue, a full decade and a half since the forces for cultural change began to ebb, to attack the movement and all it represented.

In truth, however, those of us who were swept up in a sense of new possibilities were also accomplices in the failure of our movement. Our own understanding of the full nature of the challenge of human potential was inadequate. As children of American society, with its conservative brand of moralism and its market brand of liberty and individualism, we were all too inclined ourselves to understand the deeper truth we had glimpsed in terms that fed into the hands of the cultural forces that opposed us.

We were too ready, as children of the market, to understand the idea of trusting the truth of our own feelings and deepest needs as a license to indulge ourselves. In opposing the rigid and constricting morality of the traditional culture, we were not ready enough to take on the hard work of achieving truly organic personal growth and moral development. It would have strengthened us to have a better understanding of what it means to nurture the "human potential." The search for such an understanding is a principal purpose of this chapter.

FEEDING OUR FACES

What is "individualism"? Different possible meanings are continually being confounded. Things need sorting out.

The market system fosters a certain form of individualism. The market's Hobbesian individuals have appetites seeking satisfactions. They are self-interested creatures who come together for exchange, which is to say, they use each other. The cultural conservatives also understand individualism in its Hobbesian form, and in this form they oppose it.

My critique of "the contract society" puts me together with the opponents of individualism in our belief that the way our society has unleashed and endorsed appetite is wrong for the individual and dangerous for society. In his critique of *The Culture of Narcissism*, Christopher Lasch disparages "the pursuit of happiness to the dead end of a narcissistic preoccupation with the self."[2] Robert Hogan sees the "individualistic perspective" as fostering an "egocentric" psychology.[3] The impact of this individualism on society is fragmenting. Our cultural ethos, which Edward Sampson describes as "self-contained individualism," fosters a person "who does not require or desire others for his or her completion or life."[4] Individualism, writes Alan Waterman in his useful overview of the critique of individualism, "is said to assume competitive relations with others. . . . Such social relations promote mistrust and suspicion and contribute further to social alienation."[5]

The critics of individualism are justified, I believe, in their alarm about the deification of appetite, the unbridled pursuit of profit and pleasure, in which the Hobbesian individual is encouraged. And, it must be admitted, all their critiques of the hedonism of consumer society can be applied to the countercultural movements of which I had direct experience.

There *was* self-indulgence in the "if it feels good, do it" crowd. A trip to the hot baths at Esalen could be just another way of pampering oneself, no different in nature from buying a luxury house or a fancy car. The process of healing and caring for oneself *could* become a narcissistic enterprise, with people wallowing in the therapeutic enterprise as if all that mattered in the universe were one's own precious self. "Personal growth" *could* be pursued as narcissistically as a closetfull of fashionable clothes.

"Do your own thing" *could* quite readily reinforce the disintegrative forces of our social atomism, eroding the cohesive bonds of mutual responsibility and caring in the same way as does the unbridled pursuit of gain by corporate actors in the market. I had students in the 1970s who, as "consumers" of the goods of the human potential movement, felt wholly disconnected from the fate of any part of the world around them, who felt no responsibility for seeking any goal except their own satisfaction.

The individualism of the human potential movement, with its belief in each person as the source of his or her own guidance, *could* be interpreted as being as amoral, as relativistic, as the amorality of the market. Just as the market (and its ideology) refuses to differentiate among wants and satisfactions—whatever anyone wants and gets produces "utility," which is good—so also did I see "human potential" ideas used to prevent any moral judgments. "If it is true *for you*," "if it is according to your values," then no more discussion of truth or goodness is possible. Even the Nazis, it follows, had their truths, their values, which must be accorded the same status as any other. Moral judgment, like utility, was construed—by some—as being the province solely of each separate person.

These, however, represent not the values and ideology of the "human potential movement"—not at least as I understand them—but their corruption. The critics of the movement, nonetheless, have seemed consistently to reduce the movement to its failures and perversions. This is a distortion, and it is unfair.

Should the idea of democracy be rejected because elected officials often put their own desires for perpetual reelection above the public good? Should the ideals of monastic life be evaluated on the basis of the lives of those abbots who used their positions to carve out little empires of wealth and power? I would say not. Yet it is frequently on this kind of basis that the human potential movement has been condemned.

The very notion of "personal growth," according to one critic, seems "heavily burdened with the self-contained individualistic thesis. The greatest good is individual self-expression; the group and the culture are seen as the evils that thwart freedom and independence. . . . Persons are helped to separate themselves even further from others."[6]

The idea of self-actualization, a concept from Carl Rogers's humanistic psychology, articulates a central concept concerning human potential: it is the notion that each person possesses a self worthy of nurturing, a unique set of gifts whose potential deserves to be realized. But critics, as Waterman shows, have linked self-actualization with narcissism and self-indulgence.[7] Striving for the development of the self, as these opponents of the individualism of the human potential movement understand it, is construed as inevitably fostering selfishness with "socially destructive consequences."[8] According to one such criticism:

To advocate that one should seek self-actualization and not be determined by society or other individuals seems inevitably to urge the individual to look to his or her own needs, desires, and fulfillments, in preference to those of others. It seems inevitably to suggest that what one should do in any situation is to maximize one's own benefits rather than aiming at benefits for others, or justice, or anything outside of oneself.[9]

This hardly characterizes the life of Carl Rogers himself, and it is, I believe, a significant distortion of the Rogerian idea.

If this image of selfishness is indeed a distortion, I am inclined to believe that this misrepresentation is nonetheless made in good faith. It is not, in other words, a malicious falsification motivated by polemical purposes, deliberately setting up in the name of one's opponents a position that is easy to discredit and reject. At the root of the rejection, I suspect, is a vast gulf between the parties' images of human nature; the reason this gulf leads to distortion is that it remains unarticulated. How can people fruitfully discuss "self-actualization" when their images of *the nature of the self* that is to be actualized are radically different?

What kind of entity is this "self"? That question is equivalent to, What is human nature? Implicitly, the critics of individualism share the Hobbesian assumptions about what we are—egoistic creatures of unruly appetite. The self of "self-actualization" they therefore equate with the self of "selfish." The focus on nurturing the self is understood as necessarily being in the same spirit as the pursuit of "self-interest" of the maximizer of profit or utility in the marketplace.

A different view is possible. It does not deny the reality of the Hobbesian self, but it sees us as being *more* than that. The "self" of the individual, properly understood, involves something deeper than, more important than, the selfish appetites of the Hobbesian creature.

If human beings have been endowed by their Creator with such a self, then this could provide the basis for a moral individualism. If every individual comes from nature with a core that is more trustworthy and more magnanimous than mere unbridled appetite, then one could imagine liberty in agreeable marriage with integrated and harmonious social order. Not all the voices in our liberal society, however, make it easy to discover that deeper self.

GIVE ME LIBERTY AND GIVE ME LIFE

I don't know precisely why it is that liberty is so precious to me. Those people on the right wing—and I lived among such people for a while in Barry Goldwater's Arizona—who chafe at the idea of Big Brother off in the capital telling them what to do, are, in this at least, my spiritual kin.

The issue of liberty first rose to prominence in my mind when I was on the threshold of adulthood. Actually, it was not so much liberty as its absence—capture, confinement, brutal treatment. In the final years of high school, I observed a recurrent pattern in my dreams. Not every night, but often, I would dream that I was imprisoned in some terrible or dangerous place; I would flee, I would be pursued, but, by cleverness or sheer will, I would make good my escape. Or perhaps I would be incognito in Nazi-occupied territory, in great fear of being captured, and would turn my hopes to D day, which, I knew, was soon to come.

What to make of this? Adolescence is full of confinements of various sorts. What was the nature of my bondage?

In my first year of college, the dreams intensified. The prisons were more elaborate and more cruel, the escapes more difficult. A terrifying image from one of them is still vivid in my mind, an image of men (who looked like the executioner in Dr. Seuss's *The 500 Hats of Bartholomew Cubbins*) bashing babies' heads against the stone lip of a well.

Given the life I was leading at Harvard, a hypothesis readily presented itself. My life as a freshman was one of long hours of hard work. In high school, I had striven to achieve, but now I felt I was in the big time, and I felt driven to perform at a major league level. The introspection prompted by my dreams led me to make explicit to myself an implicit commandment by which, I came to see, I lived my life: only by excellent performance in my work could I justify my existence.

But why did I need justification at all? Against what accusations was I working to gain expiation? I did not have the answers to those questions, but I had uncovered an agency within me—like an alien being—whose power shaped and dominated my life. I called him the Taskmaster.

In relation to this Taskmaster I was a virtual slave, putting more than a hundred hours per week into my studies. I also loved my studies, but this love was frequently swallowed up by other, darker feelings that possessed me. I could not escape noticing the unfree, burdened quality of my labors. (Remember when we were slaves in Egypt, the Jews remind themselves each year during the spring rites of renewal and liberation.) The burden came primarily from the *external* aspects of the relationship to the work. How will *they* judge my performance? Will it meet the perfectionistic standards of some Judge, on high, out there, above me?

Please, I had thought since I was in high school, let's just get rid of grades. Then we could just work for the love of it. But if grades there are going to be, I felt *compelled* to get good ones. Better than good. Only then would the Taskmaster give me any peace.

Like a garrison in a conquered city, Freud said of the super-ego. The Taskmaster was an alien presence in that way. In my dreams, it was I who strove for freedom in a land occupied by a foreign conqueror. I longed to feel what it would be like to be comfortable and at home with myself. I began to seek the road to liberty.

What made my freshman year especially brutal was that I was trying to please both God and Caesar. That is, I was not content just to do the work my teachers demanded; I also wanted to create out of the material of the courses something meaningful to me. I wanted to hold the stuff in my hands and listen for where I was called to take it. Sometimes, assigned a fifteen-page paper, I would write forty—the first fifteen to meet the course requirements, and the rest to give form to my own search for understanding.[10]

The rest of my college career represented two successive alternative strategies for dealing with my Taskmaster. The second year, I set aside my yearning for my own quest and became merely a dutiful student. Listening to only one voice—the one from outside—I was able to regain some strength. Then, in my last two years, I addressed the problem anew. I tuned in to my inner compass to get an idea of the direction I should go and, as much as possible, I sought out mentors who would support me in my chosen line of inquiry. By my senior year, almost all my energy went into "independent studies," overseen largely by two men (Erik Erikson and Robert Bellah). The work I was doing, coming as it was from my own core, was meaningful to me.

I was still driven, but my sense of bondage was diminished. My dreams of imprisonment were less frequent and less intense. There was no more bashing of baby's skulls; the spaces in which I ran to escape were wider. But I was not a free man.

In the meantime, my father had been diagnosed with Hodgkin's disease. He and I had always been very close; not less so because it was his exacting standards by which my internalized Taskmaster judged me.

My father also worked like a man driven. The stories of the hours he labored daily when trying to start his career as an economist were legendary, were among the tales my mother related in her weaving of family history. Eventually, he was reasonably established, and he felt he could make more room for things in his life besides work and sleep. Yet he cannot himself have felt that he was operating in very friendly territory: his magnum opus, a book published less than a year before his death, was rewritten nine times.

As my father came closer to the end of his life, he looked back, taking stock. He had but one regret, but that one hurt. It hurt him to acknowledge, and it gave me pain to hear. He wished he had prevented his work from taking over so much of his life. He wished he had *lived* more, especially that he had spent more time with his family. Listening to him at his bedside, feeling how both our hearts were aching, I understood how difficult it had been to live with my father's Taskmaster. These reflections upon his life hit me with the force of a lesson taught to a son by his dying father. "Don't follow in my footsteps," is what I took from it. "Not in this. Remember to live."

For a year before my father died—it was my senior year in college—I had a series of dreams showing that in my heart, if my father died, I would want to follow him. They were extraordinarily vivid dreams, dreams that not only would awaken me but would continue to possess and shake me after I woke up.

One night, in my his hotel room in Boston, where he had come on business and to visit me, I told my father a couple of these dreams. The words he spoke to me then echoed in my mind till their imprint was engraved. I had hardly ever seen my father cry, but he was crying then. "You *live*, kid! I want you to live! *You do that for me!*"

After his death a few months later, my father's one regret and his powerful injunction concerning my life after his reverberated together until, in combination, they blasted apart the structure of my life. My father's death occurred at the end of my first day of graduate school. Within months, I saw that I no longer had passion for that kind of work, and before the year was over I dropped out and moved west to California to seek spiritual renewal. How should I live my life? What did it make sense to do?

No work meaningful to me presented itself, so I simply earned a living and tried to find my way. (My father's mother, bewildered at my leaving the path of success, wrote me, "I hope you are becoming accustomed to your way of life.") My Taskmaster was still there, however, and he was not pleased with me. Like a runaway slave, I could find no place I could rest in peace. What was I doing to justify my existence?

My father remained present, not only in his embodiment as (a large component of) the Taskmaster, but also in the form of his painful regret and his tearful commandment to me. "Thou shalt live, and not be a slave!" In my wanderings in the wilderness, I endeavored to think through anew what life was about, and what I arrived at required the dethronement of the Taskmaster. I pushed and pushed at him, but he wouldn't budge.

I became depressed. One night, in December of 1968, I awakened from a most disturbing dream. It was on the old pattern of captivity and escape, but this time, for the first time ever, the dream ended with my recapture. My escape had failed. That night, in the middle of the night, I hit bottom.

Within that dark pit, something rebounded. From then on, I gradually regained life. I found that I was increasingly able to partake of life, in its many dimensions, without the drag of the Taskmaster's yoke.

It was only well after my rebirth that I was able to discern how I had freed myself, how I had changed the oppressive relationship with my Taskmaster. I never did succeed in dethroning him. His power was too deeply entrenched, and the structure of my character too resistant to fundamental realignment. What I had done was to humanize the Taskmaster by a single act of legislation: I redefined "work."

If the old commandment was "Work with passion and perform to a high standard," and the new dispensation was "Live!" I could reconcile the two if my work was defined as "full engagement in any meaningful activity." I broadened the Taskmaster's understanding of the tasks he should assign me. No longer would I gain respite from his complaints and demands only by *producing*, by performing tasks that were means to ends. Now I was free to "work"—that is, to be meaningfully engaged—by having a good conversation with a friend, by marveling at the smell of the woods on the hills, by listening to Bach.

By means of this trick, though I remained imprisoned, I managed to enlarge my prison into the whole world. I felt reborn free.

THE NEED FOR WHIPS

With the Taskmaster's grip loosened, will anything get done? Our moral culture suspects that in the absence of the whip—from the outside in the coercive societies of old, or internalized from without in the compulsive societies of modern times—we would lapse into self-indulgence and lassitude. This suspicion reveals a profound mistrust of the human being.

We live in a "free society," but *to the extent* that this freedom is founded upon a moral culture of distrust of human nature, the liberty we enjoy will be a narrow one: freed from *external* tyranny, but still not at liberty to flower forth in our full humanity.

Our democratic institutions are indeed something for which to be thankful. But there is some darkness lurking in the background, left there from the psychological evolution that helped to give rise to our moral culture. There is some truth to a remark once made to John Maynard Keynes by a Russian: "You don't need the police because you all have mental straitjackets."[11]

Over the centuries, our Western civilization developed itself into an enormously productive, constantly active, dynamic system of power. A reading of Max Weber's *The Protestant Ethic and the Spirit of Capitalism*, however, shows that the impetus behind this extraordinary activity may be the goad of a psychological wound. "One does not only work in order to live but one lives for the sake of one's work," said the early Protestant theologian Nikolaus Zinzendorf. (But would not our Father, in heaven, say to us rather, "Live! Do that for me!"?) Zinzendorf continues, "If there is no work to do one suffers or goes to sleep."[12] Only productive activity stills the pain, appeases the angry Master.

Free people can also be slaves. One of the patron saints of capitalism, and a founder of American liberty generally, Benjamin Franklin, gave us the pithy wisdom of Poor Richard. (There is indeed a poverty about Poor Richard, even though his expertise concerns the means of amassing wealth.) "If you were a Servant," Poor Richard asks, "would you not be ashamed that a good Master catch you idle? Are you then your own Master, be ashamed to catch yourself idle, as Poor Dick says."[13] The self in this dramatization of the internal interaction is, clearly, the Servant. It is "I" who would feel ashamed, like the Servant, rather than affronted, like the Master who catches me. This captures well the inner experience of servitude of that psyche capitalism creates in its stage of accumulation, a psyche that has brought inside itself the voice of a powerful, demanding Master.

Bondage takes many forms. We can be premature in acclaiming our liberation. Surely it is worth celebrating that we are no longer slaves in Egypt. But what if, as our legacy from laboring for Pharaoh, we have taken into ourselves the image of one of the Pharaoh's slave drivers, an alien presence to perpetuate the conquest of our true self even after the visible chains have been removed? The labors I like to regard as my own may still be but toil under the lash, constructing tombs for Pharaoh.

Where is my true self to be found in the psyche divided between Servant and Master?

People under assault defend themselves, when the self is too weak and is overwhelmed by pain and terror, by the psychological trick called "identification with the aggressor." "If I am the object I fear, then I need not be afraid."[14] This is how abused children grow up to become child abusers. This is how the Georgian boy Iosif Dzhugashvili, who dreams of vengeance

against Russians—unwelcome Russians who dominate his homeland like a garrison in a conquered land—grows up to become
Joseph Stalin, "father of all Russians," with an especial contempt
for the conquered Georgians of his native country.

With the history of civilization one of epidemic conquest and
victimization, with our societies dictated by the requirements of
power and often powerfully antagonistic to our human nature,
human development in each generation often has required coming to some kind of peace with forces one fears. What is my real
self? Many people have grown up to believe the answer to be: I am
the commander of this garrison that keeps the people of this city
in submission and obedience.

And what of those who, less overwhelmed by terror, maintain
better their identification with the inhabitants of the occupied
city? Are they able to discern readily the true nature of the conquered people? Or does the fact of conquest distort and obscure
the underlying reality?

Kipling, writing about the "white man's burden," described the
nonwhite beneficiaries of the white man's conquest as "sullen." Is
their sullenness a reflection of their true nature, or is it perhaps an
artifact of the circumstance that brings the white observer into
position to pass his condescending judgment upon them? In the
absence of myself as Master, is my true nature to be found in the
Servant whose feelings revolve, apparently, around the fear of
being caught in that state of idleness he evidently desires?

The moralists of cultural conservatism view the conquered city
of our souls and pass their judgment on our presumed natures.
Like Kipling assessing his new-caught, sullen peoples, they see a
darkness about us. Like Poor Richard's Master, they imagine it is
only the force of shame that stirs us from what would otherwise
be our naturally slothful state. "These slaves," say the Pharaoh's
overseers. "If we weren't standing over them with our whips,

they'd lie around, achieving nothing. They'd never build the tombs."

FOR THE GLORY OF GOD

Next to, of course, God, Bach is the one I admire most. The outpouring of beauty that streamed through this man inspires my awe. When people ask me whom I regard as my mentor in my own work, I answer, in all seriousness, Bach.

In order to create the marvels of his musical compositions, did Bach have to overcome the inherent sloth of his nature? Are we to believe that some Taskmaster instilled by the conquering force of civilization had to put a whip to the naturally idle being Bach was born to be? I cannot claim to know for sure. But I don't believe it.

Among the mythic constructs of the worldview of Western culture is the image of the neurotic genius. But although the internal warfare of neurosis may be expressed and, in part, ameliorated by the gift of genius, I doubt whether neurotic conflict gives rise to or contributes to genius. The expression of the gift is more likely in spite of than because of neurosis. The Soviet Union is now having to transform itself, in part because a system based on the external Taskmaster stifles human creativity. Likewise, I suggest, the internalized Taskmaster is more likely to impede than to facilitate the flow of inventive imagination.

On his works, Bach customarily penned the inscription: *Ad majorem Dei gloriam*, or "To the greater glory of God." In my picture of Bach, the God that is glorified by his magnificent creations is not some Master standing above, not some Being on high bestriding humanity as though it were some sullen race He is determined to conquer. God is rather like some wondrous spring, the Source, welling up from below. Deep within himself, in my image, Bach—whatever his culture may have taught him to see and to believe—found access to this wellhead of the sacred. The self in its flower is not a conquered city where God's garrison reigns, but a verdant village built around a sacred spring.

Bach's divine work glorifies God, in my eyes, because it reveals the clear channel Bach provided for the expression of God's glory. (In the film *Amadeus*, the envious Salieri marvels that when Mozart is composing, it is as though he were taking dictation from God.) Bach's greatness lies in his genius at making himself into an instrument. Bach stands like some marvelous organ pipe with the cosmic wind rushing through.

Producing beauty, I believe, is a natural expression of human health. The power relationship embodied by masters with whips is a reflection of the sickness inflicted on humanity by the grievous dynamics of our history.

Without goads, our civilization assumes, we would accomplish nothing. Look at what our schools do. The little children I have known have all been animated by an abundance of curiosity. One hardly needs to goad them into taking an interest in the world. They spontaneously want to explore, to take things apart, to figure them out. But our schools do practically nothing to harness this natural resource of the human self. "Learn this, whether you are interested or not," is the usual message. "As for what you're curious about, that does not interest us. You cannot be trusted to know what you should be learning." Not surprisingly, after some years of this kind of education, the native curiosity of our children atrophies. By the time they graduate from high school, all but a small handful shuffle in and out of classrooms like new-caught, sullen people.

Not coincidentally, studies have shown a corresponding pattern in the ups and downs of our children's self-esteem. Upon entering school, most of our children apparently feel good about themselves. By the third or fourth grade, a much larger proportion of our children are struggling with low self-esteem. The systems of our civilization don't think much of us, and they are good at teaching us to think likewise. Our self-esteem reads like an unfavorable report sent back to the imperial capital by the commander of the garrison.

Should I reject altogether the idea of a Taskmaster within? If I take any satisfaction from the objects of my own creation, do I owe no debt to my Taskmaster for making me ashamed to catch myself idle, for not letting me rest until I've met his standards for my work? In all honesty, I don't know the answer. Never having been free of him, I don't know what I would have produced in his absence.

I do believe, however, that what is most of value in my work has nothing to do with the Taskmaster. The real gifts have come in moments of my greatest freedom, when I was most fully and flowingly letting myself be, unconstrained by anxieties of performance and judgment. The really good stuff comes from the depths, not from above. Poor Richard's advice may be appropriate for the productivity of drones, of servants and slaves who toil in the service of a conquering ruler. But I have found idleness a most essential ally of the work of creativity.

When I come to a point where I feel uncertain of where to proceed in unraveling a puzzle, or I feel too weary to continue without strain, the worst thing I can do—for the sake of the work, as well as myself—is to try to force the process, to follow orders from above. Rendering unto Caesar the tribute he demands entails a spirit contrary to rendering forth what is from God. Far more fruitful is to stop the labor and embrace idleness. In the warmth of a hot bath, all the knotty problems seem to dissolve. In the "afterbath" of my shameful shirking, I drip a trail back to my desk to jot down the solutions that simply seeped up into consciousness when I emptied my mind and let go of all intention.

We did not survive eons of life's evolution by being inherently defective. From our ancestors' first pulling themselves dripping out of the primeval seas all the way to the crafting of our human

form, we could make it only by being inclined by nature to do
what life requires of us. The idea that we need to make war upon
ourselves to get ourselves to do what is needful is a calumny
against our nature or, at the least, is a clue that the needs involved
are not our own.

CONSUMING PASSIONS

The "spirit of capitalism," as Max Weber showed, came to earth
and was made flesh in conjunction with a work ethic based on
inner compulsion. This combination of economic system and cultural neurosis generated a degree of material productivity the
world had never seen before.

Production was, of necessity, the heart and soul of capitalism
for its early stages of development. Consumption—sometimes
even opulence—was always part of the picture. But until the level
of material wealth for the mass of the population was raised much
above the level of basic necessities, the dynamic of the system
had no need to inflame the passions of consumption.

The very success of the system in terms of production eventually necessitated a corresponding evolution in consumption. As
the productivity of human labor was magnified, the system that by
its nature will reward labor according to the value of its contribution gave more and more people more and more claim over
resources. That is, they had more and more money in their pockets. Their bulging pockets made them attractive targets for a system that, by its very dynamic, seizes upon every opportunity for
its enrichment and can know nothing of "Enough." The dissem-
ination of wealth thus stimulated our opportunistic economy to
create people like itself in the voraciousness of their material
hungers.

The psychology of compulsive work on the productive side was
thus joined by a psychology of insatiable appetite on the side of
consumption. The asceticism of the work ethic and the hedonism

of the ethic of consumerism may appear to represent one of the "cultural contradictions" of capitalism.[15] But the two are both products of the same magnetic field of economic forces, unfolding over time in the evolution of the market society.

In fact, these two dimensions of the character structure of "capitalist man" are not in such complete contradiction. Both the compulsion in labor and the insatiability in the pursuit of pleasure can be seen as symptoms of the same wounding of the psyche. It is when the connection of the self to the true source of its nourishment has been ruptured that the injured psyche becomes driven alike in its work and its pleasure.

The psychology of capitalist production and that of capitalist consumption share several important characteristics. Both represent the triumph of the power system, not the emergence of the healthy human being. And both obscure the natural wholeness of the self. The defender of the system might say that in these effects, the market system is no worse than virtually all the other social systems we see displayed in history. That is probably true. But that truth is no reason for our being complacent about our condition.

The Good Spirit

Perhaps "the pursuit of happiness" is an innate drive in human nature. But the question remains: Of what does happiness consist?

We may recall (from the previous chapter) Edward Bok's speaking, when he left the pursuit of profit to do the work of philanthropy, of the importance of things "outside the pale of the banking-house." The satisfactions, advocated by Bok, of turning one's thoughts to others lie outside the pale of the Hobbesian psychology of appetite. The pursuit of self-interest, as it is understood in the philosophy underlying the market system, involves the narcissistic self-indulgence of social atoms.

We are back to that question raised by the human potential movement and its critics: Is narcissism the natural expression of the human being in the pursuit of happiness?

The Greek word *eudaimonia* is generally translated into English as "happiness." But, as David Norton explains in his book *Personal Destinies*, this translation obscures a crucial distinction essential to the venerable philosophic idea of eudaimonism. "What the eudaimonist demands to know first," Norton writes, "is whether the gratified desire is right desire or wrong desire."[16] Right desire or wrong desire. How is one to judge? Either, says Norton, can give pleasure. But only the gratification of "right desire" gives the feeling of *eudaimonia*. That feeling, therefore, "serves as a mark, a sign" that the individual is engaged in "right living." Not for the eudaimonist, therefore, is the economists' equation of one utility with any other.

Even casual students of the classical world may recognize the Greek word *daimōn* from the story of Socrates. Socrates referred to his guiding voice as his *daimōn*. It was his *daimōn* who told Socrates, at crucial moments, the course he should take. It was not generally an easy path, or one attractive to the pleasure-seeking hedonist.

Some seek to reduce this *daimōn*, this image of an "inner voice" to our concept of "conscience." But Norton maintains the two concepts are quite distinct, pointing to a difference that is entirely germane to our inquiry into the true nature of the self of the individual. Conscience, as Norton observes, "means a voice within the individual that belongs to an authority outside him." To live according to the dictates of one's *daimōn*, by contrast, is to live in accordance with *"one's own truth."*[17]

The *daimōn* of *eudaimonia* (*eu* meaning "good") is, therefore, a part of the core of a person's self. It is homegrown, not an import. It is a natural leader from within the body politic of the personality, not a conquering invader. The *daimōn* represents, in a sense, an ideal toward which the self naturally strives. The *daimōn* provides a person "his ideal possibility," which contrasts with "his empirical actuality," that is, with himself as he is. The fulfillment of the self, in this sense, is hardly to be equated with narcissistic self-indulgence. It is a task and a challenge. "It is every person's primary responsibility first to discover the *daimōn* within him and thereafter to live in accordance with it."[18]

The philosophy of eudaimonism establishes the basis we are seeking for a marriage of a genuine individualism—one that empowers and liberates the human person—with a morality that guides the course of the individual onto the right path. Here is the key to the question posed at the outset of this chapter: whether freedom of the expression of human nature is compatible with harmonious social order.

Unlike the moralism of the conservatives, eudaimonism does not regard the path of goodness as leading to the altar of the sacrifice of the self. To be pointed on the way of goodness, a person need not subordinate the core of her nature to a stern authority outside and above her. By contrast with the individualism of market liberalism, the core of a person's self is seen as containing its own moral compass. True fulfillment is not an amoral pursuit. The nourishing of a moral human world—one in which people practice "right living"—is wedded to the true pursuit of happiness. The "true self" seeks the gratification of "right desire" and is rewarded by that feeling, *eudaimonia*, which "signals that the present activity of the individual is in harmony with the *daimōn* that is the true self."[19]

In contrast with the egoism of Economic Man, there is here a willingness to bring the ego into alignment with something deeper and more important. "There is a feeling," writes Waterman in endorsing the ethics of eudaimonism, "of doing not just what one wishes to do, but what one must do."[20] "Accept your

destiny," was one of the great Greek injunctions. In contrast with
the insatiable hunger of Economic Man to have more of what he
has not, the striving of the eudaimonist is, in Pindar's words, to
"become what you are."[21]

Happiness of this kind represents a kind of proper nourishment.
Rightly fed, each person fulfills the healthy blueprint with which
he or she was born. Improper nourishment—some of the poisonous feeding to which we civilized peoples have been subjected by
the systems growing out of our agonized history—leads us to grow
in other, misshapen ways. But the way of self-actualization is an
unfolding of one's true nature, a fulfillment of intended design.
"Living one's own truth constitutes integrity," writes Norton, "the
consummate virtue."[22]

SELF-FULFILLING

How are we to know right desire from wrong desire? This is another way of asking the question with which we began: Do people
know what is good for them?

Minutes after my baby is born, there he is in his mother's arms
sucking away at her breast. He didn't need to be invited twice.
No one had to tell him what he should do. No one needed to persuade him that the sweetness of his mother's milk tasted good.
Naturally endowed with a certain wisdom about what is required
for living, the newborn creature willingly cooperates in a family
activity that serves to perpetuate our family line. Wouldn't it be
nice if that same wisdom could be counted on for all the subsequent decisions of life?

There is an old idea—found in ancient Greek and in traditional
Jewish thought—that before we are born we possess divine
knowledge but that, as we come to life, we are induced to forget.
The mechanism of our losing our way, however, seems otherwise
to me.

The natural wisdom of the suckling infant is not a feature of the single organism alone. It represents, rather, a fit between the infant and the environment into which he or she is born (specifically his or her mother). This, in turn, is the legacy of the countless generations during which the design of the species was laid down in the relentless molding of the organism to correspond to the demands and opportunities presented by the surrounding environment.

Our wisdom will not look wise, however, if we are born into an environment that is hostile to our inborn needs.

Hostility tends to generate self-confirming beliefs. Paranoids, by their suspiciousness and their defensive rage, create enmity that confirms their belief that they are surrounded by enemies. Teachers who expect their students to fail or to misbehave tend to elicit the very conduct they anticipate. Likewise, a culture that believes in the evil or folly or amorality of human nature will counter and eventually silence the voice of natural wisdom in its members, producing people who do not have access to a reliable compass inside them to help them find their way. That is the source of our "forgetting."

We believe our society—more to the point, we are *taught* to believe our society—to be benign and humane. I think of the cry of so many bewildered parents, cut to the quick by ingratitude: "Look at all we've done for you!" But as Theodore Adorno has said, "It is part of the mechanism of domination to forbid recognition of the suffering it produces."[23]

We are each born craving someone to hold us and something to suck on. Ashley Montagu has observed how unusual are the cultures of Northern Europe and North America in how little tactile contact is given the babies born within them. Is it only coincidental that these same cultures, raising their infants on a starvation diet of physical touching, are precisely those that served as the cradle for the economic system based upon insatiable material appetites?

Early in this century, the respected American pediatric authorities sought to wean American parents away from such "mawkish" and "unbusinesslike" ways of treating their children as holding them, and rocking them, and giving them affection.

As for breast-feeding, our scientific authorities—representing to parents the same voice of "progress" and "advanced civilization" that those infant formula ads utilized in Pakistan—worked for much of this century to hinder it. When I was born, my mother wanted to breast-feed me. When she ran into difficulties during the first week at the hospital, the medical authorities in that institution, far from supporting her efforts, sought to discourage her. They made disparaging remarks likening her to a cow. Humiliated, my mother gave up.

This contempt for the natural needs and inclinations of the human organism may have diminished since that golden age of the glorification of "scientific expertise," but the war against our babies persists. The other day, my wife told me how sorry she was that she allowed the advice of our kindly doctor to make our baby's first nights home from the hospital so much more difficult than they needed to be. The baby wanted to suckle, but she had been told that it was important to establish in the baby's mind that there would be a rhythm to its feedings. So for a couple of nights, my wife watched the clock, waiting for permission to do with our son what they both longed to do.

Who can trust the messages of the human organism? Civilization and its clocks must govern the biological rhythms of the untrustworthy creature.

Our baby was going to have his own room. It was all set up. Very soon, however, he let us know that he had his own needs, and these needs were not identical with those of all other babies.

When they were infants, my two older children could be picked up and put down easily when they were asleep. Not Nathaniel. From the beginning, unless he was in physical contact with one of us, he would immediately awaken, unhappy. My wife would nurse him to sleep, and then be unable to get away. For the first six months, all his naps were spent either lying next to his mother or being carried around by one of us in some kind of pack.

Being willing to do this required of us a degree of effort, of course, and a willingness to be inconvenienced. It also required that we go against a powerful stream of counsel from people both professional and otherwise. With the exception of the people from La Leche League—one of the few organizations in our society that genuinely and radically believes in the value of human nature—almost everyone else underscored how important it was to "teach" this neonate to be independent.

Do we imagine that, during the millennia of primate and human evolution, our babies slept in their own rooms, away from their mothers? Are we to suppose that if we did not force autonomy onto our little ones, they would not in the fullness of time claim their independence on their own?

"Our daughter was just like that," the father explained to us upon hearing of our little "neo-Nate's" rather intense need for contact. "But we cured her of it. We did what the doctor said—we put her in her room and let her cry. It was hard, but she cried less the second night, and by the fourth night, she went off to sleep by herself without protest."

How hard was it? How long did she cry that first night? "Oh, about five hours. My wife had to leave the house, because she couldn't stand to hear her. But we knew we had to do it."

I'm sure the child learned, all right. But the question is, Precisely what did she learn? To summarize the lesson as, "She learned how to go to sleep by herself," seems an extraordinarily narrow and overoptimistic rendering of what must have been an extremely profound, not to say traumatic, experience.

Are we to assume that this child who, at the age of ten, seems— at play with my own daughter of that age—a perfectly normal American girl was too young to be wounded by such an ordeal? I am reminded of the remark of the German pediatric expert of the eighteenth century, J. Sulzer, who, after advising severe beatings of very young children to root out their willfulness, concludes reassuringly: "If their wills can be broken at this time, they will never remember afterwards that they had a will, and for this very reason the severity that is required will not have any serious consequences."[24]

The conservative moralists would put us into cages, thinking of us as wild beasts not to be trusted. To them, the self is a narrow and petty thing, unreliable in its concerns for the well-being of other people, indifferent or hostile toward morality, desperate to feed its insatiable appetites. And, surprise! That is not unlike the way we behave. Thwarted and wounded, the "true self" hides away, skulking in the shadows of unconsciousness like some beast on a nocturnal hunt. Into the light of a hostile world steps the smaller self our abusive culture has summoned, a narcissistic and shallow creature, angry and hungry.

We become the smaller self in self-defense. The narcissistic project of psychopathology, after all, is understood to be a reaction to a failure of love from the outside world. It begins with us as infants getting a message—from the place that, by nature, we look to for love—telling us that we are no good, that our needs are not important or legitimate, that the messages we hear from the core of our being cannot be trusted. In compensation for the injury to the feeling of self-worth that all abuse represents, the narcissistic defense strains to buttress the self with grandiose images of being the center of the universe.

In the wake of trauma, who would dare to unearth the "true self," the *daimōn*, the message from the underground spring that would be our guiding voice? To penetrate beneath the shallow structures of our defense would be to contact once again the terror and pain from which we have sought to protect ourselves. For while we were learning to be "good" boys and girls—to go to sleep by ourselves, to stifle our desires for intimacy that our likewise wounded progenitors had been made incapable of providing, to sit obediently at our desks until the almighty clock tells us that movement and spontaneity are permitted—we were also learning deeper lessons about the need to be alienated from ourselves. "If I am not the true self that is being wounded, I need not feel this agony."

Compelled to close ourselves off from the source of right desire, we are inevitably made vulnerable to the systems that traffic in wrong desire.

A SUCKER BORN EVERY MINUTE

While a hostile culture teaches us to be the smaller self that confirms its dismal expectations and justifies its abusive treatment, it also takes our natural impulses and turns them to its uses.

Twenty years ago, when I first embarked on the exposition of my own parable, I happened upon *The Parable of the Beast*, by John Bleibtreu. Early in that work, Bleibtreu presented a striking image that stays with me still. He describes the suspended life of a tick, which hangs on the limb of a tree, possibly for year after year, until it encounters the wafting of a certain chemical that indicates the presence of a warm-blooded creature below. These airborne chemicals unlock time for the tick, which responds to the scent by dropping down, presumably to the Promised Landing on the furry coat of his long-awaited meal.

That's how it is supposed to work, but in Bleibtreu's account, the scientists rigged up some simulation to emit the crucial chemical and to demonstrate the tick's chemical trigger mechanism. In the clever hands of the manipulators of nature, the tick's eighteen years of patient waiting, piled on top of a hundred million years of his species' evolution, become simply the overture to the creature's making a serious error in judgment.

By what means are we, living in this unnatural zoo, to judge which is the right and which the wrong desire?

How well the neonate knows what to do, savoring the sweetness of its mother's milk. In a few years, my little son and I will meet in the perennial Battle of the Sweets. His tongue was made to tell him that sweet tastes good, but the world his tongue was designed for presented different possibilities from those dangled before him by this brave new world through which I must help to guide him. The fruits of the ancient Garden of our Creation are still there, but they are almost buried beneath the mounds of artificial and refined sweeteners.

And the Serpent is there, in this new garden of our own creation, inviting him to taste of the candied apple dangling from the tree of ignorance of health and sickness.

A study by the Australian Consumers Association disclosed that during those afternoon hours when children constitute the largest part of the television audience, almost half the commercial messages were for food, and of these foods over 90 percent were foods that—because of excessive sugar and/or fat—were nutritionally problematic. The Consumers Association criticized the way the sellers whispered into the ears of babes such helpful teachings as the designation of Milky Way chocolate bars as "the sweet you can eat between meals." "With 73 percent sugar and 17 percent fat," said the critics, "this claim is promoting a product which has a negative nutritional value and is entirely likely to ruin the appetites of children, for whom it is promoted, for their normal meals."[25]

Can people be trusted to know what is good for them? Not altogether. Natural wisdom needs a good deal of help in navigating safe passage in an unnatural world. But our systems are not the allies of our wisdom. To them, the infant sucking the sweet milk from its mother's breast is a potential consumer whose inborn love of sweetness can be manipulated into an addiction to the sugary goods the system purveys.

There is a sucker born every minute.

WITH FRIENDS LIKE THAT

We are born unfinished creatures, dependent—by nature—upon our cultural environment to render our humanity into its finished form. The fact that our world will not be an entirely natural one— that is, one determined solely by genetically transmitted information—is itself embodied in our genetic structure.

Our *daimōn* comes, as it were, with generic instructions, relying upon our cultural teachers to help us with their application to the particularities of life among our cultural kind. However wise the inherent constitution we are given by our Founding Father, like our other good constitution it wisely does not express itself in terms that would presume to anticipate all future contingencies. For that, we are inescapably dependent on the interpretive judgment of our cultural authorities.

But since the emergence of civilization out of the already venerable cultural development of humankind, the pervasive problem of power has generated problems with the appointive process. As human society evolved in substantial opposition to the needs of human nature, our system developed a vested interest, as it were, in subverting our natural wisdom. The market system, while far from the worst offender in this painful history, is no exception.

The market is interested in using us in the two roles of producer and consumer. As producers, we ought not be too attentive to the messages from our bodies. For some years after I had completed my sentence in our educational system, I was critical of the ineffectiveness of the schooling process to which I had been subjected. The schools I attended were supposedly good ones.

Wherever my parents moved, they chose our neighborhood with the quality of the schools as the principal determinant. The best schools in the state. But I always felt that I learned less per hour spent in school than in just about any of my other pursuits. Why didn't these good schools do a better job of educating?

Then it came to me: these schools were not ineffective; they were just teaching a different lesson from those ostensibly in the curriculum. What we were taught was to subordinate our interests and impulses to the demands of an external structure; to tolerate boredom without complaint; to do repetitive, empty tasks to specifications; to regard clock-time as real and to become deaf to our biological rhythms; and generally, except in the domain of competitive sports—in which the dominant spirit is the striving to be on the right side of the cleavage of the universe between winners and losers—to detach ourselves from our bodies. At teaching these lessons, my traditional public schools were extremely effective.

The medium was the message, and the tedium of the medium was at the heart of the message. All this was "good" education, if that meant the preparation of children to take their places in a productive, industrial market economy.

In the book *Mechanization Takes Command*, Siegfried Giedion traces the ways in which the rise of the industrial economy transformed the nature and rhythm of human labor. As machinery became increasingly central to the productive process, the traditional approach to work, with its pace dictated by that of the human body, was supplanted by the dictates of the mechanical apparatus. The epitome of this process was the famous time-and-motion work of the American Frederick Winslow Taylor. "In Taylor's work," writes Giedion, "the human body is studied to discover how far it can be transformed into a mechanism." The stresses incurred by workers as "wrong or slow-working methods are replaced by rational ones . . . [and] human movements became levers in the machine,"[26] were considerable. When Charlie Chaplin got swept up off the assembly line into the giant gears, he was enacting an arduous human transformation that had been wrought upon generations of workers by the evolving economy.

Efficiency of production was Taylor's obsession. In this, he was but a visible agent of the invisible force lines of compulsion exerted by the market system. Efficient producers render the inefficient obsolete. And in the marketplace, as in Taylor's calculations, the human costs of this mechanization do not figure in. The larger gears in which the human body and its natural voice are being ground into silence are, indeed, the whole overarching mechanism of the efficient market economy.

Just as it is not the *daimōn*, but the system, that governs man or woman as producer, so also in our role as consumers is the system the enemy of our deeper selves.

What is right desire, and what desire wrong, in the search for fulfillment? The voice of advertising is consistent in its advice: "The good life in advertising is mainly characterized by pleasure," write Andren et al. in concluding their thoroughgoing content analysis of American advertising.[27] The gurus of the institution of advertising have explicitly declared the same thing. Jonathan Rowe reports that "Dr. Ernest Dichter, a pioneer in motivation research, has said that the task of advertising is not primarily to sell products, but to convince the American that 'the hedonistic approach to his life is a moral, not an immoral, one.'"[28]

The eudaimonist would maintain that the message of the market to the consumer strengthens wrong desire and is not directed to the true self, that the path to true fulfillment is not through the unbridled pursuit of pleasure, and that therefore the voice of the market is a voice of seduction.

Between the voice of the market and the ideology of the market there lies a fundamental contradiction: the ideology justifies the system by declaring us rational, while the voice of the system, heard in the medium of advertising, strengthens the system by exploiting our capacity for irrationality.

This exploitation is most obvious in the case of advertising that is directed at children. Young children, it has been discovered, do not understand what an ad is; to them, it seems to be just another form of programming. Because they "lack the capacity to understand what an advertisement is all about," they are especially vulnerable. In their suggestible condition, more than half the first graders interviewed in a study during the 1970s "wanted every toy or game they saw advertised on TV."[29]

No philosophy of the rational actor—from the Greeks to modern times—has maintained that children are equipped, unprotected and unguided, to take full responsibility for themselves. This capacity, rather, is a supposed asset of maturity. Yet the medium of advertising has been as adept at finding, as it has been determined to capitalize on, the chinks in the defensive armor of *adult* rationality.

The medium of television, says Jerry Mauder, a former advertising executive, puts viewers into a state of consciousness like daydreaming or meditation, a state in which we are in "the right mental condition for the placement of images." The many changes in focus and viewpoint of the TV image are so difficult to keep up with, he says, "you just submit to it."[30] This facilitates a kind of persuasion different from that of rational discourse.

Even before the dawn of the flickering television screen, the ad men were utilizing the comparatively unguarded paths of visual imagery to bypass the critical faculties of consumers. Roland Marchand, in *Advertising the American Dream*, describes how advertising created "icons" with their visual images of products. As Margarita Laski had noted that the creators of advertising had wanted to see themselves "as delivering not only the goods but the Goods,"[31] so did it pay industry to divert the deepest spiritual values of our culture from the realm of the sacred to the goods they were peddling.

This usurpation could not be carried out openly, however, without provoking the outrage and resistance of the very people whose reverent obedience to their marketing commandments they were endeavoring to secure. The use of certain words was therefore abjured, says Marchand, words such as "'worship,' 'pray,' 'bless,' 'revere,' 'bow down to,' or even 'adore' to describe the attitude the consumer should take toward the product." Words have an explicitness in our awareness that more readily will evoke our critical judgment. The ad men could enter our spiritual consciousness more safely on the less explicit, hence less defended, path of the visual icon. "Illustrations did not observe such limits, and their subtlety in inducing a reverential attitude from a reader made it harder to discount their appeal to the proper degree."[32]

Marchand provides examples of the use of "visual clichés" to make products "into virtual idols"; for example, the use of the numinous aura that painters had used for saints and Saviors would now surround the latest vacuum cleaner. The bounds of the permissible move relentlessly forward. Now Toyota has ads on television using Handel's "Hallelujah Chorus" to convey the wonders of driving their automobile. With such devices, advertisers were "creating a secular iconography for the age. . . . As an ad in *Printer's Ink Monthly* offhandedly noted in 1928, advertisements were 'beginning to occupy the place in inspiration that religion did several hundred years ago.'"[33]

Through this medium of communication, the economic system could fasten its insatiable lips to the body of our culture and suck out for its own nourishment the ancient spiritual energies of our cultural heritage.[34]

Nothing sacred, only profits without honor.

THE CULTURE OF SEDUCTION

That it bypasses the critical faculties is not, by itself, a basis for condemning the guiding voice with which the market whispers and shouts continually in our ears. All great artists, all full-bodied communications, operate at many levels. If our religious teachers or our psychotherapists or our dramatists were limited to the terms of completely explicit, fully rational discourse, our cultural sphere would be flat, the realm of our consciousness impoverished.

What distinguishes the teaching of the market is the cynicism of its manipulation of the student. The teacher is really a con artist. What the teaching of the market purports to be doing and what it is actually doing are very different things. Here is another quote from a giant of advertising, in this case Ernest Calkin, back in those bald-faced golden days of 1926: "The happiness of the reader should be the real topic of every advertisement. The happiness of the advertiser should be carefully camouflaged."[35] But of course it is not the consumer's happiness that is the *real* target of the advertiser, it is the consumer's *money*. A fool and his money are soon parted. And the market is ingenious in the cultivation of our folly.

It is not just the means and motives but ultimately the effects of the teachings that justify the condemnation of the market as a teacher. What it teaches as the road to the good life does not lead there.

In his provocative and highly personal exploration of our possessive culture—*About Possession: The Self as Private Property*—John Wickse turns to Jean Jacques Rousseau to illuminate the futility of the pursuit of happiness through the possession of commodities and the cultivation of the pleasures they offer. Rousseau criticized the hedonistic and possessive approach to life, saying it buys pleasure without happiness. "Pleasure without happiness occurs when false and superfluous desires are perceived as true needs."[36]

There are clues that indicate that the gratified desire is the wrong one (just as the feeling of *eudaimonia* serves as a signal of our being on the right path). Rousseau's observation about the craving for goods to possess is one such clue about the misguidedness of the market's approach to the good life. Not having these goods, wrote Rousseau, is for modern man "more cruel than possessing them was sweet." People are "unhappy to lose them without being happy to possess them."[37]

What is disclosed here is not the liberty of free people but the bondage of the addict. As Alan Watts—a man who evidently drank himself to death—once said: "You cannot get enough of what you don't really need."

In part, the market in its teachings reflects and expresses a spiritual confusion that is a long-standing part of our culture, a confusion that the economic system did not itself deliberately create. In that sense, its teachings could be misguided without revealing bad faith. But let us not forget the camouflaged happiness of the salesman for the sake of which he is willing to sacrifice the happiness of the buyer. The lack of integrity is an integral part of the picture.

A wonderful illustration of this sacrifice of the buyer is found in Eugene Linden's *Affluence and Discontent: The Anatomy of Consumer Societies*. In this story, Linden himself was the salesman. It was Linden's job to sell encyclopedias. Specifically, he was selling the *New Standard Encyclopedia*, which Linden describes as "the worst encyclopedia being marketed" in that year. Considering the five-hundred-dollar price tag on the set, as Linden says, one would think that if a salesman were successful in getting a blue-collar family to consider in principle the purchase of an encyclopedia, "they would shop around" before committing to the one offered. "But," he tells us, "this was not the case. In the thrall of the sales pitch, people did not behave rationally."[38]

How could the salesman induce people into such a large and unwise expenditure? Linden offers his explanation. He begins with the status anxiety of the working class in the America of that time (1968), where "it was culturally insupportable for a workman to work with his hands and feel good about it." Next,

Linden explains the meaning of children in the American mythology, as the means "for the American to redeem his life." Children, he says, "are the materialistic equivalent of the Hindu notion of reincarnation."[39]

Upon this foundation, the salesman can build his manipulative structure. The first step is to provoke the buyers' anxieties about their own achievements, and the next is to offer a numinous fantasy of the children's success, attached, of course, to the purchase of the product. What the salesman sells, Linden explains, is a "convenient fiction" to enable the buyer momentarily to set aside the insecurities the salesman has worked to exacerbate. "What the customer buys with his purchase," we learn from the former salesman, "is a ticket back to the dormancy from which he has been aroused."[40]

This racket, as Linden outlines it, is the commercial equivalent of the extortion extracted by gangsters selling "protection." When the gangster sells protection, what he protects the buyer from is the threat the seller himself creates. When Listerine virtually manufactures the fear of "halitosis" with its advertising campaign, when the sellers of that previously mentioned stationery evoke images of malicious talk behind one's back, or when the encyclopedia salesmen induce a family of limited means to pay five hundred dollars to be allowed to sink back into the relative comfort that preceded the salesman's knock, something similar is being transacted.

There are a couple of important differences. Whereas the gangster creates the threat out of nothing, the voice of the market is more likely to strengthen fears already present. What do my friends really think of me? Is my life a failure? On the other hand, over the course of years and then generations, a persistent effort by a powerfully pervasive system can eventually harvest the fruit from orchards of insecurity and fear that the system itself originally planted.

The other most salient difference between these two forms of the protection racket is the greater ability of the legal extortionist to obscure the nature of the transaction. The shop owner who forks over a monthly payment to his "protector" is under no illusions about what he is buying. The gangster may use circumlocution—"We wouldn't want some fire to break out accidentally"—but he has no need to "stimulate an unconscious association in the buyer" as does Linden's encyclopedia salesman. The power of the process of the extortion that our economic system can legally employ for its enrichment derives from its ability to hide what is happening. By manipulating the unconscious, by creating a transaction in which one side is aware and the other unaware, the market's system of selling can pull off that dream of the con artist, so splendidly dramatized in the film *The Sting*: to fleece the mark without his ever knowing he was touched by the shears. From the mark's point of view, the communication was really about *his* happiness, while the happiness of the seller was successfully camouflaged.

"The purchaser," Linden concludes, "is activated by the sales pitch into performing his role in a consumer society; a sales-resistant family on a shoe-string budget is transformed by the pitch into an avid consumer of the unnecessary."[41]

WHO NEEDS PROTECTION FROM THE PROTECTION RACKET?

Now, the wary reader may feel at this point that he or she is being manipulated by polemical overstatement into buying an unwarranted conclusion. The first objection might be that it is not really true that the buyer is unaware of the seller's intentions. Americans generally know what selling is about. We grow up laughing at the Music Man and the way he manipulates a town's concerns about the moral fiber of its youth into a desire to buy band uniforms for a fictitious musical program. And, secondly, more sophisticated Americans have generated a substantial literature, from Vance Packard to Roland Marchand and Stewart Ewen, exposing the manipulations of the advertising industry. So who needs protection from the protection racket? And who needs yet another critique of the voice of the contemporary American salesman, the ad man?

A good answer to the first, and partially valid, objection is provided by Ivan Preston in his book on "puffery" in advertising and selling, *The Great American Blow-up*. Preston is exploring the legal protection our society affords puffery, that is, protection of the right to make claims that are not true but, according to our law, are not "deceptive." Puffery is illustrated by claims such as the *Chicago Tribune*'s representing itself as the "world's greatest newspaper," or Blatz describing itself as "Milwaukee's finest beer."[42]

No one would disagree with Preston that "you can't always 'be sure if it's Westinghouse' . . . [or that] State Farm isn't 'all you need to know about insurance.'" But the law and the advertising industry disagree with Preston's objection that such debasement of communication constitutes deception and is a threat to the public. What does "finest beer" mean? "The regulator's answer is that it means nothing." And people know they ought not to pay attention to such claims. Why protect the intelligent American public from such transparently "meaningless" verbiage? In the words of the chairman of *Advertising Age*: "How far down the road of idiocy do we go to 'protect' the person who would consider such a phrase a guarantee of superiority?"[43]

But Preston's counterargument seems to me irrefutable. And it applies to all the methods used by the advertising industry: *if it didn't work, the masters of selling wouldn't use it.*

The courts, Preston tells us, upheld the right of a car salesman to say that a car was air-conditioned even though it wasn't. The court said that it was permissible to make such a statement because the claim was "obviously false." But, Preston retorts, "if

buyers always noticed the falsity, then why would the salesman
have bothered to say it?" Likewise, Preston sees through the disclaimers of the advertising industry that it isn't fooling anybody
but a few idiots, saying, "The line would not be used if Blatz felt
it had no effect."[44]

A 1971 study by a market research firm, R. H. Bruskin Asso-
ciates, bears out the soundness of Preston's assumption that the
mavens of marketing know what they are doing. Twenty-two percent of a sample of U.S. citizens regarded as completely true, and
36 percent as partly true, the statement that "State Farm is all
you need to know about insurance"; "You can trust your car to the
man who wears the star" elicited corresponding figures of 21 percent and 47 percent; 43 percent and 30 percent for "Perfect rice
every time"; and so on. "Puffery's continued existence in mass
media" Preston concludes, "shows that advertisers think it effective with a substantial portion of the public in obtaining reliance
and altering purchase decisions."[45]

The puffery problem stands emblematic of the way the voice of
the market reverberates generally in our minds. Even where there
is no "meaningful" claim in terms of logical assertion, we can be
persuaded to act on the basis of "propositions" we would never accept—such as the "proposition" that this vacuum cleaner, pic-
tured here surrounded by a nimbus, is imbued with divine
properties. Even were we to "know" that there is more worth
knowing about insurance than one particular company, we may be
more likely, because a claim to the contrary is echoing in our
minds, to act as though we believe otherwise.

Human consciousness is a complex amalgam of processes, following different rules and operating at different levels. Skillful advertising composes correspondingly complex messages that
operate on us both within and beyond our awareness. Depth psychology has made it clear that the island of conscious awareness
does not control the drama within our psyches. The best we can
achieve is to open the flows of communication among the voices

within us and to mediate their various points of view toward the achievement of integrity.

But this achievement is opposed by the system of selling. It is precisely the *lack* of communication between conscious and unconscious that makes us vulnerable to subtle manipulation. Thus, the system seeks to stay ahead of our awareness. As the American public grows more sophisticated, the ads become less blatantly manipulative, but no less so for that. It is only to the extent that we remain weakened by the lack of integration that the voice of the system can keep us from hearkening to the guiding voice of the *daimōn* and can confuse us enough about our needs that we will part with the resources at our command in exchange for the unnecessary.

The relationship between the voice of the market and the American people is a power relationship. The battle is over the control of resources, but, given the nature of our system, with its protection of liberty, the battle is inevitably fought on the terrain of our hearts and minds. The outright theft practiced by coercive systems is forbidden; the system must *persuade* us to part with our money. And part of the winning strategy of the system is to persuade us that we are so powerful in our liberty that we have nothing to fear, that not only are we masters in our own psychic house but that the system stands as our servant ready to do our bidding. In this perspective, the idea that we buyers "know" what the sellers are up to—in puffery, and more generally—is part of what we have been sold, part of the voice in our minds whose credibility signifies the system's ongoing success in winning the battle.

It is in the perspective of the contest of power raging over control of our minds that a useful response can be given to that second objection: that the manipulative work of advertising has already been adequately exposed by insightful people. Indeed, good work has been done. But in battles over hearts and minds, the battle must be ever waged anew. One does not say, "Church? I went to church once, so why go again?" One returns, to hear old and important truths articulated anew. We celebrate our liberation from bondage in Egypt not once, but every spring, as the earth too renews itself from the cold forces of darkness that bring confinement and death to the animal and plant life of the land. So it is also if we are to be freed from the subtle captivity of the system whose voice bids us erect the tombs of a consumerist society.

A cardinal rule in war is, "Never underestimate your adversary." Advertising serves, as I have said, as the voice of the market system. The market system, in turn, is the most powerful institutional system in our liberal society. For over a century, this dynamo of social power has worked to develop the technology to persuade us to approach life in the way that further enriches and empowers the system, whatever it does or fails to do for our own fulfillment.

Surely, we are not powerless. Nor are we complete fools. Unlike the tyrannies of old, our power system must convince us, and we will not buy into just anything. That is why we get a much better deal than those who lived under the old systems of exploitation, systems that needed to provide only subsistence to its human livestock. Our opportunistic and noncoercive system also supplies us with a lot of what we want.

But we ought not to be naive and equate what we buy with what we want. The same system that in the course of a century has developed global instantaneous communication, and vehicles that can land on Mars, should be presumed to be comparably formidable in the tools it brings to bear upon us. As Preston says, "Selling goods is one of the most expert acts ever developed on our continent."[46]

A MIGHTY BAD TEACHER

When a persuasive technology of the highest order is backed by material resources of enormous magnitude, the result is perhaps the most powerful educational influence in American society. Advertising messages pervade our consciousness. The average American, according to George Will, is exposed to three thousand advertisements every day. These work to influence all of us, but the greatest concern should doubtless be the molding of the thoughts and feelings of children in their most formative years. "We now want kids' involvement with Kool-Aid to be wherever they are," said the senior product manager for the sugar-laden beverage, speaking of his company's getting its trademark on dozens of children's products and events, "at home, at play, at school."[47]

The comparison between advertisement and school as teachers of our children comes to mind. Even back in the 1950s, David Potter, in his famous book on American national character, *People of Plenty*, noted with wonderment that in this nation more money was spent on advertisement than on educating our children through the high school level. In recent years, one frequently hears disturbing findings about how the average American child spends more time in front of the television than in the classroom, and a good deal of that TV exposure means highly effective instruction by the teaching voice of the market system.

Money and time spent do not capture the whole of it, however. It is one of the virtues of the market system, unlike our educational system, that the industry demands of the professionals they hire that they deliver the goods, that is, that their methods work. The act of selling, as practiced on TV, is considerably more expert than the act of teaching students in the classrooms of this continent.

We should not be surprised, therefore, with findings like those recently reported by the Center for Science in the Public Interest. CSPI found that eight- to twelve-year-old children, in a survey of Washington, D.C., and nearby suburbs, were able to give the names of more different brands of alcoholic beverages than of presidents of the United States. It is not just name recognition, of course, that is being taught. Along with such knowledge, the ads impart attitudes. A study conducted by the American Automobile Association Foundation for Traffic Safety concluded that "beer commercials lead children to believe that drinking is safe and associated with masculinity."[48]

A powerful teaching institution is engaged in the enterprise of inculcating beliefs. There is nothing extraordinary about that. Every culture works to inculcate in its members beliefs that are congruent with participation in social life. What is alarming about the voice that the market system seeks to instill in our minds to shape the way we live is, first, the nature of the beliefs and, subsequently, what this implies about the nature of the relationship between teacher and student.

Whether the advertiser is trying to persuade us that beer-drinking is manly, or that Milky Way is a fine thing to eat between meals, or that using infant formula is an advanced and sophisticated way of nourishing one's newborn baby, the overall theme is constant and plain: Meet your needs by purchasing our product. The overall effect of a profusion of such messages is to inculcate that philosophy of life we have already explored: hedonistic in its equation of material pleasure with fulfillment; impulsive in its emphasis on appetite and immediate gratification; and atomistic in its characterization of pleasures as purely private matters. The voice of the market, in other words, works to shape us into those pleasure-worshiping Hobbesian egotists that the upholders of our civilization's moral tradition tell us need to be kept in cages of authoritarian social control.

What does it mean that the most powerful teacher in our society seeks to induce us to believe that this is what life is about, that we should take this approach in our pursuit of happiness?

It would be almost comforting to believe that the values the advertisers are transmitting, whether misguided or not, are their own. After all, by their choice of what to do with their considerable creative intelligence—getting rich by manipulating people—they do seem to be affirming the great importance of material riches in their own lives. And Roland Marchand depicts the early ad men as being the early embodiments of the speeded-up, modern life-style they were to help spread across the country with the images of American life they rendered in their ads.[49]

Even if this is partly true, however, it would be naive not to recognize that deliberate distortion and deception are a central part of the communication process. As Michael Schudson says, in *Advertising: The Uneasy Profession*, in their creations the advertisers are promoting "values that, on a personal basis, few advertisers or copywriters would affirm for themselves or their children." The teacher teaches what he himself does not believe. Advertising "speaks to people as no decent person would speak to a friend."[50]

It is an educational process in which the student is simply a means to the teacher's ends. The voice of the market is not trying to hurt us, just to use us. It is not hostile to our true welfare, simply indifferent. Because we are not complete fools, the market sells us many useful and life-enhancing goods and services, and many advertisements can be seen as helpful communications that serve to bring together rational buyers and worthwhile products. But to the extent that we can be made fools—and this is no small extent, particularly when we are in the hands of a power that can work to misguide us over generations—the system will gladly sacrifice our happiness (or true welfare) to increase its own camouflaged happiness (enrichment). Our minds, our beliefs, our ways of living, are simply the means by which the system can get us to open our purses to them.

To the greater glory of the Almighty Dollar.

Is such an exploitative and abusive teacher a historical anomaly, or have other kinds of cultures produced equally bad teachers?

People have been cruelly exploited and abused in other, non-market societies. When we look at the grisly accounts from Amnesty International, the market's effort to persuade children to eat junk food does not seem to rank up there with electric prods inserted up bodily orifices. Madison Avenue persuading us to buy the unnecessary is less cruel than the Inquisition torturing people for believing the forbidden. Our manipulative Big Brother seems quite benign compared to the one that not only sought to undermine all the religious wisdom of a people's cultural heritage but actively forbade religious instruction and punished those who tried to keep the faith.

The teaching of traditional religion itself was often inseparably intertwined with the apparatus of injustice and tyranny. For centuries it served power to teach people that God would reward those great virtues of staying in one's place and meekly accepting one's hard lot. In the Western world, when political and intellectual revolution managed to break the stranglehold on the human mind of authoritarian and doctrinaire systems, an enormous amount of bitterness welled up to the surface, directed against what was then regarded as the "bad teacher" of the old order: the Church and its clerics. Bad teachers are nothing new.

The teachings of advertising, however, seem extraordinary in the totality of their indifference to the students. Potter, after describing the way advertising seeks to inflame desire and envy, compares advertising with two other institutions, the church and the school. Whatever the present and historical shortcomings of these institutions—and they are considerable—Potter is probably correct in judging that both "have been very self-conscious about their role as guardians of the social values and have conducted themselves with a considerable degree of social responsibility." By contrast, he says, advertising suffers from "an inherent lack of social responsibility." What makes this institution so troubling is that it "has in its dynamics no motivation to seek the improvement of the individual or to impart qualities of social usefulness."[51]

What makes advertising so unadulteratedly manipulative is, I believe, the same social dynamic that makes our situation seem to us comparatively so benign: our system is founded on an ideal of liberty. To the extent that this liberty is understood in the terms of the contract society, as permitting each to serve only himself and requiring no one to care about another, this liberty grants to mighty economic power the license to use and to manipulate by any available means—short of force and outright fraud—whomever it can reach. By the same token, because our liberal society protects us against exploitation by violence—by the slave driver's lash or by armed robbery—persuasion becomes the indispensable tool of exploitative power.

Where the baron of old could come and seize our harvest, leaving just enough for us to survive to plant next year's crop, the captain of industry must make us *choose* to give him our bounty. The opportunities of power thus induce today's baron to make the copywriter's pen as mighty as the bloody sword wielded by the minions of yesterday's. And because we all see ourselves as freely making our own choices, and doing as we please, we regard ourselves as free men and women acting in pursuance of our own interests and values.

We are indeed fortunate, as we believe, but not as fortunate as we believe.

FREE TO BE YOU AND ME

Can free people be trusted to know what is good for them? It proves to be difficult to address this question without addressing the prior question: What is freedom?

In the liberal tradition, the essence of freedom has always been freedom *from* an oppressive authority that compels us to do what is against our will. Liberating humankind from such coercive power has indeed been a significant step along the path of liberty. But there is more to the exercise of power than raw coercion; what comprises the "will" that would be free is correspondingly less self-evident than liberal theory supposes.

That the market system exerts power on a society's evolution by constricting the range of genuine options was the thesis of *The Illusion of Choice*. As in the bounded universe of Einstein's theory, the society evolving within the market's field of forces can appear to proceed in its chosen direction indefinitely without ever coming up against a palpable and insurmountable obstacle, but can nonetheless all the while be diverted by the boundedness of the market's universe.

Similarly, the market system shapes the "will" of its members, so that each individual believes each choice to be his or her own. Power does not need a sword to work its way. Is the encounter of the growing human mind with the advanced technology of market persuasion, armed by billions of dollars in airtime and billboard space any less a mismatch than the encounter of the unarmed serf on foot with the mounted knight in armor?

The liberal society of the market tells us freedom means the liberty to indulge the whim, desire, or craving of our selection. Choose your pleasure. So, we are free to have it our way at Burger King or to let McD's do it all for us. As men and women free in this sense, we experience the "self" as a repository of desires. And the champions of morality in this system, seeing us flock to junk food and titillating TV, are confirmed in their belief that human nature cannot be trusted, that the self, unfettered by authoritarian structures, is self-indulgent and base.

This analysis of the workings of the market affords a broader view of how people can be subordinated to power. But we are in need of a correspondingly deeper understanding of what it would mean to be free. Such understanding is offered by eudaimonism. To be free, says the eudaimonist, is to be able to live in accordance with one's *true self*.

To be free in this sense would require that one's cultural environment had not succeeded in alienating one from that true self— a requirement that suggests either that the free individual lives in a nourishing cultural system or had succeeded in liberating him- or herself from the bondage of an oppressive one.

The person who lives in accordance with the true self is free in a different sense from the shopper in the mall with a hundred dollars to spend. The shopper enjoys a broad range of external choices and is at liberty to consult that part of the psyche from which come the desires to which the market caters. The freedom of the eudaimonist is not so indeterminate, and its essence is not the length of the menu that the external world puts into one's hands. Rather than scanning a limitless horizon of options, the person living in the service of the true self feels, like Luther breaking from the Church to follow his calling, that "I can do no other." Rather than looking to the outside for options, the eudaimonist listens to an inner voice that points out the path that should be followed.

The distinction between these two kinds of freedom is articulated by Norton. One kind of freedom he calls "caprice," which he defines as the "freedom to do whatever one freely wills," and which is "predicated upon the mere absence of restraint." The kind of freedom "endorsed by eudaimonism," by contrast, "is not caprice but strictly freedom of and for self-determination."[52] This freedom is defined by a *presence*, the presence of an inner voice, one's *daimōn*, that guides one according to knowledge of which desires are right and which wrong for the realization of one's true being.

The freedom to "become what you are," in the phrase of the ancient Greek poet Pindar, is not an easy one to live up to. It demands discipline. Bringing forth one's individuality means ordering one's inner polity according to sound judgment of what is right for one's growth and what is wrong. Unlike the individualism of the market, which Norton describes as "smug" in regarding "individualism as a fait accompli,"[53] that of the human potential movement—properly understood—is an accomplishment.

Taught to regard one's self as a mechanical given, we neglect
to attend to our true self and become vulnerable to outside voices
telling us that we can "have it all," and that we should "do it now."
Persuaded that immediate gratification is a sufficient guide to
right desire, we fall easily into the grip of consumerist hedonism.
Traditional morality has always been suspicious of a life of immediate gratification. Its position was cleverly lampooned by the
Victorian writer Samuel Butler: "Morality turns on whether the
pleasure precedes the pain or follows it. . . . Thus, it is immoral
to get drunk because the headache comes after the drinking, but if
the headache came first, and the drunkenness afterwards, it would
be moral to get drunk."[54]

The eudaimonist concurs that a concept of "utility" that focuses excessively on the immediate is not of much use. The question to be asked is not simply, How do I feel? but, Where will
this ultimately take me? What is the utility of junk foods and junk
reading, if I recognize that the aftertaste tomorrow derives from
the truth that "You are what you ate"? It is not that plunging voluntarily into pain is virtuous. The point, rather, is that laying the
foundation for one's true, lifelong enjoyment of "utility" takes
effort. The greatest satisfaction in life comes from the realization
of the true self, and this takes effort.

Effort is not the same thing as pain for a healthy organism. The
little son who, two years ago, knew to suck on his mother for
nourishment is now practicing his climbing techniques over the
back of the sofa, with considerable exertion. No one had to assign him such exercises in motor control. His climbing is a natural
expression of his being. It is when we are ill or injured that effort
is a strain. In distress, we seek ease and comfort.

In a society that truly nourished us, one that fortified the
healthy human organism, we would not so readily participate in
the shallow consumerism of contemporary America. When one

becomes accustomed to a diet of whole foods, junk foods no longer taste so comforting. They taste like junk. When one has a healthy appetite for life, when one is hungry to engage the realities of our existence, the additional work required to experience a Shakespeare play is not a strain, and the mindless sitcoms on network TV do not soothe and amuse. They annoy. When the core of one's own individuality has been encouraged, the homogenous shopping malls do not seem a sanctuary to seek out when the going gets tough. They seem barren. When one is getting what one really needs, one does not feel unable to get enough of our countless superfluities.

HANGING TOGETHER AND FALLING APART

When the wave of liberation washed over Eastern Europe recently, we celebrated their release from totalitarian bondage. We also indulged in a few rounds of self-congratulation. Our way of life has been vindicated, we told ourselves, as the nations freed of Soviet occupation rushed to become capitalist democracies. We welcomed these new-uncaught, rejoicing peoples to our world, which we describe to ourselves in terms of liberty.

Well, yes and no. We do enjoy real liberty, and our political economy has a great deal to offer that is of tremendous value. But we are far from wholly free, and are the less free the less we recognize our own forms of bondage.

When the human potential movement arose to encourage each person to blossom forth in his or her fullness, our civilization's truncated vision of what we are rose up to condemn the quest as an indulgence in selfishness and narcissism. If our society is not to degenerate further into the morass of narcissistic atomism, according to our society's predominant morality, the self needs not to be liberated but to be fenced in and restrained by commandments from on high.

Here are the lineaments of our chains made visible. Our injuries have made us petty creatures, and have blinded us to our true nature.

When Vaclav Havel, only recently released from his prison cell, was chosen to lead the people of Czechoslovakia on the path of liberty, he spoke to his people of the legacy of bondage they all bore within them. Their experience of tyranny, he told them, had left them "morally ill." Living in "a decayed moral environment," Havel told his countrymen, had taught them

> not to believe in anything, not to care about one another and only to look after ourselves. Notions such as love, friendship, compassion, humility and forgiveness have lost their depth and dimensions, and for many of us they represent merely some kind of psychological idiosyncrasy, or appear as some kind of strange relic from times past.

The whole world was moved to hear a head of state speaking spiritual truth to his people, summoning them to recover their "depth and dimension," reminding them that genuine liberation is not just a matter of dismantling the oppressor's garrisons within their land but has a spiritual dimension as well. The bondage enters the soul, making the deep values of the true self seem but relics of some world long dead.

When the Children of Israel were freed from enslavement in Egypt, the Lord found that it was necessary for the generation of slaves to die out, wandering in the wilderness, before the way to the Promised Land could be opened to them. The bonds of slavery constricted their hearts and minds and disabled them from participation in the new life of liberty in the land of the father of their tribes, Israel.

Our own bondage makes many of us believe that it is only through the commandments of authority, only under the lash of the overseer, that we can be domesticated for social living. We imagine our state of nature to be one of Hobbesian solitariness, the pressure of our selfish instincts to be continually straining against the yoke of having to take anyone into account but our own hungry, greedy selves. Our wounds persuade us that these symptoms, which Havel diagnosed as "moral illness," are the natural traits of human individuality.

An empirical study shows us to be quite otherwise. Alan Waterman culminates his exploration of *The Psychology of Individualism* with a report on his investigation into the correlates of individualism. The "individualism" with which Waterman is concerned is the kind we have been exploring, the kind characterized by the pursuit of self-actualization and by the cultivation of attention to an internal guiding voice. Waterman finds the moralist's apprehensions about the consequences of this kind of individualism to be wholly misguided.

The critics of the human potential movement have feared that this cultivation of the self "would contribute to mistrust, manipulation of others, and unscrupulous competition." But Waterman's data showed, on the contrary, that the cultivation of the self—in producing higher self-esteem and less defensiveness, and in providing a more solid basis for feeling good about oneself than the process of invidious comparison—yielded "a reduced likelihood of treating [others] in manipulative and exploitative ways."[55]

The view of the self as an inherently petty thing leads critics to believe that individualism, by creating "atomistic self-containment, narcissism and atomism," would make its adherents "unlikely to engage in cooperative and helpful behaviors." But Waterman's findings show "it is just those persons most expressing the [individualistic qualities being measured] who are the ones willing to participate in mutually rewarding activities and willing to be helpful to others."[56]

Similar results were found when the researchers tested a hypothesis about the quality of the human relationship established by different groups of people. Contrary to the misgivings of the critics, "Individualists appear more capable of sharing their personal feelings, of being emotionally supportive, and of committing themselves to the people with whom they form relationships."[57]

The well-nourished, healthy self is a very different creature from the wounded self our bondage has produced. What it feeds on, and what it is prepared to feed back into the world, is quite different, in terms of spiritual nourishment, from what the smaller, injured self craves with its compensatory appetites.[58] When we go deep into the self, it turns out, when we embrace those depths from which we have become alienated, we do not end up still further removed from one another. Rather, we break through into a place where a deeper sense of connection and caring opens up.

Narcissism, we should recall, is a defense for the emotionally malnourished. Loving others comes best from those who know how to love and honor their own selves. And that knowledge, in turn, comes from growing up in an environment that loves and honors us for our true selves. To believe we must choose between the nourishing of ourselves and the creation of a harmonious society is to shackle ourselves to systems that wound us.

The true self can be trusted to be, not an amoral social atom, but a responsible part of a larger whole. One way of understanding this is to recall that our state of nature was not solitary but communal. In the beginning, we survived primarily by the net formed by the caring bonds among us. To go to the core of the human self, therefore, is to contact a being that has been crafted, more than for anything else, to contribute to the well-being of a closely knit community.

The infant suckling its mother's breast will grow up to suckle her children, or to guard and provide for his offspring and their mother during their extended period of vulnerability and dependency.

INTO THE SELF AND BEYOND

There is another possible way of understanding how the nourishing of the true self, rather than encapsulating a petty ego, reveals our deep connectedness. Perhaps the *daimōn* that, in Norton's view, leads to "personal destinies" should be understood as something more than our own personal guide. Perhaps the cultivation of what, from one point of view, is our own *individuality* is, from a larger perspective, a form of fidelity to or alignment with a *transcendental* force.

The idea of God enters into Norton's exploration of eudaimonism only to differentiate his views from those of Kierkegaard. To Kierkegaard, says Norton, eudaimonism is ultimately impossible because, the person's "individuating principle" being from God, there "is no way [the individual] can contribute out of his own resources."[59] Norton would have us claim our own individual powers.

But a different view of God permits a different understanding of our *daimōn* that weds Norton's respect for our resources with Kierkegaard's sense of our connection with a transcendent guide. What if God is not just a power above us? What if our "own resources" are understood as being themselves manifestations of God? The *daimōn* that would guide us might then be at once our own and the voice of God.

We are not each created in a vacuum, islands unto ourselves. Our individuality exists for itself, but not just for itself. It is also part of the larger stream of humanity that has momentarily washed us onto the shore of life. We are each called upon to realize the particular ideal embodiment of humanity that is our own unique potential as part of perfecting the larger enterprise of human life on earth.

Digging deep, we break through into that sacred underground aquifer that connects one well with all the others. Here we find liberation—liberation in the knowledge that being truly free to be ourselves and being the Servants of God are the same thing. *Habits of the Heart* reports the experience of an American student of Zen. "I started Zen to get something for myself, to stop suffering, to get enlightened. Whatever it was, I was doing it for myself. I had hold of myself and I was reaching for something. Then to do it, I found I had to give up that hold on myself. Now it has hold of me, whatever 'it' is."[60]

NATURE AND NURTURE

I believe in the sanctity of human nature. That is the heart of it. Deep within us, I believe, we are endowed by our Creator with a guiding voice that is sound and wise. What is necessary in the development of moral and trustworthy human beings is not the construction of cages to restrain the wild beast but the proper nourishing of our sacred core.

It matters whether one believes this or not. It matters quite visibly in my daily life in what I do as a father. What do I want my young daughter to become? And how should I understand my role in bringing about that result? My answer is that she is, potentially, a beautiful rose, and I am but the gardener. The beauty is already in the seed, let alone the bud, and my role is to keep the plant healthy.

By contrast, much of our cultural heritage, as I have been arguing, sees our inborn tendencies as evil growths that must be lopped off. We needn't look so far as the "poisonous pedagogy" Alice Miller describes as shaping Germanic culture and bringing about the monstrous possibility of Nazism. The psychoanthropologist Howard Stein describes the upbringing of children in the heartland of America in not altogether dissimilar terms. In the culture of the American Southwest, the child is regarded as a wild creature that must be broken as a bronco is busted, Stein reports, its will made to submit unequivocally. "Only perfect will-lessness," in this cowboy subculture that plays such a central role in the self-image of America, has been acceptable from children in their relations to the authorities on high, their parents and God.[61] Human nature is seen as something in conflict with the moral life, something that must be overcome.

It is true that, in America, this view has been consistent with a kind of "rugged individualism" that places a high value on liberty. But even the individualist dimension of this culture, which is the other side of the same coin from the authoritarian hostility to the child's nature, rests on a philosophical foundation in which the idea of human nature has been emptied of its moral component. In the political philosophy of John Locke, R. H. Tawney says, "Nature had come to connote, not divine ordinance, but human appetites." The liberal vision that said that "self-interest [though amoral] should be given full play" was not based on a view of any innate human tendency toward goodness.[62] It was, as we saw in the previous chapter, a belief in the ability of the system to make paradise out of parts steeped in vice.

The liberal vision of naturally appetitive individuals and the pious vision of the war of God against the ingrained sinfulness of the human soul share a darkness in their image of our nature. That darkness is pervasive, showing up sometimes in unexpected places. Recall Barry Schwartz's telling account of the "battle for human nature." After delineating the common structure among economic, behaviorist, and evolutionary thought, Schwartz complains that "this picture leaves out any consideration of morality, of how people *ought* to be as opposed to how they are."[63] In this single phrase, it would appear that Schwartz forfeits the whole battle. The picture of human beings as maximizers of appetite satisfaction, Schwartz seems to be conceding, captures what we *are*. It would seem to be up to nurture to make up for the amorality of our nature.

What does it mean to assert—contrary to the dark vision of our nature that is so pervasive—that the "is" of human nature contains within itself the "ought" of how we should live? What does it mean to say that our natural core inclines us toward both the good life for human beings and toward a well-woven moral fabric for the human community?

I am not arguing that we arrive in the world fully formed moral beings. Nor am I maintaining that the nurture we receive from our cultural environment has no important contribution to make. The realization of the "true self" is more complex than that. And so is the matter of dividing "nature" from "nurture."

The limits of an oversimplistic view of the meaning of human nature are suggested by the example of the famous "wolf children" of an earlier era. These children, believed to have been raised apart from human society, among animals—though quite possibly they were, rather, the victims of confinement and neglect by human "caretakers"—were grotesquely disabled creatures. There is no reason to believe that a human infant raised apart from a healthy human environment would turn into a Rousseauian "noble savage" of any sort.

But we are entitled to include some proper nurture *within* our concept of human nature. We are not simply sprung from seeds, like those fuzzy parachutes unleashed by the milkweed and borne by the wind into the wider world.

Consider the rhesus monkey: what is the nature of this creature? A few decades ago, the psychologist Harry Harlow, at the University of Wisconsin, conducted some famous studies in which newborn infants of this species were separated from their mothers at birth. The experimenter placed these unfortunate animals individually with artificial mothers of different sorts: some were placed with "mothers" made of cold wire caging, while the monkeys in the other, luckier group were each placed with surrogates covered with the cozier drapings of terry cloth. Harlow found that those that, in their first formative weeks, received no tactile comfort from their surrogate caretakers developed into profoundly maladjusted adults. They were incapable of relating positively with other members of their species, their incapacity extending into the inability to mate and reproduce successfully. Even just the addition of terry cloth to this tactilely barren and emotionally impoverished setting proved enough to spare the creatures such profound social maladjustment.

Is the nature of the rhesus monkey to be understood purely in terms of the individual's genetics? Is the monkey born with its nature complete? Of course not. Such a view of the creature's "nature" would lead to the preposterous conclusion that those unfortunate wretches rendered by the manipulations of the experimenter incapable of relating to their own kind, or of passing along life, were as valid representatives of the species' nature as the monkeys found living socially in nature.

It makes more sense, I would maintain, to say that the monkey is born with its nature requiring *predictable aspects of nurture* for its completion. The newborn monkey has not been structured to be born as a unit entire unto itself. Its design is founded on the assumption—not unreasonable in the absence of external interference from someone like Harlow—that from birth it will be in the presence of other furry creatures like itself, especially a mother that will hold and nurture it. It is part of the *nature* of a rhesus monkey to be a social being and to be capable of effectively reproducing and rearing its young—even though the *realization of that nature is dependent upon adequate nurture.*

We human beings, too, like the baby rhesus, have embedded in our nature a birthright concerning the social environment into which we will be born.

At a pivotal time in my intellectual and spiritual development, I encountered a marvelous book by the anthropologist Colin Turnbull. Entitled *The Forest People*, this book was a vivid portrayal of life among the Pygmies of the Ituri forest in Africa. These people are among the few hunting-and-gathering peoples surviving into our times. Though it is, of course, something of an oversimplification to assume that their way of living discloses for us how our ancestors lived many millennia ago, they do afford a clue of sorts. What was so moving to me in *The Forest People* was the revelation of the full-bodied humanity and dignity and vitality of these people.

For writing such a book, for describing the human reality he encountered in the anthropological field in such vivid and experiential terms, rather than in the usual desiccated and deadly discourse of most anthropology (as if either the observers or the observed were aliens from some other planet, rather than each group sharing the common bond of their humanity), Turnbull became for me something of a hero.

It was subsequently very disappointing, a few years later, to come across a later piece by Turnbull. This one reported about a group of people called the Ik. The state of affairs among the Ik was abominable. Human relationships had broken down. The members of this society showed striking indifference to the well-being of their fellows, each person seeming to be captivated by that paradoxical combination—not altogether unfamiliar, in less extreme form, to students of modern society—of complete selfishness and a kind of despairing indifference to his or her own fate. The culture and social order of the Ik having been shattered by the encroachment of other, more powerful cultural systems, this diseased society, as depicted by Turnbull, appeared to be on a downward spiral of moral chaos, heading into oblivion.

What disappointed me was not the news of this human tragedy, though reading about the suffering of these people was certainly anguishing. What disappointed me, I recall, were Turnbull's reflections on his diverse experiences in the field—with the Ituri Pygmies, on the one hand, and with the Ik, on the other. Each of these tribes, said Turnbull, should be understood as embodiments of our human nature. Equally. As though health and disease have the same status as a reflection of life's design.

Surely, just as the rhesus infant has the right, for the completion of its nature, to anticipate that it will be born into the loving arms of a furry mother and not the cold carcass of wire mesh, so too does the design of human nature incorporate the foundational assumption of an intact, healthy human society. The Pygmies were born into such a society, and as such reveal to us something about the natural design of human life. The Ik were flailing in the midst of cultural wreckage. Just as the subsequent inability to reproduce of those monkey babies isolated with wire mothers proves that their environment had warped and thwarted the unfolding of their nature, so also does the manifest unviability of the Ik's way of life at the time of Turnbull's observations, as their fractured culture slid toward extinction, demonstrate that their plight is no mirror of human nature.

Accidents happen. Babies are born brain-damaged, having strangled on their umbilical cords. Societies are fatally wounded by catastrophes. The design of life is not proof against mishap. But neither is the nature of the design made manifest by the carnage of such catastrophe.

Human nature is what unfolds when healthy people grow up in a healthy society. The "true self" is what unfolds in a person whose nurture makes good the promise of our birthright to a society that is intact and that operates in harmony with the innate needs of the human being.

Where Is the Blueprint?

Can people be trusted to know what is good for them, and to act in a way that promotes social harmony and integrity? They can if they are born into the right kind of society, one that nurtures the development of the true self.

One might suspect tautological thinking here: the "right" kind of society nurtures the "true" self, which, in turn, inclines toward the right desire. But my position here, far from being tautological, is in substantive disagreement with major aspects of our mainstream worldview.

I believe the true self to be the natural core of the human being. Character, I concede, has to be built—just as the actualization of the self is a challenge and not, as in Norton's characterization of our predominant form of individualism, a fait accompli. The question is, Where is the blueprint? Much of our culture assumes the blueprint for good character must be *imposed* by society upon the growing organism.

In his interesting philosophical critique of narcissism, Eugene Gendlin investigates the assumption, widespread in our psychology, that the levels of the psyche deeper than the ego are chaotic and autistic, while the ego itself is understood to be a socially designed construct. Gendlin's exploration is a "critique of narcissism" in that he is challenging the idea—concomitant with these assumptions—that all the psychological processes that are "earlier than the ego" are narcissistic. But it is the shabby, wholly disrespectful view of our inborn psychological structure that is most pertinent to our present point.

The image of our primitive humanity as essentially chaotic Gendlin finds articulated in Freud. But he traces back further to Kant, and especially to Nietzsche, the "metaphysical assumption that *order is something imposed on something else.*" In Freud, this metaphysical assumption that "organization can come only from domination" leads to a view of the id as a wellspring of chaos and autism. "The ego is an organized entity," wrote Freud, "whereas the id is not." At "the core of our being," he said, is the "obscure id, which has no relations with the outside world."[64]

Freud's own work, as Gendlin also notes, constitutes a rather thorough disproof of his own metaphysics, for discovering the

organic intelligence of the unconscious was one of Freud's greatest contributions. But Freud remained trapped in his reactionary
assumptions about the nature of order as domination. Perhaps
this is part of the reason Freud was much less attuned than his
sometime associate Carl Jung to the potential of the unconscious
as a guiding voice with spiritual wisdom.

It is astonishing to imagine how people could conceive our
primitive, natural being to be an inchoate mass of disordered impulses, related to nothing but its narcissistic impulses. Our ancestors have been on this planet for millions of years, bearing with
them into each generation an organismic readiness to survive in
a complex world. Order is the very essence of the design of life.
It is true of each of our cells. How could it not be true of our natural minds? Even before there was human consciousness, there
was ordered awareness. There was the integrity of the animal
body knowing what to do in the world. This "animal body," as
Gendlin also notes, is in itself the source of a "very complex be-
havioral order."[65]

It is a measure of how far we have been alienated from that organic wisdom that a dominant line of thought in our civilization
could conceive of the order in our functioning as dependent on
"whatever order the prevailing [external] power imposes."[66] To
suppose that the structure of our ego consciousness must be simply an "alien form" imposed upon the body is to imagine that we
somehow survived the eons leading to civilization without knowing what we were doing. What a strange, nonevolutionary view
of how our Mother, the Earth, worked so patiently to make us
. . . not perfect, but far closer to perfect than any order our civilization has yet learned to give to any of its creations. Untimely
ripped from life's natural territory, this ideology condemns us to
the reactionary and oppressive dominion of external powers.

Society must inevitably be like the garrison of an alien conqueror within us, this ideology tells us, for the city of the psyche,

like the sullen peoples of the imperialists' imagination, is incapable of self-government. The ego must be the pharaoh's overseer, because our organic being is not up to doing the work of life.

And what of human freedom? In the wake of a philosophy like Nietzsche's, Gendlin says, "the Western hope for 'free individuals' was viewed as . . . inherently impossible." Since the order in our psychological structure was "considered to be the creation of past domination," the only kind of "liberation" possible was deemed to be through "new domination" in the form of the imposition of "social engineering."[67]

The baby in my lap is not going to "build character" if nothing whatsoever is imposed from the outside. His mother and I will be sure he learns limits. We do not regard the idea of meeting his needs as meaning catering to his every whim. Nor do we think that nurturing the core of his being means yielding to every fit and tantrum. In my observation, the children whose parents make this kind of mistake are deeply relieved when they find some authority that, until the children have completed the task of gaining sufficient control over themselves, will give them limits. In a variety of ways, children tell us that they need *both* to have their *real* needs met and to have their environment place limits on them. The need for limits is one of the needs inherent in the child's nature.

For parents to provide such limits I regard neither as unnatural nor as a replacement of the child's nature by the structure of domination. Providing a child with some kind of limiting is, in my view, as much a part of nature as giving tactile contact to a baby rhesus. Adults with a proper sense of self-respect and with a healthy relationship to both their own impulses and their own discipline are the natural fruit of a healthy human community, and will naturally not let their offspring tyrannize them or others. Nor will they encourage their little one to be a slave to every wish that crosses his or her mind. Such building of character therefore seems to me to be part of the unfolding of the blueprint of our human nature.

By the same token, though the child needs some external authority to help it find its true self, and to distinguish right desire from wrong, the order that characterizes that self is not that of an "alien form" of power displacing some inherent chaos. I try to help my gifted daughter, Terra, recognize those gifts that are among the blessings of her natural endowment and to honor these more than some of her pettier impulses. But I see this merely as a kind of pruning to make more room for the full flowering of the rose that is her true self, what the life force is trying to embody in her. The blueprint for her blossoming was there in the seed, and is not to be imposed by my power or anyone else's.

Perhaps I overstate my case. Perhaps the blueprint for our ideal, true self is not wholly contained in our natural design. Perhaps the "intact, healthy human society" that is our birthright is not sufficient to bring forth our "ideal possibility." Perhaps there is *some* irreducible element of culture *overcoming* our nature in living up to our *daimōn*. Perhaps. I am not sure.

What is irreducible in my argument, however, is a conviction that the natural core of the human being is sacred, that from the wellspring of our nature issues forth the *principal ingredients* of the best of our humanity.

NATURE CALLING

This conviction is integrally connected with a crucial moment in my life, the moment I received my calling. One day in 1970, when my spiritual renewal was gathering momentum after the dark days following my father's death, I was in a landscape where marvelous natural beauty was side by side with the ugliness and pollution of our industrial society. Feeling at that moment unusually open to responding to both the beauty and the ugliness, I was plunged by this contrast into turmoil. A question welled up in my mind: To which of these worlds do I belong?

Here I am thinking thoughts, employing one of the most sophisticated languages civilization has devised. If I identify with my consciousness, must I concede fundamental allegiance to this civilization that seems to trample under the wheels of its juggernaut so much of what is beautiful and sacred?

Coming up against that thought, my mind wheeled and turned. My mind swam to a place of thought beyond words. I felt that I contacted a place in myself way beyond history. In my gut, from that moment, I knew that what I really am is an animal walking upon the earth. This is my real identity, part of the core of my true self—a creature breathing the air, with his feet on the ground, a temporary channel of the stream of life that has been flowing across the earth for time beyond our comprehension. I felt a profound sense of the sacredness and beauty of that stream, and of the core of my being to which it had given rise.

It was immediately after this realization that something happened that has set the course of my life ever since. No sooner had I discovered my true nature than I was given my calling.

In the course of a moment, or maybe two or three, I felt that I was being shown something. It is the only time in my life that it did not seem to be just "me thinking," but rather something sending me a message, conveying to me the images that crossed my mind. I called that something "the Source," and I felt it to be a pulsing and vibrating energy that radiated from the leaves of the trees, that shone in the face of my companion, that is the source of life's unfolding miracle.

What I was shown was a vision of what happened to our species over the past ten thousand years; of how humankind, through its creativity, had stumbled into a process of the evolution of civilization that then unfolded according to a logic of its own; of how the sacred stream of our humanity was then diverted by the concrete channels of this civilization, like a river turned to alien purposes by the California aqueduct; of how we have suffered from this new and still uncontrolled experiment of the living system, this still-cancerous eruption, this evolution emerging out of evolution.

Along with this vision came a charge, an assignment: to develop and articulate what I had just seen. Having thrown aside Pharaoh's overseer, I had become open to other guiding voices. Having contacted the core of my being, I became able to hear in what form I might contribute to the wider world. It was a labor of love, despite the pain at the heart of it, a work of devotion. More than a decade later, it was published as *The Parable of the Tribes*.

ON THE WHOLE: THE PROBLEM OF THE SOCIAL CRITIC

Is it not both unfair and unreasonable to be so critical of our liberal, market society? This question occurs to me as, night after night, I watch and read the news and am led to say, sometimes right out loud, "We sure are lucky to live in this country and not in that one." Consider the threat of dictatorship or anarchy, the scarcity and corruption, in the Soviet Union; the starvation and brutal civil war in the Sudan; the poverty on the denuded hills of Haiti; the stagnation and political upheaval of Argentina; the grim dictatorship in Burma; and on and on around the globe, where people's lives are beset by peril or despair or privation from which at least most of us here in America (and in the other liberal market societies of the West) are sheltered.

It is the Christmas holiday season as I write this. After a sumptuous dinner at a Turkish restaurant on Christmas Eve, a treat from my wife's mother, we return to her apartment and catch the last part of *It's a Wonderful Life*. How different is the moral climate of Jimmy Stewart and Donna Reed's little town from that of the society I am depicting in these pages. Even if Jimmy Stewart's small town of caring people is somewhat overdrawn, so, of course, is my portrait of the contract society and the Hobbesian social atoms of amoral appetite.

I believe in the reality of both Americas.

Every year, by revisiting films like *It's a Wonderful Life*, America confirms a beautiful vision about itself. The savings and loan is not just about squeezing profits, as the greedy Mr. Potter believes, it is about people helping people. It is an institution through which communities can work to make themselves and the families within them decent and whole. As the angel shows the main character, the acts of compassionate people, acting through their corporate roles, do matter, and the bread they cast upon the waters does return to them.

The continuing popularity of such films is itself proof that the heart of America still beats for more than new Chevrolets. These movies function as myths in our cultural system, made so not just by the Frank Capras who make them but by the millions of people who watch and weep over them every year.

There on the other channel another such myth is playing: *Miracle on 34th Street*. Kris Kringle enters the world of American commerce, as well as the lives of a few individual people whose hearts need opening, and brings salvation. When the Santa at Macy's sends customers to other stores to find the gift that is just right, he elicits at first the predictable Hobbesian outrage from the management. But then it proves to be a marketing stroke of genius, as a public thirsty for someone they can trust to be concerned for *them*, not just his own profits, rewards the store whose Santa genuinely cares about the children and their Christmas joy. Give and ye shall receive.

These films were made in an earlier era, one to which idealistic and euphemistic images came easily. They don't make 'em like they used to. Sometimes I feel nostalgic for that era that was so good at expressing ideals and whose mythic expressions still help me contact my love for America. Nothing so fortified my native patriotism as the World War II movies of my childhood years.

But on the other hand, perhaps it is just as well that the rose-colored glasses of that earlier time have been set aside. Perhaps it served a struggling nation, when FDR was its leader, to have news media compliant with the president's wish to have his confinement in a wheelchair made invisible to the public. Having newsreels that, when we see them today, have the look and the sound of propaganda, however, came at a steep cost. All over America, there are people dying of cancers from careless nuclear testing, from chemical dumping, from cigarettes sold with medical endorsement, from asbestos whose manufacturers kept its hazards secret—crimes abetted by an implicit social contact to idealize and support the structures of power in our society.

As we now enter the 1990s, the costs of having had as president in the 1980s an actor from that era of staged idealism are coming due for payment. In getting the government off our backs, the president and his men let the savings and loans run rampant, as if to do so would unleash Jimmy Stewart to build a decent community; what was really unleashed were Charles Keating to buy influence and Neil Bush to get a loan he'd not be required to repay. Now, as the chickens come home to roost, we discover our goose is cooked.

My father used to talk of "grabbing the bull by the tail and looking the facts squarely in the face." It may not be a pretty sight, but I think it is that—more than the rosy vistas of self-idealization—of which we remain more sorely in need.

It is a matter of balance. We need to be committed both to appreciating what is good in America and to improving what is not. At some point, the greater danger might be that we, as a society, are so obsessed with the faults of our system that we disable ourselves from preserving the treasures of our heritage. At that point, the greater service would be lauding the baby rather than harping on the pollution in the bathwater.

That is not, however, where America—or indeed our industrial civilization as a whole—now stands. Ronald Reagan's politics of denial notwithstanding, we stand at a point in our history where the rose makeup of Hollywood idealization has flaked off and there is widespread uneasiness about what the face of our society has and will become. But the system still lumbers on, essentially unreconstructed. As if in a slumber, we go through the motions; acting as if we still believed in the orthodox faith, we have not yet roused ourselves to confront the need for thoroughgoing spiritual and institutional renewal.

When I was a boy, I would hear our leaders speak of America as the world's greatest nation, a land of promise and principle. Today's leaders speak the same phrases, but I do not think they are either spoken or heard with the same conviction. It is not just that our competitors have gained on us, in some ways overtaking us. More than that, I believe, there is a sense as the generations go by that we are challenged to move beyond the old answers. (Indeed, with the passage of time those old answers cumulatively generate new problems.) And we sense that we have not yet met that challenge.

Is American society great? My answer is, compared with what? When I watch the news, I feel lucky to be an American. In the annals of civilized history, American society—and, in general, the liberal market society—is in many ways a noble and successful experiment. But in view of all that is seriously and dangerously amiss, it is a foolish indulgence to invest our emotional energies in cultivating an idealized image of ourselves.

Idealizing what we are stands in stark contrast with *striving toward an ideal that we might become.* We can celebrate how well we compare with other sorry spectacles in the agonized history of civilization. Or we can challenge ourselves to strive to move toward a truly whole and nourishing civilization. The contrast is between the complacency of congratulating ourselves and the inspiration of moving closer to our godly possibilities.

Just as each human being has a *daimōn*, an "ideal possibility" that he or she can work to actualize, so too do we as a whole species. This *daimōn* of humankind is speaking in our ear all the time, summoning us to the task of making a healthy civilization that nurtures whole people. We can hardly begin to envision, from the present stage of our tortured social evolution and from the constricted state of consciousness our traumas have engendered, the beauties of which humanity is capable.

The *eudaimōn* of our kind guides us only rarely with glimpses of our potential species-actualized destiny. More often, its voice goads us by showing us how far short of our full human potential we fall. Every time we open the core of our being to experience the pain of our world's being so out of joint, the *daimōn* of humankind is spurring us to undertake the work of healing.

Thus, while it is not a pleasant task to confront the moral confusion of our times, it is part of the sacred task we are called to do.

CHAPTER 5

The Wages of Sin

'Tis all in peeces, all cohaerance gone.
JOHN DONNE

THE HOLY AND THE DIABOLICAL

It is the essence of living systems that they comprise assemblies of matter and energy composed with exquisite order and wholeness. The moment a human life begins, the embryonic being begins taking materials derived from its mother's groceries and constructing a body whose integration is of mind-boggling complexity. Each individual human form is an expression of a design developed by the species over eons, and will depend for its nurturance and completion on the larger human community in which it is embedded. And the viability of the entire human enterprise, in turn, rests on the encompassing biosphere, whose elaborate cyclings of the stuff of life and whose protective and homeostatic arrangements make the whole planet like one pulsating body.

The preservation of wholeness is a matter of life and death. The moment a human life ends, the web of interconnections is torn, and disintegration returns the stuff of life to dead pieces. Those times when whole communities of species have been wiped off the face of the earth have been—until our present perilous moment in life's evolution—times when events beyond the control of the living system, such as the crashing of a meteor onto the planet, have badly broken the pattern of life's interconnections. Part of the core nature of those values we call sacred is that they serve and are filled with life. They preserve us and connect us with

166

those meanings that animate us. If life is at the heart of the sacred and if wholeness is of the essence of life, then it follows that the idea of wholeness is absolutely vital to our comprehension of the realm of the sacred.

Our language confirms that this is so. The word *holy* is connected at its root with the word *whole*, as well as with those words describing life in its intended form, *hale* and *healthy*. Opposed to the work of wholeness is the diabolical, from the ancient Greek word *dia-ballein*, to "throw apart" or "separate."[1] Breaking things up is the Devil's work.

This juxtaposition between the holiness of bringing things together in health and harmony and the working of the diabolical in driving them apart is captured in a famous description of the nature of sin. According to the theologian Paul Tillich, at the heart of sin is the problem of *separateness:* in the state of sin, one is separated from oneself, separated from one's fellows, and separated from one's God.

In Tillich's theology, it is the human condition to be in this state of sin. These separations are inevitable. But surely, human beings are capable of living at various points along a spectrum running from the holy and whole at one end to the diabolically separate at the other.

In the domain of the human soul, the holy state we can envision is of a person at peace with him or herself. It may be inevitable that a human being will have weaknesses, but one need not be ruled by them. The whole person, rather, can be like the hexagram for "Peace" in the Chinese classic the *I Ching*: the solid lines form the foundation on which the broken lines rest, and the Judgment says, "The small departs, the great approaches."[2] Such a person has integrity, honoring that which is from God by living in the service of his or her greatest gifts.

A world of the holy is one that is marked by love and intimacy within the smaller community and by harmony and justice in the wider society. Each person in the just society gets what he or she deserves. The society protects its treasures for those to come, each generation knowing that it is part of a larger whole streaming through time. Parents cherish their children, who embody the continuity into the future of the gift of life; and children cherish their parents, to whom they are indebted for the receipt of that gift.

In this holy vision, human beings live in harmony with the rest of creation. The needs of the human realm are made to align with the health of the living earth. People recognize their status as being not apart from the rest of the biosphere but a part of it. The clever animal's knowledge of the laws of nature includes an appreciation of that fundamental ecological law that says, "A creature that wins against its environment destroys itself."[3] *Homo sapiens* is wise to the proper limits to his place in the great scheme of things.

How we live, of course, is very different from this vision of a holy human order. Diabolical forces both within and around us are at work driving the pieces apart, till all coherence may be gone.

A FAUSTIAN BARGAIN

The order of our market society does confer upon us many benefits. We are rich beyond the imagining of our ancestors. But at a cost. The forces of the market conspire to "throw apart" much that is holy. For this reason, our placing our destiny in the hands of the market system appears a kind of Faustian bargain.

Faust is the prototypical mythic figure who sells his soul to the king of diabolical forces in exchange for great powers.

On their face, the old legends surrounding the figure of Faust concern the rise of science more than the rise of capitalism. The myths emphasize Faust's pursuit of unholy knowledge more than great riches. Faust as an emblem of evil, of man on the path toward damnation, was useful to the defenders of orthodox piety against the opening of the human mind to the path of intellectual adventure, against the threat to dogma represented by humanism and by the beginnings of the scientific enterprise.

The time and places where the myth of Faust grew in the cultural imagination, however, suggest a connection with capitalism as well. The historical magician around whose actual life the legend of Faust formed dwelt in the Germanic culture of Martin Luther, dying a few years before Luther nailed his theses to the door. In this world, it was not only the pursuit of free thinking that appeared to be the Devil's work. "All around him Luther felt the irresistible attraction and power of capitalism," Norman O. Brown writes in *Life Against Death*, "and interpreted it as the Devil's final seizure of power in this world."[4] The forces of legend swirled around Germany throughout that century but eventually received their finest artistic articulation through the pen not of a German but of an Elizabethan Englishman. In Marlowe's England, the expansion of what Francis Bacon, in his *Novum Organum*, called "the human empire" was the result not only of the new knowledge but also of the new engine of economic development. Two centuries later, Goethe wrote his masterpiece *Faust*, a complex psychological and spiritual exploration of human ambition and yearning. As Marshall Berman clearly shows in his *All That's Solid Melts into Air*, a major element of the story of Goethe's Faust is a "tragedy of development," in which the hero, pursuing the opportunities given him by means of his deal with Mephistopheles, becomes an agent of that economic process of development that sweeps all aside.

The connection between the Faust legend and the market system is suggested in the very structure of the story. The pivotal event in the tale, after all, consists of an act of exchange: a man sells his soul in exchange for certain powers. A bargain is struck. A deal is made. The prototypical interaction of the marketplace serves here as the means by which the protagonist becomes inextricably enmeshed in the world of the diabolical.

It is, of course, too extreme to say that capitalism represents "the Devil's final seizure of power in the world." Yet the phrase does capture an essential element of the picture. For in giving the soul of our society over to the forces of the market, we have allowed the wholeness of the order in which we live to be thrown apart.

BREAKING UP

The rise of capitalism and the rise of science do not just happen to occur together. In essential ways, they were expressions of the same spirit, the same approach.

From a positive vantage point, each represented a victory of freedom and openness over the oppressive restraints of archaic civilization. Where the old order imprisoned all members of society in their traditional social roles, the market opened the way to exploration, and innovation, and social mobility. Where the old regime imposed dogma upon pain of persecution, the new science allowed all questions to be asked, opening the entire cosmos to free inquiry.

But freedom can be dangerous if there is nothing to guide it. Freedom from oppression is essential for the healthy growth of the human spirit. But when freedom entails a disconnection from all order, a perilous kind of chaos ensues. In the form in which they emerged, both science and capitalism have tended to break down the capacity of people to see and to experience the larger orders of which they are part.

Both systems employ a relentlessly analytic approach to the world. It is by breaking the whole into its constituent pieces that the world can be mastered.

The thrust of Western science has been that the whole is but the sum of its parts. Variables are to be isolated. This is the

essence of Galileo's experimental method. When we have so organized the world that the mass of an object can be manipulated
quite separately from its velocity, we will be able to see quite
clearly the relationship between force and acceleration. Bits and
pieces. The need to break things down into the infinitesimal
drove both Newton and Leibniz independently of each other to
develop a new mathematics, the calculus. The source of the
metaphor for Newton's clockwork universe is derived from an
assemblage any piece of which can be taken out, viewed separately,
and replaced with another identical—interchangeable—part.

The problem with a science that is lopsidedly analytic is that
it cumulatively destroys our capacity to see things whole.
Pursuing this approach for some centuries, we end up with a university blind to the universal. The universe of discourse has nothing "uni" about it, having been splintered into so many fields, each
of which has been broken down still further into specialties that,
in the irresistible logic of throwing things apart, disintegrate into
innumerable subspecialties. A kind of intellectual speciation occurs, so that minds working in different areas lose the capability
for cross-fertilization. Mutually unintelligible languages develop,
cursing our towering structures of information with the bane of
Babel. In the worldview that is unbalanced in its devotion to
analysis and its neglect of synthesis, the network of interconnections is lost. Disabled from seeing things whole, we more easily
fall into the illusion that nothing is holy.

Capitalism manifests the same analytic tendency. "Individuals
have to be defined as *barely* as possible so that all their characteristics, skills or capacities are potentially saleable." Everything
must be separable so that everything can be sold. Everything becomes reduced to the status of a commodity, so that nothing can
stand in the way of the advance of the productive empire. The
system's reductionist vision reduces everything to the terms of
its own measure—money—making all values interchangeable as

parts in its clockwork mechanism. Land and labor and capital are just factors of production, and those dimensions of interconnection and wholeness that do not feed the system of production are invisible and without value. "What is required is for the individual to be isolated," writes Abercrombie in articulating Marx's critique, "bare and separable from social ties."[5]

One of our most eloquent contemporary critics of the market's calculus, of its ceaseless undermining of the systems of interconnection that preserve the health of living systems and the meanings of human life, is Wendell Berry. In his book *Home Economics*, Berry laments in particular the disintegrative impact of market forces on the rural communities to whose values he himself is so deeply attuned: "The industrial economists cannot measure the economy by the health of nature, for they regard 'nature' as simply a source of 'raw materials.' They cannot measure it by the health of people, for they regard people as 'labor' (that is, as tools or machinery parts) or as 'consumers.' They can measure the health of the economy only in sums of money."[6]

IT'S NOT NICE TO RAPE MOTHER NATURE

The problem with making a pact with the Devil is not, ultimately, that it is forbidden so much as that it is misguided. Our allegiance should be to God not because we are supposed to be on His side but because the order of God is on ours. The pact with the Devil is a bad bargain.

The figure of Greek myth King Midas might be seen as a spiritual ancestor of Faust. He gets his wish, that everything he touches should turn to gold. But his wish embodies his unholy ignorance of the vital flows that connect him with the world and sustain his life. His greed becomes his undoing, as his food turns to inedible gold. Unholy wishes with diabolical consequences.

We are part of a living system on earth, a system that drew out of the dust of the earth a seething, interconnected body composed of many organisms, of which our species is but one. This system not only created us but continues to sustain us. Every breath we take—drawing upon an atmosphere that the biosphere itself composed—affirms our ongoing dependence on the health of the whole living system.

Yet, at an accelerating rate, our civilization is breaking apart the network of interconnection and exchange on which all life on earth depends. In our Midas-like ignorance of the nature of life, we sate our lust for wealth while we erode the foundation of our existence. We forget that a creature that defeats its environment destroys itself. "Winning against" is not part of the holy order of life. The idea that existence is a Hobbesian war of elimination is itself an artifact of the diabolical processes that corrupt our thinking.

We live on a dying planet. Nowhere is this more painfully visible than in the jungles of the Amazon, where for a few years of gold the forces of the international economy are laying waste a living order that it took hundreds of millions of years to create. "My dream," says Gilbert Mestrino, a Brazilian politician, into the newsman's camera, "would be to look at this enormous, empty land, and find man, work, and the rational use of resources."[7] It is, of course, only through a reductionistic vision like that which measures everything through profit that such a land—seething with an incredible diversity of life, with species not yet counted or named—could appear "empty."

All kinds of diabolical forces throw apart the wholeness of nature as it is rendered in the consciousness of this "rational" man: "I come from a Christian background," he continues, "where Christ taught us that man should take from nature what sustains him. Therefore, I just cannot accept the preaching that man can die but the tree cannot. So, if one day, the world must be destroyed, the last to be destroyed should be man."[8]

It is a rationality escaped from reason that could conceive of the living order as an elimination tournament. Ignorant of the sacred web of interconnection and synergy that makes the bio-sphere—were it not, perhaps, for the disruptive impact of our civilization—a virtual perpetual motion machine, Mestrino imagines that we can win against our environment. To win is to be the last to be destroyed, in this diabolical vision. To see the world thus is to forfeit the chance, afforded us by the holy order of the biosphere, for eternal life—or at least as eternal as the survival of the sun in its present form, which is to say, another half dozen billion years.

This Brazilian's vision is a message from the forces of destruction. "One day the world must be destroyed." The last to be destroyed is man, triumphant that he has first laid waste the planet, in the "rational" effort to sate his greed.

The foremost psychologist of the wellspring of greed, Melanie Klein, has written that "at the unconscious level, greed aims primarily at completely scooping out, sucking dry, and devouring the breast." Greed is that "impetuous and insatiable craving, exceeding what the subject needs and what the object is able and willing to give." Its aim, she says, is ultimately to destroy the breast.[9]

In an insatiable craving for more than they need, those who run our modern economy seek to scoop out more than this living planet, in its generosity, spontaneously offers us. It is no coincidence that those, like this Brazilian, who rationalize our unbridled greed are killing our Mother, the Earth.

THE DELLS

This Brazilian politician may be more extreme than the mainstream of our economy in his relation to nature. Or perhaps he's simply more baldly explicit. Nonetheless, a central element of the market system in general is the spurious type of rationality that subverts the wholeness of the natural order and the relationship between the human and the natural.

The land, writes Karl Polanyi, "invests man's life with stability; it is the site of his habitation; and it is a condition of his physical safety; it is the landscape and the seasons. We might as well imagine his being born without hands and feet as carrying on his life without land." And yet, the market economy works "to separate land from man and [to] organize society in such a way as to satisfy the requirements of a real-estate market."[10]

The question of the place of the land in our system of values was much on my mind when I lived, some years ago, in Prescott, Arizona.

Of the many beautiful places there, my favorite was an area called the Granite Dells. The Dells convinced me that there is something to the idea shared by the American Indians and the ancient Greeks that in some special places, spirits dwell—that to visit these places is to make a spiritual journey.

From a distance, the Dells form a seam stretching across the plain, rounded rocks glowing pink like flesh fresh from a hot shower. Up close, this rocky core of primeval hills provides a perfect place to climb and jump, and to witness how when nature destroys its own creations, it is simply forming a new kind of beauty. In the low places, the worn away pieces of granite make a soil where cactus and pine and oak grow. And at the very bottom, by the creek, a ribbon of leafy cottonwoods shows how soft rocks can become.

One of my friends when I lived in Prescott was a man born and bred in the area, born to the family business of investing people's money and bred to the individualist creed for which the region is known. After wise-cracking with each other, we would settle into some good-natured ideological argument. I remember the day his belief in the sanctity of private property and my belief in the sanctity of the earth collided. He ended up defending the position that, if some individual owned the Grand Canyon, he'd have a right to turn the place into a parking lot.

Neither of us won the argument in the other's eyes, of course. But when I went to the Dells many years later, on a trip back to

Arizona, I remembered that history has its own way of declaring winners in arguments such as ours.

There were the Dells again. Still eerily majestic, still filled with a thousand secret places where spirits whisper. But there, in the very middle of the place, where I used to enter the Dells on a trail of rabbit tracks and coyote scat, a great gash was laid open. Dynamite and bulldozer had swept aside the rock to open the way for a large steel structure rising in the hollow. To my eye, this building, with its glinty hard surfaces, seemed to have no relation to the place where it stood, except that it could only stand there at the expense of the place. But I wondered whether that kind of "expense" had any place in the calculations of those who owned the spot. Or did the builders simply figure that they could profitably trade on all that surrounding beauty?

As I became choked with the pain of that sight, I recalled that ad against littering in which an old American Indian looks at a site strewn with beer cans and styrofoam cups, a tear running down his well-chiseled face. In the ad, the Indian stands as a spirit of the land itself, a land that once was his, but his in a different sense than we make it ours today. Hardly able to look at that gash in the Dells, I thought: that watchful spirit has far more to weep over than merely the ill-tended droppings of our economic system.

WE ARE THE FLOOD

In the grip of a system that breaks everything down into commodity form, the earth is violated. The living planet is dismembered, as land becomes real estate, forests become lumber, oceans become fisheries and sinks. In the midst of our wealth, we think ourselves the winners. We do not notice the "High Voltage" signs surrounding the biosphere. We forget that no creature can get away with trespassing against the holy order of life for long.

Meanwhile, we continue to practice the economy of destruction. Separation is the essence of sin; thus the economy that separates man from nature is an economy of sin. And the wage of sin is death.

As I watched the program on TV, it struck me as a matter of life and death. A map of Europe showed a vast deciduous forest that once stretched from the Urals to the Pyrenees. Then, five thousand years ago, the clearing of the trees began. The verdant area on the map shrank bit by bit—until but the tiniest patch remained. Bialowieza, on the Polish-Russian border, a mere remnant of an ancient kingdom of nature.

Then they showed us the kingdom, the fragment of it that remains: the bison standing beneath the towering trees, blowing steam above the drifted snow; the hooves of wild horses pounding through the lighted clearing; acorns blossoming into oaks. It was a vision of Eden, a world ancient and primeval yet as fresh as the day of creation. Everlasting, were it not for us. Now an island in danger of being swallowed by the waves of humankind.

The Garden of Eden wasn't a place we were kicked out of. We cut it down around us. We weren't sentenced to death. We invited death in. Having escaped the regime of nature, we engineered a coup d'état. But no creature can win against its environment for long.

If you throw a frog into hot water, it will know to jump out. But if you put it into water and only slowly raise the temperature, you can boil a frog to death. And it stays put, like a pouch of Green Giant frozen vegetables.

We're boiling ourselves slowly in our environment. Long ago, the green mantle that adorned the birthplace of civilization became a rough and rocky desert. But it took so long in human terms, no one noticed. We prosper like profligate heirs, spending the capital of soils and forests and creatures it took countless generations to accumulate. But will our kind be thriving still after another five thousand years? The huge reservoir of life is evaporating, but we need a time-lapse mentality to see the bubbles rising around us.

There is another image for our kind: Noah, the steward of life's replenishment. His ark was like a seed, encapsulating the bursting energies of life. Rid of its toxins, the Thames again dances with salmon. That dot on the map at Bialowieza may not be an island about to be washed over but a seed from which the whole can grow. Freeman Dyson envisions us sending out seeds of life into the vast sea of the lifeless universe. We, the creatures with the freedom to invent, may yet prove a boon to the struggle of life against death.

But for now, we are not filling the ark. It is we who are the flood. Spilling out of our channels, sweeping tropical forests away, extinguishing the precious flame of countless species, washing off the topsoil of the abundant American prairies.

And if we choose to play the flood, who is there to play Noah?

WE DIDN'T KNOW

There is an institute that brings Jewish high school students to Washington to see the national capital and to grapple with some of our major national issues in the context of their religious traditions and values. I have been invited on several occasions to be the one to speak to these young people about the environment. "Be provocative," I have been advised.

What do we think, I ask the students, of those Germans who did nothing during the Nazi era while millions of people were murdered in the death camps? After the war, many of those Germans claimed, "We didn't know." Do we accept that as an excuse, absolving them of all responsibility? No, we suspect that they knew or, if they didn't, it is because they chose not to. They averted their eyes to the horrors of the holocaust, to the people dragged away in the night, the trainloads rumbling through the countryside, the foul-smelling smoke descending on the land. Doing nothing, they abetted the crime.

And we—are we not like those Germans? There is another holocaust going on all around us, as one species—ours—makes war upon all the others of the earth. We are killing the planet. Won't we also claim we didn't know what was happening? The sun still rose, we'll say; the trees still sprouted their leaves in the spring. All seemed normal. But if we don't know about this holocaust, is it not simply because we choose to avert our eyes? If we were attentive, we would notice the gathering wave of reports from around the world, of deserts spreading, of extinctions accelerating, of waters dying, of climate and atmosphere being transformed by careless human activity.

We choose not to know, thus freeing ourselves to continue "business as usual." Our first priority, rich as we are, remains economic growth, even though we can now see clearly how much of what we call growth is merely spending the capital of the biosphere that it has taken billions of years to accumulate. When the going gets tough, the tough still go shopping, consuming resources to satisfy momentary whims.

The Germans had a better excuse than we do. For them to have opposed the Nazis' terrible genocide would have been to put their own lives at immediate risk. Those who did more than turn their backs we rightly regard as heroes. But we—what heroism is required of us? We are free to restrain our material appetites and live in simplicity. We are free to campaign openly and loudly for changes in our national policies. We can uphold the holy and be personally secure at the same time. But how many of us make that choice?

The kids generally find this challenge provocative enough.

In one of the great scenes in the Bible, Samuel goes to David the king. David, in his lust for a married woman, has used his royal power to have her husband sent off to a place in battle where he is sure to meet his death. Samuel poses to David a question of justice: What should be done with a rich man who has great flocks of sheep but, when he wanted to slaughter one to provide a banquet, stole for the purpose the only sheep owned by a poor neighbor of his? David is outraged at the rich man and declares the man should be put to death. Samuel then springs the trap shut: "Thou art the man!" says Samuel. It is an effective rhetorical device.

A World of Social Atoms

It is not only the integrity of the biosphere that is thrown apart by the forces of the market system.

The advocates of the market are bedazzled by the proficiency of the system in assigning prices to a myriad of goods and services, effecting a kind of miracle of computation. The disparate choices of countless actors are distilled into so many curves of supply and demand, representing the costs and benefits to those actors taken as a whole. The resulting prices reveal the relative value of the various competing commodities, and this information serves to channel the distribution of resources into an optimal "market basket" of products. This is what economics teaches. But its picture, unfortunately, is incomplete.

The market has a systematic bias. Not all the costs and benefits of a given transaction enter into the market's calculations. The costs to those who live downwind of a steel factory, and are compelled to breathe in what the factory exhales, do not enter into the price of a ton of steel. Not unless collective political decisions correct the economic system's blind spots. The costs to my neighbors of my selling my land to a developer with plans for a shopping center are also neglected when I make my deal. According to the market system, what I do with my property is none of your business.

The reality is that we are not so neatly encapsulated from one another as the atomistic economics model would represent us as being in order to justify the neglect of our interconnections. Virtually everything we do has some impact on those around us. The web of our interconnections is intricately interwoven. But these connections are systematically ignored in the calculus of the market.[11]

The market is therefore consistently biased in favor of the transactors over those who are bystanders to any given transaction. It is only the costs and benefits to the buyers and sellers that enter into the supply and demand curves that determine price. While the parts are minding their own business, the business of the whole deteriorates.

The costs of the market's blind spots are enormous. And they weigh unevenly. They weigh unevenly, first, in falling more on some than on others. Those who transact less are victimized more. Even if the uneven distribution of wealth were just, those with less wealth would still be the victims of injustice from the market system. This is because in their relationship to the market, the role of the unconsulted third party looms larger for the poor than for the rich. Lacking the means to transact, the poor benefit seldom from the system's solicitude for transactors. Spending more of their time on the sidelines, they are more acutely the victims of the system's disregard of bystanders.

But, in some ways, all are victims of the market's uneven ability to register value. To say that the system attends to the needs of transactors but ignores the needs of bystanders is also to say that the system takes care of only some of the needs even of the rich. For everyone in the market society, their needs as social atoms are more readily taken care of than those needs that relate to their interconnections with a larger whole. Even those whom the market provides with private opulence are condemned to enjoy it in a world that is falling apart.

All the contracts in the contract society tend to have too few signatures on them. Representing us each as social atoms, as islands entire unto ourselves, the system disables all of us from being able to mind important parts of our business. The human community is fractured, its coherence gone. Unless we make collective decisions to correct these fragmenting biases of the market, our economy will do the Devil's work.

THE LETTER AND THE SPIRIT

The story of Faust is about the pitfalls of a particular contract—a pact made with the Devil. But at a deeper level, the tale may be suggesting something diabolical about the whole contractual approach to the human striving for fulfillment.

One of the most entertaining films I ever saw was a modern comedic version of the Faust story. Made in the late 1960s by members of the British comedy review *Beyond the Fringe*, the film was entitled *Bedazzled*. In the film, a miserable and sexually frustrated man sells his soul to the Devil in exchange for the fulfillment of a certain number of wishes. The hero's great desire is to find sexual fulfillment with a particular woman—a waitress at a diner where he is a short-order cook—after whom he lusts but who has no interest whatever in him. Armed with a handful of automatically granted wishes, our hero would seem to be assured of the gratification of this simple desire.

But the comedy of *Bedazzled* grows out of the hero's inability to phrase his wishes in so airtight a fashion that the Devil cannot simultaneously grant his wish and perpetuate his frustration. In one case, our hero forgets to stipulate that the woman will requite his love. When the hero corrects that oversight, the Devil puts them into a situation where she is married to his best friend so that their guilt makes their mutual attraction a source of pain. In the final sequence, the hero crafts a wish that sounds complex and meticulous enough, but the Devil finds a way out. The hero having neglected to stipulate that he and his beloved will be of opposite sexes, the Devil makes the two of them nuns living together in a convent. By the time it is over, our dispassionate amusement and our sympathetic frustration are both quite intense.

Perhaps this funny story has no deeper meanings. But I believe that it draws its energy from its resonance with some profound spiritual problems in our civilization.

The Devil is shown to be the master of the contract. He wields the letter of what is stated to defeat the spirit of what is intended. At one level, this may indicate our sense of the pitfalls of a contractual approach to our efforts to get what we need from one another. Our deals effect specific exchanges. But are we getting what we really want from our network of social interaction?

The contract society is predicated on the definability of what we want. Our orientation to what can be defined and measured reveals a kind of idolatry. It reflects our cultural tendency to embody values in concrete things. "*This* is what I want." The requirements of human fulfillment, we believe, can be specified. Value can be reduced to the explicit and quantifiable terms of money.

Thus on one level the saga of frustration in *Bedazzled* may serve as a reminder that it is the letter that killeth, while the spirit giveth life. Not just in the matter of contracts, but more generally in the way we make of concrete, objectifiable *things* the objects of our desire. The hero trying futilely to specify the terms of his fulfillment may have an important message for a consumerist society that is seeking fulfillment through a never-ending sequence of bedazzling commodities.

STRANGERS

Separated, one person from another.

We are bombarded by messages encouraging us to purchase products that, the ads imply, will make us look important, will imply high status, to the people who see us. Wear expensive clothes, and you'll make a big impression. The fact that you can afford a high-priced item will say a lot about you. "When people saw [basketball star] Walt Frazier driving the avenues of Manhattan in his Rolls Royce, they may not have known exactly what his income was, but they could be reasonably sure that, whatever his job was, he was probably very good at it."[12]

In discussing the consumption of "observables," Robert Frank notes that the utility of such expenditures is much greater in a place like New York City than in some small town. "When someone we know very well shows up with an expensive new car . . . we are not suddenly led to believe that his ability is much higher than we previously thought. On the contrary, if we know that the car is beyond his budget, we may question his judgment in having bought it."[13]

The more the people who see us are people who already know who and what we really are, the less sense it makes to use material objects to impress the world around us. Conversely, it is in a world of strangers that the display of the trappings of high status is most likely to persuade the audience of one's importance. But what is the real value of such persuasion?

Frank seems to buy the idea that the displays of big-city folks are rational. You'd better have a fashionable car if you are a lawyer, or your potential clients may conclude that you are not much sought after. (The dilapidated car of the TV detective Columbo seems part of his strategy of misleading his suspects into underestimating him.) If you're single, it makes sense to spend a lot on clothes and cars to make a favorable first impression in the unforgiving singles markct.[14]

There may be grounds for such arguments. What strikes me most about the phenomenon of spending to impress strangers, however, is how sadly misguided it appears as a strategy for getting the real nourishment that human relationships have to offer. It is not from strangers that we get what really matters but from those with whom we are connected by intimate ties. Who cares what strangers think? The answer may be, more and more people are learning to care, to focus their concerns on a social world of strangers. It is in "stable environments with long-standing social networks" that observable goods are less important, Frank says.[15] But with the progress of the modern market society, such environments are progressively undermined. The ties that bind are rent. The more intimacy becomes impossible, the more do human relationships come to consist of strangers making impressions on each other. Fortunes are spent maintaining images, as social life becomes more like a parade of celebrities, a perpetual night at the Oscars where people come to see and be seen.

The glitzy outer surface of things becomes more important as contact with the inner being is lost. We are separated from one another, and alienated each from him- or herself.

Stuart Ewen quotes a young woman from Peru on the difference between what style means in New York from what it meant in the traditional society of her upbringing. In Peru, she said, style had been "the way in which the inner being of someone is expressed." In the modern metropolis, style "has become something people think they could buy," a display of a "glamour of images without bottom, without real meaning." Now, she says, "I . . . begin to understand why life seems so meaningless to many people in a big society. . . . [For] we are betraying our own self, selling our own inner being."[16]

But we are most profoundly *social* beings. How are we to know our inner being in a world that is too estranged, too thrown apart, to mirror our self back to us? Psychoanalytic theory has shown how our fundamental relationship with ourselves is an internalization of the way the world, in our earliest years, related to us. A world in which the connections among people are in a state of sin is one in which each person will have difficulty saving his own soul.

We become strangers even to ourselves.

FAMILY BUSINESS

The !Kung Bushmen of the Kalahari desert work a few hours a day to provide their subsistence, having the rest of the day to play with their children, to dance, and to enjoy the world around them. Anthropologists suggest that in this the Bushmen are typical of hunter-gatherers,[17] implying that for most of our time on earth, we *Homo sapiens* have not been pressed for time. We might not have had much in material wealth, but we had time for each other. Contra Hobbes, our lives were not so solitary or brutish.

In 1989, *Time* did an article on time. It seems that we Americans have less and less of it. "According to a Harris survey, the amount of leisure time enjoyed by the average American has shrunk 37% since 1973." One of the principal casualties of the increasingly pressured and frantic pace of time is family relationships. Edward Zigler, a psychologist at Yale, describes the costs paid by children: "We have eight-year-olds taking care of three-year-olds. We're seeing depression in children. We never thought we'd see that 35 years ago. There is a sense that adults don't care about them."[18]

Many forces doubtless contribute to this fraying of familial bonds in favor of productive work. But I detect the powerful pull of the magnetic force of the market system. As we saw in chapter 2, "Everything Money Can Buy," the system continually teaches the greater importance of those transactions that register in the market over those that don't. A man staying late in the office is contributing to our national wealth. But a man romping with his little ones—of what economic use is he?

Not to worry, the market can help remedy the deficit in parent-child contact engendered by the focus on economic ambition. "Hallmark, that unerring almanac of American mores, now markets greeting cards for parents to tuck under the Cheerios in the morning ('Have a super day at school,' chirps one card) or under the pillow at night ('I wish I were there to tuck you in')."[19] Everything money can buy.

A recent article in *The Christian Science Monitor* described the emergence of the latest service industry.

Not so many years ago, the idea of hiring strangers . . . to honor an elderly father on his birthday or to take a widowed mother to brunch on Mother's Day would have been unthinkable in many families.

Today, the existence of this service, and services like it, measures what relatives no longer can do—or will do—for relatives. From paid child care (rent-a-parent) to this type of paid elder caring (rent-a-daughter), responsibilities that once would have been considered part of an unwritten family code—this is what a family does for its members—are now of necessity being turned into commercial transactions.[20]

So we read about adults hiring surrogate family members to show their elderly parents a good time and hiring others to take care of their small children from morning till evening. The same system that renders an old-growth redwood forest into so many board feet of lumber can turn human relationships into a commodity as well.

In their study of how families relate to material possessions, Csikszentmihalyi and Rochberg-Halton discovered a difference in attitude between two different kinds of families. They found that families characterized by "warmth" in their interrelationships were less likely to crave material possessions as ends in themselves. It is "cold" families that become possessed by the "autonomous necessity to possess more things, to control more status, to use more energy." The "cold" family seems to "breed [this kind of] terminal materialism by not being able to cultivate the basic symbolic skills and rewards of human existence."[21] The "emotional isolation" in cold families, these researches report from their findings, also "prevents members of these families from getting involved in broader community affairs." They seek their consolation in *things*.

We can see that some of the forces unleashed by the market system operate in a mutually reinforcing fashion. The market's success in eroding human connections among family members promotes terminal materialism, with its insatiable appetite for the kind of "goods" the market specializes in. The addiction to consumption, in turn, further strengthens the power of the economic system.

We are driven apart, and our hunger for meaning is channeled in directions that feed the system better than they feed us. "Meaning, not material possessions, is the ultimate goal in [the lives of the American families studied], and the fruits of technology that fill the contemporary American home cannot alone provide this." Eat of the fruit of material abundance, proposes the Serpent, with his Faustian bargains, and you will enjoy the highest standard of living ever known. But fulfillment in our lives is about connection, whereas the path of separation is cold and dead. It is the holy vision that offers true fulfillment. "People still need to know that their actions matter, that their existence forms a pattern with that of others, that they are remembered and loved, and that their individual self is part of some greater design beyond the fleeting span of mortal years."[22]

TOLERATING SIN

"A free society," writes Michael Novak, in defending capitalism against attacks made in the name of morality, "can tolerate the public display of vice because it has confidence in the basic decency of human beings, even under the burden of sin."[23] But the market does more than tolerate vice. It actively fosters addictions. The advertisements for tobacco and liquor are often, and correctly, adduced as examples of the system's working actively to seduce people from the path of health, to undermine the integrity of the organization of the person by subordinating good judgment to misguided appetite.

Of course the liquor industry doesn't want its products abused, we hear on *Wall Street Week* from someone who works closely with the industry.[24] The cigarette companies, in the same pious spirit, all insist that, in their massive expenditures on advertising, they are merely fighting one another for market share.

Such disclaimers are incredible on their face. It has been observed that it is no coincidence that the only two areas in which the advertising industry claims that its efforts do not increase consumption are those, like the promotion of tobacco and alcohol, where the wages of addiction so clearly are death, and where legal constraints on advertising loom as a constant threat.[25]

In times perhaps less hypocritical, more than half a century ago, the head of the United Kingdom Brewer's Society told a private meeting, "We want to get the beer-drinking habit instilled into thousands, almost millions, of young men who do not at present know the taste of beer."[26] The ways that contemporary advertising uses images, a study has found, "appear to feed into the alibi system and the denial mechanism of alcoholics, leaving them vulnerable to damage."[27] The system exploits the vulnerabilities of these people rather than working to strengthen their character.

In this, the marketing of addictive substances is but a more extreme and clear-cut example of the wider phenomenon: the addiction to material consumption. A genuine teacher helps provide real nourishment for real people. But it is a diabolical teaching that leads people into the trap of unfulfilling addictions, leaving them wondering, "Where's the beef?"

In a free society, it is often said—and often quite rightly—that the best remedy for bad speech is not restriction on speech but more speech, good speech. Setting aside the question of the extent to which commercial messages are entitled to protection under the first amendment, or to what extent it is legitimate even in a free society to constrain the more pernicious aspects of seductive advertising, it seems to be clear that we in America today use "more speech" very inadequately to remedy the ills that advertising creates.

In elementary school, my children were taught in strong and effective ways to beware of strangers who might seek to lure them with candy into their cars. The schools brought in social workers to talk to the kids; they showed them films. But nowhere in their schooling have they been warned against this other, far more pervasive form of seduction. Countless hours, week after week, our children are "taught." They are presented diverse material, much of it useless. But with a few exceptions, all of this instructional speech to our children contains not a word to help them decipher the language of manipulation by which the economic system seeks to use them for its purposes.

Of course, the power behind the seductive use of advertising is far greater, far more capable of molding school curricula, than the political power of child molesters. In the long run, however, which group does the more damage to our nation's children?

CELEBRITY

In a world of commodities, what is of value is what sells. This tends to be as true of our God-given gifts as of everything else. So it is that we continually see many of the most gifted among us appearing in commercials, lending their luster to products whose manufacturers wish to trade on the prestige that visible achievement confers.

A few years ago, Madonna reduced still further the distinction between artistic performance and commercial message when she and Pepsi collaborated on a new vehicle: "A two-minute Pepsi commercial framing the release of Madonna's new single, the title track of her new album, 'Like a Prayer.' "[28] We had seen how songs—long meaningful to a wide audience—would subsequently be turned to commercial purposes. "You Are the Sunshine of My Life" became a love song to Minute-Maid orange juice. But Madonna, that phenomenon of artistic marketing who seems in recent years always to be at the top of the lists of highest-paid entertainers, was willing—for a fat sum of money—to combine the debut of "Like a Prayer" with Pepsi "visuals." To paraphrase an old line, you cannot pray to both God and Mammon.

The ad had its international debut during *The Bill Cosby Show*.
At one level, as the article in the *Boston Globe* observed, this was an
irony, because Bill Cosby has been a celebrity with a long-time
commercial relationship with Coca-Cola. But from my point of
view, there seemed something fitting in the Madonna-Cosby connection. I remembered my disappointment, and bewilderment,
at seeing Cosby's forays into making commercials.

I had been an admirer of Bill Cosby. An extremely gifted comic
talent, he seemed also to have a genuine concern for children.
Much of his work seemed to provide constructive guidance to his
young viewers. That same sense of admiration and trust that I
felt for him doubtless made him attractive to advertisers. If Cosby
tells us to buy something, people will be inclined to think, it certainly must be good for us. Then, there he was on the television,
selling instant pudding and Coca-Cola to kids. The same avuncu-
lar figure, with the same easy way of making little children laugh
and cuddle with him, was now telling the kids to consume sugar
and caffeine.

Why? Surely Mr. Cosby's purely artistic endeavors make him
enough income to live more than comfortably. What made the
extra dollars important enough to sell to millions of children
products that a wise parent would want his or her kids to avoid?

The *Boston Globe* write-up of the Madonna Pepsi commercial
was entitled "Madonna sells her soul for a song." Of course, in
making such a pact with the forces of the market, Madonna is re-
markable mostly for the success and brazenness of her efforts to
enrich herself. The whole world of celebrity in America shows a
deepening confusion about values and about the integrity of the
human soul.

In an earlier time, there was a significant distinction in the public mind between fame and notoriety. The famous had done something laudable, while the merely notorious were well known but
of ill repute. Mere notoriety was something that "respectable"
people would eschew. Now that distinction is disappearing. In a

society whose values are collapsing into the terms of mere buying and selling, the chief remaining distinction is between products that have achieved widespread name recognition and those
that have not and are thus doomed to oblivion.

How much will he or she command on the speaker's circuit?
In such a perspective, Gordon Liddy (notorious as the most
bizarre of the Watergate break-in crew) and Jessica Hahn (who
leaped into public visibility for having allegedly been seduced by a
notorious religious hypocrite) became celebrities, media stars,
who join the gifted in the high-priced people market. Anyone
who can get into *People* magazine is automatically held in respect,
if not awe.

In such a world, the gift becomes but one more commodity
that people can use to rise into the firmament of the rich and visible. The gift is a mere instrument of human ambition.

In a different view, the gift is not something we are given as
much as something we have to give the world. It is a privilege and
a responsibility—just as the *eudaimōn* is a challenge—conferred
upon us by the life force that has created us. The fulfillment of
the gift represents what the life force is trying to achieve through
us. It is not ours to use for our own purposes so much as we are its
to use for purposes that transcend us. In a vision of human life lived
in accordance with holiness, each person seeks to live in accordance with the spirit of her gift.

Not all celebrities are willing to sell their souls. An article on
the sports page told of the decision by the football star Bubba
Smith to stop appearing in beer commercials. "The moral implications of what he was doing had gotten to him."[29] When he was
serving as grand marshal in the homecoming parade of his alma
mater, Michigan State, he heard the crowds of students yelling not
the old football songs but the beer commercial slogans, "Tastes
great!" and "Less filling!" Later, at the game, it seemed to him
that almost every student in the stands was drunk. That's when
he decided to quit.

When he notified his beer company of his decision to stop appearing in their commercials, "company officials reportedly took it to mean that he wanted more money. But that wasn't it at all. He simply wanted to take a giant knot out of his conscience."[30]

How many Bubba Smiths are there, and how many Madonnas? The problem is, in terms of the impact of such "role models" on society, it doesn't really matter. The way our world is set up, certain kinds of people are made far more visible than others by our system. Children growing up in our society *see* Madonna making it big by selling herself. But it is precisely when Bubba Smith makes his decision to follow his conscience, rather than make his prestige a commodity for sale, that he ceases to be visible.

Perhaps our society should invent a way to display those celebrities who say no. Perhaps an organization can be formed whose membership consists of celebrities who make advertisements only on a *pro bono* basis and only for nonprofit purposes. If membership in such an organization came to confer prestige and respectability, and if this organization could command media attention, then our children might have role models of conscience as well as those of greed.

When I look in the mirror, I see a few hairs on what I now call my forehead. They seem out of place, but I know the history. They are stragglers left over from a hairline I had a quarter of a century ago. They are like a Bialowieza woods standing against the tide of history. The state of our moral environment may be similar. Values other than those of the market endure into our times, but we should be aware of the danger that they are merely vestigial. In the life cycle of a man, the recession of the hairline appears to be irreversible. But the moral decay of a society need not be. If our sacred values are to predominate—if, like some Bialowieza that might turn out to be a seed to restore the whole, these values are to have a chance of making a comeback—we need to recognize and to hold in check those systemic economic forces that work to break them down.

SHOP OF HORRORS

In a morally confused society, it may be difficult to distinguish the eudaimonic from the demonic.

For my children and me, one of our favorite films is a musical from the 1980s, *Little Shop of Horrors*. Rendered with extraordinary creative energy, the film explores the issue of ambition and the conflict between integrity and temptation. It is also the most acute treatment I know of the Faustian motif in relation to contemporary capitalist society.

The first song sets the stage. It is about life on "skid row." This is a place where life is dead-end, where relationships go nowhere. A sense of deprivation is pervasive. The song also introduces our hero, a nebbish named Seymour, an orphan with a job in a flower shop where he's treated "like dirt." He sings about his uncertainty that God has any purpose for him. Seymour concludes with an entreaty that someone help him escape his life at the bottom of the social ladder. Upward mobility seems the only way out of utter hopelessness.

Seymour's calling seems to be connected with his interest in exotic plants. One day, after a total eclipse of the sun, in the inventory of a Chinese plant vendor a strange plant appears that had not been there before. Seymour buys it for $1.99, and names it Audrey II after the young woman on whom he has a crush, and who also works in the Little Shop.

In the next song, "Some Place That's Green," we meet the heroine, Audrey (I), and learn of her dreams. She, too, longs for success, defined in her case not by achievement but by conventional middle class life. In this life, she sees herself as cooking like Betty Crocker and looking like Donna Reed. The happiness she yearns for entails marriage to Seymour, but her only way of describing it is through a set of objects and a material life-style that have been defined for her by the mass media. She imagines her house smelling of Pine-Sol, looking like a picture out of *Better Homes and Gardens* magazine. Unfortunately, it can only be a dream, she thinks, because she is trapped in a relationship with a dentist, a sadistic person, a man who is, as he soon tells us, "a success." His song tells us the secret of his success, his pursuit of a twisted kind of calling. After telling us about his childhood practice of torturing and killing animals, the dentist tells us that his mother had assured him that he would some day find a way to make his sadistic impulses pay. And so he becomes successful by inflicting pain.

Meanwhile, even Seymour's unsatisfactory situation is threatened by the growing commercial failure of the flower shop, whose owner, under the best of conditions, only barely tolerates him and his clumsiness. This situation is turned around, however, by the placement in the shop window of Audrey II. The strange plant seems somehow magically to attract free-spending customers.

But there is a catch. Seymour has discovered that there is only one thing that will keep the plant alive. He asks the plant what it wants from him. Blood? Just then he accidentally pricks his finger, and thus inadvertently learns that, yes, it is indeed human blood that Audrey II requires to stay alive.

This seems acceptable enough at first, in view of the material success the plant is bringing. But eventually the plant has grown to the point where it needs more blood than Seymour can provide from cutting his own fingers. At this point, the plant has its own song, which it sings in the rich baritone voice of a streetwise black man.

"Feed Me" is the name of the plant's song, and it is entire human bodies he wants to be fed. He sings to Seymour of the wishes he can grant for material success: the plant dangles before Seymour tempting images of celebrity, material wealth, access to women.

This is Seymour's first temptation to sell his soul for material success. Being a decent fellow, he hesitates. But then the dentist drives up with Audrey I, and Seymour sees him physically abusing her, and agrees with Audrey II that the dentist does indeed look like plant food.

First the dentist, and then the shopkeeper, are devoured by the plant—without Seymour's actually having to murder either of them. Seymour is thus not fully compromised and is able to retain our sympathy.

Big-time success comes knocking at Seymour's door, and he then confronts his second temptation. Notably, it revolves around the question of whether or not to sign a contract. The contract will make him a celebrity. Because of the giant plant, Audrey II, he will have his own TV program on plants, his picture on the cover of *Life* magazine, and all the fame and fortune he craves.

Again, Seymour hesitates. Though he yearns for the financial rewards offered him, he declares that the plant is too dangerous to be kept alive. No, he says to himself, he will not sign, because that would mean more killing. But then—as with the first temptation—the image of the woman he wants, the plant's namesake, serves again to drive him to stay with his Faustian deal. This time it is because of his fear that her love for him is dependent on his material success, which, in turn, depends on the plant's survival. He signs.

Eventually, his increasing closeness with Audrey and his increasing recognition of the catastrophic danger Audrey II poses to the planet combine to embolden him to confront the plant and renounce their partnership.

By now, however, the plant is enormous and possesses power far beyond Seymour's ability to counter. The plant sings from its sense of its own power, telling Seymour that the time has come when he will have to submit to the plant's dictates. The plant now reveals to Seymour that he has been dealing with forces far beyond his ken. Seymour has no idea of what he has been dealing with, the plant tells him menacingly. The plant, describing itself as bad, further reveals itself as a truly alien being—from outer space— poised to take over the earth.

In the pursuit of his ambition, our hero has enlisted the help of an alien, unholy power. This power, he discovers, has been less at his service, ultimately, than it has been using him for its own designs. It has harnessed his ambition and his yearning for love— his desire for material success and his confusion about the basis of human connections—as part of its own plan to take over the earth.

In the end, as with Goethe's hero, Faust, Seymour is delivered from his pact with the diabolical. In their final confrontation, while the plant toys with Seymour on its way to destroying him, Seymour manages to electrocute the plant. Having thus redeemed himself, Seymour is free to walk away with his love, with the Audrey that is of this world.

Two Economies

The market economy is not run by the Devil, but its operation does have diabolical effects. The market is not some unearthly invader of our human world, but neither are its workings a direct expression of human will, and thus, in this respect, the system acts as a force alien to us. It is not that the system is malevolent, for the system is but a structure with no meanness or ill will to it. Yet the system—if we leave it, as we have, too much on automatic pilot—does work over time to destroy much of what we hold sacred.

This, of course, is only part of the picture, and emphasizing only the negative, as I do here, produces a caricature. This system also clothes and feeds us. It gives great scope to human creativity, conferring considerable liberty in certain directions. The market is indeed a marvelous mechanism for granting certain of our wishes, and many of these wishes partake of the holy. But even if the market has considerable virtues, it is most important for us to confront its congenital defects. For if one fails to cure a grave disease in vital organs, even the healthy parts of the body cannot save the whole from death. Complacency is a luxury we cannot afford, for our civilization has yet to achieve a form that can live in harmony with the living energies within us and around us.

It is all a matter of the system's ability, and inability, to perceive value. The market's virtues are precisely in those areas where the system is capable of registering what is important. But the market has blind spots, and over time the cumulative effect of those blind spots is to throw apart the holy order of things. Like a vehicle whose steering wheel is constantly pulling to one side, the market system on automatic pilot deviates more and more from the path that wholeness and viability require. Because our efforts to correct the skewed vision of the system remain quite inadequate—because the laws that the United States and other capitalist societies have tried over the past century in their attempts to take the system off automatic pilot remain far too weak and incomplete—the system continues to do the Devil's work. The market's combination of power and skewed perception warps the evolution of the living systems it contacts.

Despite our present environmental laws, the market system still consistently undervalues what comes from nature. It is in the nature of the system to treat everything as though it were worth what we paid for it. The earth came free, so we treat it like dirt. Speaking of dirt, the price in the marketplace for a bushel of Iowa corn takes no account of the bushel of Iowa topsoil lost to erosion through the farming practices the system itself rewards. Clean air and water are treated as worthless—until this skewed accounting system renders them scarce. (In Mexico City today, people are paying a high fee to go to fresh air salons to sit and breathe air free of noxious pollutants.) Even scarcity does not impose a true understanding of nature's value. The price of oil in the market reflects only the cost of getting it out of the ground and to the point of use—as if it were the expense of writing the check and not the reduction of the balance in the account that measured the true cost of the transaction.

In the human realm as well, distorted perception undermines the wholeness of living systems. The focus on transactions, with a corresponding neglect of the multiplicity of our interconnections, splinters the communal order. The preference for what is bought and sold over other "goods" human beings exchange with each other—infant formula over mother's milk, a father's paycheck over his playing with his kids—degrades the integrity of the family. The equation of price with value seduces people into believing that whatever sells is good, sowing confusion in the moral order.

Is this what Luther sensed when he felt, in the rise of capitalism, Satan's final seizure of power in the world?

Wendell Berry recounts a conversation between him and his friend Wes Jackson about the causes of "the modern ruination of farmland" by the present "money economy," with its inadequate ability to *comprehend* the values at stake. What kind of economy would be comprehensive enough, Berry asked his friend? "He hesitated a moment, and then, grinning, said, 'The Kingdom of God.'"[31] Upon reflection on his friend's answer, Berry tells us, he has found this term indispensable.

The problem with our economy, says Berry, "is exactly that it is not comprehensive enough, that . . . it tends to destroy what it does not comprehend, and that it is *dependent* upon much that it does not comprehend." What is needed is an economy that leaves out nothing vital. This is the Kingdom of God, where even "the fall of every sparrow is a significant event." In this comprehensive system, "everything that is in the Kingdom is joined both to it and to everything else that is in it; that is to say, the Kingdom of

God is orderly."[32] That is to say, the order of this Kingdom is a holy order.

What are we to do? Nothing we can devise can match the harmony and completeness of the Kingdom of God. No system of laws will ever bring the human economy into total alignment with every dimension of the complex order of life on earth.

In a way, that is precisely the point. To begin with, it would be a great error to use the impossibility of *complete* success in rendering our economy comprehensive enough in its vision as an excuse for not making every effort to correct its defects as best we can. Then, beyond that, the very recognition of the inevitable imperfection of all our human creations is an important step in the healing of our world. It is the step of *humility*.

No one in our society can propose radical criticisms of the market economy without recognizing that he or she is challenging a system that a major part of our cultural ideology has virtually deified. One senses the risk of incurring charges of heresy, for "free enterprise" is at the heart of our civil religion, "the American way of life."

This deification is a form of idolatry, for the market system is but a machine of human creation. It is not the Kingdom of God. To imagine that we should entrust our fate, and the fate of the planet, to a mechanism we ourselves created represents a kind of spiritual folly, a kind of arrogance. It is this arrogance, embodied in powerful economic actors in our society, that constantly hampers all our efforts in the political system to correct the system's most blatant and dangerous flaws. It is this folly that threatens to make us the agents of our own destruction.

Our long-term survival requires that we respect the wholeness of the living system of which we are part. Berry writes that "the difference between the Great Economy and any human economy is pretty much the difference between the goose that laid the golden egg and the golden egg."[33] To forget this is to condemn ourselves to the fate of the man in the fable who, greedy for more than fit into the order of life's processes, slit open the goose to get all the eggs, only to end up with no eggs and no goose either.

Humility is not a form of self-punishment, putting oneself down. It is a recognition of one's true place in the great order of things and, as such, it is a way of taking care of oneself. It is of the essence of the Faustian bargain that the person who makes the pact with the Devil fails in this kind of humility and seeks, with the aid of the diabolical, to get more than is in a human being's place to get. This has been true since that first Faustian bargain in Eden, where our progenitors believed the Serpent's tempting promise that they would "become as gods." What happened in Eden, rather, is that they unleashed death into what had been a paradisiacal existence.

In the stories, the Faustian deal generally turns out to be a bad one. The pact usually leads to death and damnation. But this ought to be seen not so much as a *punishment imposed* for dabbling with evil but as a *natural consequence* of putting oneself out of alignment with the order of things.

Berry proposes one more principle to describe the order of the Kingdom of God: "Though we cannot produce a complete or even an adequate description of this order, severe penalties are in store for us if we presume upon it or violate it."[34]

Sounds like a matter of "High Voltage."

FINALE

The Real Thing

THE EROSION OF REALITY

Reality seems nowadays to be in ill repute. In reality, according to many, there's no such thing as reality. We make our own reality. Our world is merely what we render it to be. The self "never finds anything outside itself but what it has put there."[1]

In this view, it is inevitable that we will live in a man-made world, for it is we who are the creators of our own realm of experience. The relentless expansion of the human empire can bring with it no meaningful loss, for the idea of there being something of irreplaceable value out there beyond us, something sacred that was "put there" by no human agency, has no standing.

The erosion of the belief in a reality that transcends our beliefs erodes also the distinction between the symbol of something and the thing itself. Since the meaning of things is equated with what we *believe* them to mean, the loading of symbolic meanings onto an object performs a virtual alchemy upon it. If we are persuaded that the base stuff that is packaged for us possesses a golden aura, it is argued, it is for us as good as gold. So long as we come to believe that Coca-Cola, as the slogan went, is "the real thing," our cup runneth over with reality.

BUYING THE IMAGE

Symbols are undeniably powerful.

A woman sharpshooter was a guest on the TV game show *Truth or Consequences*. She hit coins that were tossed in the air to serve as targets. But then she was offered the grand prize if she would shoot out the eyes on life-sized photographs of her children. She refused to shoot.[2]

Under hypnosis, a subject is touched with an object no hotter than room temperature. Told that the object is a red-hot poker, the subject may develop a blister.

Similarly, there are those who maintain that we need have no concern about any discrepancy between what those who package our commodities persuade us they are selling us and what they are *really* purveying. The meanings heaped upon the back of the product become, indeed, part of what we incorporate when we consume the good. As George Will writes in a column defending the advertising industry against its critics, "the advertising completes the product, which in a sense is what the consumer feels about it."[3] The image, says Campbell, is part of the gratification.[4]

Tobacco rolled in a paper tube is not yet a completed product. It is only finished when the marketers tell us that these cigarettes signify that the woman smoking them has "come a long way, baby," while these others make a guy a Marlboro man, like the rugged cowboy on horseback with a handsome, weather-beaten face to go with his earthy sheepskin coat. The positive gender image is part of the gratification.

With the symbol in hand, the consumer can appropriate the imputed symbolic properties of the object and thereby transform himself or herself. Kingsley Amis writes that one of his characters possessed a "curved nickel-banded pipe round which he was trying to train his personality, like a creeper up a trellis."[5] Grant

McCracken refers to this—the capacity of an object of consumption to exercise leverage to move the consumer and his way of life—as the "Diderot effect," after a story about the effect on the author Diderot of the receipt as a gift of a dressing gown whose stylistic connotations were at variance with his previous self-image and with the assemblage of possessions he already owned. The appeal of the Diderot effect, says McCracken, is powerful "in a culture that believes there is a 'whole new me' to be discovered in untried consumer options."[6]

What does McCracken make of this belief? In his book *Culture and Consumption,* he appears to join Will and Campbell in their respect for the power of these wholly man-made realities. McCracken offers an interesting and rather sophisticated analysis of the way meaning is transported and attached to things in societies like ours. Advertising he describes as a "conduit through which meaning is constantly being poured." The set of meanings with which advertising works arises from the larger "culturally constituted world." (This is the world that makes a woman wish to think she has come a long way and motivates a man to want to see himself as like the rugged cowboy on horseback.) The advertiser works to move meanings from that culturally constituted world to connect them to consumer goods. It is the artistic task of the advertiser to get the viewer/reader, the consumer-to-be, to perceive "an *essential equivalence* between [that culturally constituted] world and [the consumable] object." The goal is to get the consumer to experience "a metaphoric identification of sameness."[7] The consumer then buys these meanings along with the product. Values of manhood are to be perceived as essentially equivalent to the cigarette. This brand of lemonade will transport you into an America of coherent community and intact families, for the liquid and the nostalgic image are metaphorically the same.

As McCracken summarizes the "trajectory of the movement of cultural meaning in modern, developed societies," "Advertising

and the fashion system move meaning from the culturally constituted world to consumer goods, while consumer rituals move
meaning from the consumer good to the consumer."[8]

It has often been suggested that consumerism serves in our culture as a kind of religion, with shopping malls and department
stores as virtual temples, and so on. Here, with McCracken, we
hear a discourse that does indeed seem to accord to our culture
of consumption such a function. The realm of our collective
meanings is mediated to us by a kind of priesthood, the advertisers, and through our creation of our own "rituals" of consumption, we bring into our lives this meaning made flesh.

What could be wrong with that? Meaning is, after all, where we
find it. Is it not?

FALSE SOLUTIONS

Worshiping an idol does not make it God. The placebo effect is
real and important, but the power of placebos does not make
them the essential equivalent of real medicine.

Part—but only part—of what is wrong with the packaging of
reality by our commodity culture lies in that old idea of seduction.
To seduce is to lead astray, and the idea of leading astray presup-
poses that some paths are better than others.

If we believe that reality is merely whatever we make it, then
we can find no standard to judge one way of packaging meanings
as superior to another. Without a transcendent point of reference by which to set our compass, we are set adrift and have no
moorings to help us resist the pull of cultural forces that would
sweep us along for purposes of their own.

A famous advertising executive, Ernest Dichter, wrote in 1960
of the growing concern of the consumer for what a product "will
do for his 'soul.'" "Many of our studies have shown that people
are groping for real values and discovering that they lie primarily
in self-development and in the realization of self-potential."[9]

How is this concern to be addressed? The advertiser, of course, is not going to ask, How are souls to be saved? The issue for the priests of the commodity culture is, rather, How can this concern for the soul be exploited? "To the extent that the modern advertiser can tie in this trend with a new car, new refrigerator, or even a new form of cigarette or tonic for tired blood, he will outshine his competition."[10]

The meanings from our culturally constituted world get attached to the goods, but what happens when they are absorbed into our lives through our rituals of consumption? Do the goods deliver the goods? Though we are persuaded to buy products in order to fulfill our needs for such things as love and friendship and pride, how can mere commodities possibly meet these needs? As J. F. Cavanaugh writes in his book *Following Christ in a Consumer Culture*, "Since none of these deepest human hopes can be fulfilled in any product, the mere consumption of them is never enough; 'more' of the product, or a 'new improved' product, is the only relief offered to our human longings."[11]

This recalls Alan Watts's statement, the most profound I have ever heard on the subject of insatiability and on the spiritual bases of addiction: "You can't get enough of what you don't really need." It implies, of course, that there is a reality in relation to which there are some things that we *really* need and others that we really don't.

The Sufis have a saying that thirst is a clear proof of the existence of water. To our commodity culture that, in McCracken's word, is continually "pouring" meaning from one realm to another, we must say that just because it says Water on the label—even if the priesthood of persuasion makes us believe it—that doesn't mean it will satisfy our thirst. There is no substitute for the real thing.

The commodity culture tells us it is offering "real food for real people," but we end up malnourished. It is not only because our systems want us to buy what we don't really need, however, that what we are dished up is a spiritually denatured kind of food. Seduction is really only the beginning of our problem.

THE WILD AND THE DOMESTICATED

Nothing can really fill us up but the encounter with reality. Reality is really plenty, for our very being in this seething and awesome world is an incomprehensible mystery. We are continually poised at the edge of perception both overwhelming and astonishing, if we but choose to turn to open our eyes and look. Even the breaking of bread is a wonderment.

This confrontation with our reality is the real food, but we have a limited capacity to stomach it. It requires a kind of strength of the organism to be open to experiencing the majesty of this cosmos, the mystery of our humanity. Only to the extent that we feel a certain sureness of our footing will we feel safe in allowing ourselves to be swept off our feet. Only to the extent that we are at ease with what we are will we feel enlivened rather than frightened to recognize how ever-strange are this world and we who live upon it.

There is always the temptation to domesticate the wildness of our reality. For such domestication, there are many techniques. Habits and routines of all kinds serve this end—addictions most of all. Give me more of the same, so I can tell myself there is nothing strange to cope with, nothing that demands of me that I confront the newness of every moment. Keep the spontaneous and the creative in check, so that the free-flowing and unpredictable aspects of living energies will not disturb my fearful comforts. Make everything bite-sized and soft, so I need never worry that in coming to life I bit off more than I can chew.

We all, I believe, engage to some degree in this work of domesticating our experience. Indeed, it is a necessity. With none of it, life would not be orderly enough to work, or comfortable enough for us to bear. It is one of the functions of all cultures, therefore, to abet us in this work of taming, to provide a kind of breakwater to give us safe harbor for our lives, protecting us against the constant pounding of the wild waves of our true condition, as we are beset on every side by miracles and mysteries. With rules to give order and rituals to afford repetition, with roles to construct our conduct and definitions to contain our confusion, culture makes us more at home in the world.

But every culture, if it is to serve us worthily, must also do the opposite—encourage us to adventure forth into the open seas of life. A culture is to be evaluated also by its success in providing us with access to the reality that transcends it. If we are cut off from that transcendence, if we are deluded into thinking that the mysteries have all been solved, our lives lose the source of their vitality. If we are persuaded into mistaking our culture's renditions of the sacred for the sacred realm itself, we become idolaters.

It is here that we uncover a more subtle, but perhaps also more profound shortcoming in the workings of our commodity culture than its deliberate deceptions and seductions. It appears to be an attribute of this culture of the market that it tends, as if by an unintended kind of Midas touch, to denature our real food. The very act of turning something into a commodity seems to impose upon it a regime of excessive domestication. This economic system, with its tendency to reduce everything to its own terms, seems peculiarly unable to permit entry into a reality that surpasses it. The commodity culture tends to drag us into the shallows.

MANY MANSIONS

One of our most effective getaways into the elemental realm of mystery is contact with the creations of diverse cultures.

We arrive on the earth with a marvelous indeterminacy, awaiting our culture's rendering of the human image to complete our form. As we mature as products of a particular culture, we inevitably harden into a particular way of being human. This necessary completion entails an inevitable cost: all the other forms we might have assumed in our development, all the other spiritual places we might have explored through our way of processing life's energies, all the other kinds of music to which we might have danced through our lives, are inevitably foregone. We come to inhabit but a corner of the spacious palace of our human potential.

The diversity of human cultures offers us a way of reclaiming, in part, what we have lost. Each genuine message from a different cultural (or even subcultural) system opens a door into another of the many mansions of humanity's house. "This is also what it can be to be human," the messages from different cultures tell us. "This also was in your potential to embody." We are reminded not only of what we did not become but also of what in some sense we still are. For there remains within us a mysterious wellspring of humanity that transcends the image into which we have hardened in the kiln of our particular culture.

The freedom and tolerance of the particular cultural system of Western society allows us considerable access into this precious reservoir of cultural diversity. Not only is our society multicultural in the living flesh, but there are no texts from other times and places that are forbidden us. No one is burned at the stake for engaging in unorthodox rites, no one stretched on the rack for passing through the portals of an ashram.

De jure we are free to walk through the gateway into many cultural worlds. *De facto* it is more difficult. There are forces operating to keep us away from the liberating discovery of the strange and the unfamiliar. Some of these forces may well be our own fears. But some may be systemic.

PACKAGED GOODS

One of the most vital kinds of music I know is klezmer, a soulful kind of music that arose in the Jewish culture of Eastern Europe. Recently, the Public Broadcasting System showed an excellent documentary on klezmer music. In this program, there was some discussion of what happened to klezmer as it became fitted to the needs of commerce: "The music was no longer the music. It was turned into a commodity. Tunes were chopped up into segments and given these abstract names. Because the record companies, in order to have titles to print in their catalogues, suddenly needed the music to fit into little packages. The music was no longer a context within a society. It was now something to be sold by Columbia and Victor."[12]

To some extent, the very fact of packaging a good inevitably transforms it. Even the wildest beast, hacked up and wrapped for display in the meat department, becomes a domesticated thing. Even the most profound book, put on a syllabus and served up in a college course, can become an innocuous text. By virtue of being reduced to fit into a predetermined slot in our structured world, anything can be rendered smaller than its true self—like some object seen through the wrong end of a powerful telescope—and thereby be robbed of its power to break open the gate into mystery.

"The Loss of the Creature"—that is the phrase Walker Percy uses in his lament about how, in our society, the way we organize and package things reduces our capacity to encounter reality for ourselves. Because of the mediation of various experts and packagers, the member of our society loses his capacity to confront objects and events "as a sovereign person, as Crusoe confronts a seashell he finds on the beach."[13]

"A sovereign person." Sovereignty among nations implies that each is master of itself. Above sovereign nations there is no authority to dictate their course. Sovereign nations confront one another in what Hobbes called "the state of nature." The frontier between the sovereign actor and the surrounding world is charged with the intense electricity of the unknown and unpredictable.

Having lost our sovereignty to the authorities that package our goods, we live in a more domesticated, more denatured landscape. Percy draws an analogy: "In the New Mexican desert, natives occasionally come across strange-looking artifacts which have fallen from the skies and which are stenciled: *Return to U.S. Experimental*

Project, Alamogordo. Reward. The finder returns the object and is rewarded. He knows nothing of the nature of the object he has found and does not care to know. The sole role of the native, the highest role he can play, is that of finder and returner of the mysterious equipment."[14]

It is not the packaging alone that intrudes between us and the encounter with the mysterious and alien object that washes up on the seashore of our cultural imagination. The music of klezmer might have been chopped to fit the demands of the package, but the voice of the melancholy and lyric klezmer clarinet still sang through. The process of turning cultural expressions into commodities, however, often involves other, more pernicious transformations, the way cheese can be processed into something not alive enough to spoil while it sits on the shelf awaiting purchase.

The anthropologist Edmund Carpenter tells the story of his contact with a Velveeta-like message from a culture that, were it not denatured, could give us entry into human spaces uncharted in our own culture. Carpenter was approached by a publisher to examine an anthology of Eskimo poems that was to be published.

> When I examined the sources, I found most were anthologies and these, in turn, drew from earlier anthologies. The final versions were often three & four generations removed from the originals and, not infrequently, remarkably different from them. Each anthologist had modified the poems to fit his own temperament, above all to fit his audience, until successive editings had eroded all traces of the originals.
>
> Since most people don't know what poetry is, least of all Eskimo poetry, and couldn't recognize it if they saw it, the anthologist's task is clear: give them rhymed sentiments sprinkled with Elizabethan pronouns.[15]

The call of the wild—the world whose utter difference from ours can serve as a sign of the terra incognita into which every people, every life, must venture forth—is overdomesticated into the yipping of a harmless house pet.

In part, this denaturing of real food is a function of the pull of demand. "This is what they want," says Carpenter of the audience for the pseudo-Eskimo poems. "This is what they get."[16] Why blame the system for giving people what they want? There are a couple of answers.

What we want is a function of our spiritual condition. If it takes a kind of organismic strength to find adventure attractive, then a system that works to weaken us can help create the demand for the bland. If, as Carpenter says of the phony Eskimo poetry, "The real thing may stick in the throat, but this goes down without a cough,"[17] the constricted condition of our throats may be a sign of how much we have had to swallow to fit into our own culture.

Beyond that, the world of commerce has a dynamic of its own that may be antithetical to the vastness of the spiritual spaces that human existence opens before us. The same system whose bulldozers flatten hills so that square factories may be set down on level places will also find it better for its purposes to have the cultural landscape leveled also. It makes it easier to work with. This is the system, as Siegfried Giedion shows in *Mechanization Takes Command*, that worked to teach people to eat the gummy, processed mass-manufactured kind of bread that best suited the needs of the expanding production system. This same system prefers having cultures standardized and homogenized in a single vat. Culture as Wonder Bread is easier to wrap up and distribute for the mass market.

It is the unique and not the habitual that can open the sky above our minds, but money is to be made from what can be reproduced on demand, from what can be manufactured in quantity from a formula. The adventurer into new realms, once having placed her destiny into the hands of the tourist industry, is unlikely to stumble into one of those transformative encounters that can befall one, as in an E. M. Forster tale. *If It's Tuesday, This Must Be Belgium*, the title of a 1969 movie comedy, captures well how thoroughly the adventure into the vast world has become just another scheduled TV program.

An astute observer of consumer culture, Rosalind Williams, has written of the damaging effects of the "commercialization of the imagination." Under its influence, she says, "the dream of Utopia becomes Disneyland."[18] The sky closes; the horizon shrinks.

Disneyland itself is discussed by Carpenter as a world constructed in the same spirit, or lack of spirit, as was the world of the Eskimo for that anthology. Both worlds—one to be constructed within walls, the other composed between book covers—represent to Carpenter the same false and comforting re-creation of the familiar to displace the real and mysterious. "Twenty cultures were chosen, scattered among tundra, desert and jungle, but even though the people dressed in different clothes and ate different foods, they were all alike, members of a single culture. That culture was *our* culture." Is Williams's commercialized Utopia, then, just what we see looking into a kind of mirror, just the image of ourselves? Not precisely. The twenty cultures of Disneyland were not exactly reduced to *our* culture, but "more accurately, [to] our clichéd image of ourselves that might be called the Hallmark greeting card view."[19] Diverse cultures are not only collapsed by homogenization but are further flattened by the bulldozer of cliché.

The commercialization of culture is not confined only to the theme parks that are constructed within the property lines of the entertainment industry. In his classic, *Small Is Beautiful*, E. F. Schumacher observed the impact on "the poor countries that sell themselves to the international tourist industry." There are effects at the material level—"luxurious airports, high-rise hotels, six-lane motorways"—that make the strange land like the places the tourists left behind. But then there are the spiritual effects on the native peoples, when they "wind up as bellhops and souvenir sellers, desk clerks and entertainers, and their proudest traditions . . . degenerate into crude caricatures."[20]

When processed by the market, in whose hands cultural diversity becomes but one more commodity for mass consumption, humanity's house may come to consist not of many mansions, but of one pleasant hotel whose essentially identical rooms are decked out with different finishing touches. A picture of a peasant with sombrero in the Mexican room, a burgher with lederhosen in the Bavarian.

DREDGED UP FROM THE SHALLOWS

The problem is not only that the commercialization of the imagination reduces many different cultures to a single one but also that it reduces them to a superficial version of culture. For people to have a shallow vision of culture condemns them to a superficial understanding of the nature of their own lives.

In his exploration of the way different cultures are rendered into so bland a form that they go down "without a cough," Carpenter is reminded of art forgeries: "Often forgeries, at the time they are made, are widely accepted but when fashions change, their fraudulent nature suddenly becomes clear & people wonder how anyone could ever have been misled by such obvious misrepresentations." Carpenter offers a solution to this puzzle. "They were misled because what they saw was themselves."[21]

But I would say that the problem goes deeper than that. Had they really seen themselves, they would not have been duped. The problem arises from buying a superficial image of what we are that reduces us to far less than the reality. The ancient spiritual injunction Know Thyself is at the core of the issue. The best mark for the con man is the person who is conning himself.

The issue is not cultural diversity per se, as an end in itself, but the state of our spiritual awareness. The stereo-optical vision offered by different versions of ourselves is only one way of perceiving the great depth of our humanity. There are others. Not only any single culture, but also any single human soul can provide a vision of the vast realm of sacred mystery that resides within us. "Just sink one well deep enough."[22]

Both the supply side and the demand side—the producers and the consumers—collaborate in reducing cultures to clichés. And on both sides, a spiritual failure is at work. The tourists shy away from the spiritual challenge of going to the deep well. The sellers of novelties in which nothing is really new are themselves like water bugs that can move quickly by making a floor out of surface tension. They barely even get wet.

Where in the human spirit is the culture coming from? That is the question we should ask of the cultural places we visit.

When someone like Bach goes to the well, he brings back the real thing. Steeped in a profound musical tradition deep in the roots of his family background and his German culture until he had incorporated that tradition into his very fiber, Bach added his own genius to channel those resources into a flowering of extraordinary beauty. In Bach, the well went deep enough for his whole being to gain expression. Neither the fact that the *Magnificat* is a kind of packaging nor that this creation is thoroughly bound to a particular culture diminishes the profundity of the contact such a composition gives us with the realm of the sacred.

Those who package culture as a commodity for our consumption, however, are often coming from much shallower waters. Not just because they lack the depth of a Bach, but because they are not standing in the same relation to their creations. I picture a Bach, or a Shakespeare, as the channel for forces that go far beyond their conscious egos. The whole idea of "genius"—like that of the *daimōn*, or the muse—originates in a sense of a spirit at work that is not one's own. (The first meaning given *genius* in the

Oxford English Dictionary is, from the Latin, "The tutelary god or attendant spirit allotted to every person at his birth, to preside over his destiny in life.") The artist, with the muse at his shoulder, is the channel for something that goes deeper than consciousness, for forces that transcend one's own deliberate control. Production of culture for commerce, however, promotes a different, more superficial mind-set.

Production for commerce is predicated on control. It prefers what can be manipulated and predicted. The orientation of the empire builder does not honor the forces that elude his domination.

Another difference concerns the producer's relation to his creation. What is important for me as producer/seller is not *my* relationship to the product but the *buyers'*. If they buy it, that's good enough. My creation is not "for the glory of God."

Consequently, the realm of culture in a commercially dominated world tends to become full of messages in which the speakers themselves do not really believe. This is true not only of advertisements, whose dishonesty we have discussed. It is true also of presumably more artistic creations like movies and books. If *Three Men and a Baby* made lots of money, we simply owe it to ourselves to milk it further with *Three Men and a Little Girl*, whether we have anything to say in it or not. As long as the suckers are willing to pay for them, we'll keep churning them out—maybe eventually we'll make *Three Old Geezers and a Woman*.

How many of the books published today are the best their authors could write by the standards they themselves apply in judging a book for their own reading? A couple of generations ago, there were a number of publishers—even in big-time publishing—who were in business to publish the kinds of books they themselves would wish to read. I had a conversation with an elderly gentleman who still publishes that way and who—distressed at the transformations he has witnessed in the industry, as the workings of commerce make the bottom line the bottom line—describes himself as one of the last of a "dying breed."

The problem is not just that culture becomes directed to the masses, and that a "lowest common denominator" degrades the level of cultural communication. More than that, something happens to the spirit of a culture when it is created by people who don't believe in it.

Ordinary people, with their everyday experiences, have a depth and richness in their lives and, often, in their creations. One sees this in the rich texture of folk cultures, the wood baskets of Appalachia, the quilts of Nebraska, the hymns of the Shakers. Everyone dreams in poetry. The unconscious of the average person has greater connection into the wellsprings of meaning than the calculating ego of the sharpest operator. When I was a boy and my father a professor at Michigan State, the most exciting events of my life were my outings with him to college athletic events. I remember well the electricity in the field house, where we would watch MSU basketball games with the screaming of some thousands of college students and the stirring music of the college band. The physicality and drama of the game, and the spirited passions we shared as a crowd, made these outings for me vibrant visits to an elemental world.

The memory of those occasions returned to me the other day when a friend persuaded me to go to see a professional basketball game played by the local team, the Washington Bullets. The level of play in the game itself was, of course, incomparably higher. But what struck me more than the excellence of the players was the manipulative packaging of everything else about the game. The management had evidently thought through what would make the event "fun" for the fans. They had decided what we would watch on the big screen above the court. They governed when and how we would cheer, using that big screen to flash us instructions on what to shout. For the interstices of play, they had arranged various games for us, announced with false emotions by the ever-present announcer and accompanied by some Muzak deemed suitable for an athletic arena.

The whole choreography of our experience left little room for the spontaneity of the fans, or for a shared sense of creation by the crowd experiencing itself as a collectivity. But it was the posture of the choreographers that felt the most alienating. Quite unlike the college band and cheerleaders, these orchestrators of our enthusiasms stood far apart from us, a kind of Big Brother dispassionately trying to manipulate our fervor. That they presumably wanted us to enjoy ourselves, that the manipulation was largely benign, could not redeem the experience. There was something deadly about the combination of the intrusiveness of this Big Brother and the unmistakable feeling that those who were so present in our experience were not really *with* us. The shallowness of the spirit engendered by this manipulative detachment gave the experience the smell of death. Human creations are not wholly alive unless their human creators invest all of themselves into them.

NAMES WILL NEVER HURT YOU

Naming things is in itself a form of packaging. To know what to call a phenomenon is to have domesticated it a degree, to have brought it by a kind of magic under some control. Placed in the midst of that brave new world in Eden, Adam's first purposeful activity is to set about giving names to all the other creatures. Named, they are less wild.

Not all names are equally domesticating, however; some remain close to the mystery of our lives, while others are as removed from the organic and the elemental as the cheers flashed on the screen at the Bullets game.

Consider the names of places. Some grow out of the rich adventure of people's lives. They are part of the story of genuine experience and, for me, they can actually add to the enchantment of the land. Driving across Arizona, we cross Dead Man's Wash and wonder about the tale that lies behind this name. What macabre discovery did the original settlers of the area make that led them to refer to this place as the "dead man's wash," until the name eventually stuck and became official enough to be put on a sign, once the era of signs arrived? By contrast, one senses that Sun Valley—the name given to the huge retirement community swirling on a plain near Phoenix—did not grow out of the lives of anyone, certainly not of any of the people living there. It smells like part of some public relations package concocted by management to lure in other people from cold and cloudy climes, people dreaming of Pine-Sol scented rooms in some place that's sunny.

The late twentieth-century landscape is covered with places whose names have no organic connection with anyone's lived experience, neither builders nor dwellers. Rancho Buena Vista for a little Mexican flavor, Eaton Estates to hearken to the life of the English country squire—naming as the selling of clichéd fantasy, making the dwellings for the moneyed masses into a kind of live-in, suburban Disneyland. A plastic rose by any other name would smell as little like a rose.

My wife spent part of her growing up years in Jacksonville, Florida, living in a neighborhood called Cedar Hills. Not a hill, she tells me, was in sight. But it sounds good. Perhaps the power of suggestion would persuade people, by a kind of placebo effect, that living there would elevate their lives. Likewise, there are hundreds of Fairviews and Linda Vistas with no vista to be found. They are all part of the effort to enchant the world, but it is futile because the process does not grow out of the genuine magic in our humanity.

Walks in older places remind one that real people partaking of the mystery of real life create a more genuine kind of enchantment. In the Maryland countryside—not far from the Sunnysides and

Meadowcreeks that have been laid down in recent years—there winds Price's Distillery Road, giving testimony to life in another era, when both the Prices and their road served to transport their neighbors. There are roads named after fords and ferries, where people crossed running waters, and mills, where their grain was ground to make their bread. The names grew out of the reality of their lives, like the names the Indians gave to one another as they grew into them.

When I want to be moved, I am likely to walk the earth. In pursuit of this walk of life, I have learned to be a reader of maps, learned to see from how people have carved up the space for their settlements where the spirit of the people is likely to animate the place. A friend of mine has maps of Italian cities on his walls, and one can tell by just looking at the lines where the magic places in the cities are to be found. The old villages in America are almost always worth exploring, growing as they did organically, over time, like the rings of a tree. How different these places are in spirit from those prototypical villages of our time, the ubiquitous shopping malls, which spring to life fully formed from the forehead of some architect hired by someone who may never set foot there.

DISCOVERY

The mystery of reality dwells within us, but we do not possess it. We can be the channels of magic, but we are not its masters.

A man and a woman, coming together, can create the miracle of a new baby. But it is not of their design. Can you imagine what a baby would be like if its parents decided instead to build it with rational, conscious decisions? Even the deliberations of a blue-chip board of directors could not package much of a baby for the parents to buy.

To allow other people to design and package our experience for us is just as deadly a proposition. The mystery that breathes and cries and gives wonderment is unlikely to survive. Others may help to guide us into the encounter with mystery, but ultimately we must plunge into the waves for ourselves. To allow the priests of packaging to act as our constant intermediaries is to narrow ourselves, to limit what we hear of the music of the transcendent to a mere echo.

It is often said about stereophonic equipment that the system can be no better than its speakers. They are like a valve whose opening limits how much can flow through. You can have the whole Mississippi River behind the valve—the clearest signal, the best amplifier—but if the valve is small, only a relative trickle will come through. Those who would manage our experience, being just human, are smaller speakers than the signal can drive, and they yield a music less than our ears can hear. So often, when we encounter the best of human speakers—like a Bach or a Shakespeare—the interposition of intermediaries diminishes the discovery. Not only the market but also our educational institutions work to eliminate surprise and exploration and discovery. Preplanned, prepackaged—"If It's Tuesday, This Must Be Shakespeare"—the experience is diminished, narrowed, as if seen through the wrong end of the telescope. Walker Percy writes that "the citizen of Huxley's *Brave New World* who stumbles across a volume of Shakespeare in some vine-grown ruins and squats on a potsherd to read it is in a fairer way of getting at a sonnet than the Harvard sophomore taking English Poetry II."[23]

Why "stumbles across"? Herein lies another part of the mystery of reclaiming the mystery. It is not only a matter of not allowing others to act as masters of one's experience. Even to seek to make *oneself* lord over the dominion of one's experience can bring alienation from the realm of the sacred.

Like the babies we create, the reality we might apprehend far transcends the dominion of our mastery. If we found in the world only what, in Merleau-Ponty's phrase, our self had put there, our world would be a paltry place indeed. It is what we did not think to put there that can most open us up and bring us to life.

Philip Slater writes of the problems created by our wealth: "One of the main reasons wealth makes people unhappy is that it gives them too much control over what they experience." Wealth becomes a kind of Midas touch, as the wealthy "try to translate their own fantasies into reality instead of tasting what reality itself has to offer." The result of making oneself the God of one's own creation is "enervating and disappointing."[24] It is a spirit that transcends our mastery that giveth life.

Slater goes on to talk about a more rewarding kind of tourism than the controlled and predictable kind that many use their wealth to obtain, and that the market packages for us. "Whenever a traveler 'rolls with' the adventure and lets it take him where it will," Slater writes, "the outcome is usually enjoyable: kindly strangers or a sense of humor turn misery into joy—wrecked plans open doors into worlds previously unknown. This is what travel is all about—adventure."[25]

This pertains, of course, not just to travel. Life in general is such a journey. It is quite true that adventure needs to be balanced with comfort, discovery with predictability. (The sight of starving and bleeding Kurdish refugees in the mountain passes of northern Iraq reminds one of the value of having *enough* control over one's experience.) Nonetheless, Slater's conclusion offers a general truth: "If you risk nothing, you get nothing."

THE BEST SURPRISE

Remember Holiday Inn's ad a few years back? "The best surprise is no surprise at all." It was their promise that if you visit some new place, they'll make it seem like some place you've been before.

It always raised in my mind the question, Is life to be lived as an adventure, or do we want to live in a more familiar, domesticated landscape? I thought of that, traveling with my family a while back. Each town had the same bouquet of neon flowers sprouting along the highway: Wendy's gold, Pizza Hut red, the plastic yellow sun rising over Day's Inn.

We knew what we were getting when we sat down. "No surprises" has its points. It's not for nothing that folktales around the world are peopled with travelers who wake up stripped of all their goods, if they wake up at all.

For these giant corporations, it doesn't pay to do us in or to feed us garbage. The recent book *The Evolution of Cooperation*, by Robert Axelrod, talks about when it pays to be "nice." It is when you'll be dealing with the same folks again and again. If it's going to be just a one-shot meeting, you'll get most if you can snatch a traveler's purse.[26] If you are going to see the fellow over the years, it is best if he'll open his purse to you every time you meet. Burger King knows, if you get mad at them in Denver, you'll stay away from them in St. Paul. So these giants relate to us more as dairy cows to be milked regularly than as beef cattle raised for one unpleasant surprise at the slaughterhouse.

But there are costs to the unsurprising way we graze through this late twentieth-century landscape. Something happens to a burger when you're making 40 billion of them, or whatever the Burgermeisters at McD's are up to now. You might risk food poisoning with the old mom-and-pop burger, but you might also get real food. Better to have eaten and lost than never to have eaten at all.

What bothers me most, though, about living with these giants is, What kind of a relationship can you have with someone that bestrides the whole world with multimillion-dollar legs? Not the kind of company I like to keep, however comfy the stalls in their big barns.

With some of my friends, when I call them at work, the switchboard asks me, "Who are you with?" I know what they mean, but

I'll answer, "Well, my cat's asleep here on the sofa." You see, you're hardly anybody if you're nothing more than yourself. Or they'll ask, "What's your organization?" And I'll say, "Alphabetical," or, "First I make a list of things to do."

My joke surprises the party on the other end of the line. Sometimes she laughs. Sometimes it seems she'd prefer no surprise at all.

I like dealing one person to another, not taking too seriously the corporate entities that are only our creations. Maybe it's my roots. I don't come from a tradition where a man might marry his Church. Where I'm coming from, it's just us people and that One much bigger than us. Just one giant, anyway, we should be eager to live with. And the encounter with that One, when it comes, is always a surprise.

BEYOND HUMAN

In this discussion of the entry points into our transcendent reality, all the ways of access we have considered are through the human sphere. Cultural diversity, the workings of genius, the texture and pattern of ordinary life as people create it for themselves— all these are man-made signs of the mystery that permeates the reality of our existence. There are other realms of the sacred, of course, that are not of human creation—Nature, for example. Here is the living body of the earth that gave birth to us and that, as it continues to surround us, remains present as a reminder of our mere creatureliness and of the miraculous beauty of life.

One of the most difficult life transitions I ever had to make was when I moved from Prescott, Arizona, to Tucson. Tucson is a nice enough city, as modern American cities go, but my arrival there sent me into mourning. During four years of living in Prescott, the living earth there had become my beloved. Every day, I could walk out the front door of my little house in the mountains and walk in almost any direction into nature's beauty.

With every step a decision was required, where to place the foot in relation to the rocks, on which side of the tree to pass, whether to climb the hill or wander down the willow-lined wash. The interaction between feet and terrain comprised a dance between the explorer and the earth. Every adventure was full of surprises, like the fragrant and heavy white flower that I discovered between the teeth of an unexpected, rocky cave. Never before—and, unfortunately, never since—had I felt such an ongoing, intimate contact with the sacred.

Then I had to leave my beloved. I moved to Tucson and lived on a street running north and south, just above another running east and west. When I walked out my front door, I had two choices: go left or go right. The smooth and flat walkway bound me to the side of the straight road. Venturing off the straight and narrow was forbidden by the proprietorship—sometimes made flesh by fences, sometimes not—of the rectangular lots into which the land had been subdivided. There were trees and flowers to be seen, where people had decided they should grow. Emerging into this land after Prescott, I felt as if my spirit were departing, like nitrogen bubbles coming out of the blood when a person has the bends.

Tucson was rapidly filling in whatever gaps existed in its human empire, but here and there I would come across open lots and would drink in the magic created by the spontaneous arrangement of palos verdes and prickly pear and stones. Even the human contribution—the inviting openings of footpaths, made by adventurous city-dwellers, through copse and rocks—added to the organic pattern.

But, after Prescott, these special spots comforted only like portraits of a loved one who has passed away. After some months of grieving, the pain passed away, and though my life had lost something cherished and essential, Tucson began to seem the natural place to be. I felt I had become "normal" again, like the Sufi in the story who, out of the pain of his loneliness, drinks the water that had made all his neighbors crazy. I had entered into a spiritual space more suitable to ordinary life in contemporary America.

In a chapter entitled "The Illusion of 'Ordinary Life,'" Rene Guenon says that the idea of ordinary life, with its modern "materialistic attitude," is understood "to mean above all a life in which nothing that is not purely human can intervene in any way."[27]

It was when I had become acclimated to the Tucson landscape that the dream became recurrent, the one about the sacred groves of giant trees reduced to a mere remnant of their former domains and threatened with being destroyed altogether.

We have some good reasons for entering into our bargain with civilization. Man does not live by the enchantment of natural beauty alone. But it is important that we not forget that something sacred is lost if the human empire, in its pervasive ambition, gives insufficient respect to the sovereignty of nature.

In an article on the Bedouins in Israel, George Moffett III quotes one of these once-nomadic Arabs on the sense of loss that has accompanied their moving into the settled life provided for them. "The hills I looked out on as a child had the rounded shapes of tents and camels," says Ali Al Asad, principal of a secondary school in the Bedouin village of Lagiya. "Now the soft contours have given way to the stark cubes of the block houses. Now we're thinking in cubes; we're thinking in frames that are already made."[28]

There are at work in the human system many forces that tend to drive relentlessly toward complete human dominion over the natural world. But great dangers do indeed attend the over-domestication of the world in which we embed ourselves. Aside from the ecological catastrophes about which even "practical"-minded men are beginning to concern themselves, perils of a spiritual nature must not be ignored. As Wendell Berry writes:

Where is our comfort but in the free, uninvolved, finally mysterious beauty and grace of this world that we did not make, that has no price, that is not our work? Where is our sanity but there? Where is our pleasure but in working and resting kindly in the presence of this world.[29]

DOMINION

Nature survives in America. On this continent, so completely wild and untrammeled just a few centuries ago, some remnants of nature's ancient empire remain. But living nature is threatened in both body and in spirit.

The blows to the body hardly need recounting. Our great national forests are managed by people who act less as protectors of the land than as agents of those interests—in lumbering, in mining, in ranching—that see these forests merely as a source of natural capital that can make them still wealthier.

The injuries to nature's spirit are more subtle, but we should now be readily able to recognize them, for in part they have to do with that problem of packaging. As Gregor von Rezzori writes, "The few places [in America] where nature is regarded for its own sake, as nature—the Grand Canyon, Niagara Falls, Kings Canyon, Yosemite, Yellowstone—are kept in cages, like animals in a zoo."[30] All part of man's dominion.

From the point of view of the "consumer" of this natural beauty, the problem is the same as with other forms of tourism, the contrast between the eye-opening act of discovery and the vision-constricting effects of looking through the wrong end of the telescope. "García López de Cárdenas discovered the Grand Canyon and was amazed at the sight. It can be imagined: One crosses miles of desert, breaks through the mesquite, and there it is at one's feet." For sightseers, on the other hand, "The thing is no longer the thing as it confronted the Spaniard; it is rather that which has already been formulated—by picture postcard, geography book, tourist folders, and the words *Grand Canyon.*"[31] A part of this is inevitable, of course, for we cannot all come upon the wonders of the world unexpected. The problem can also be exacerbated by people who think they have seen the Grand Canyon when, disgorged by a bus, they get a picture of themselves standing in front of a wall at the South Rim, with the canyon a labeled beast looming behind them in its cage.

Perhaps the more important issue concerns the spiritual state underlying the "production" of natural wonders as a commodity for consumption, underlying indeed the whole approach to nature as an asset from which diverse commodities can be produced. It is the mind that would imagine itself master of the earth, that would seek to imprison cosmic forces in cages of its devising, that is the key to much of Western civilization's diabolical enterprise.

In his book *The Illusion of Technique*, William Barrett explores the spiritual implications of the Cartesian dualism that, he says, underlies our technological era. The issue is the stance of the "conscious Ego"—the only thing whose reality Descartes found beyond doubt—toward the surrounding cosmos. At the heart of the enterprise of this conscious ego is the project of reducing the objective world entirely to its own terms. "It impoverishes the object of all qualities except those relevant to its own purposes," says Barrett.[32] (Von Rezzori, in the same passage where he speaks of Yosemite-in-a-cage, writes that through American eyes the land appears "as an object of enterprise, a building site for some bold undertaking that might be blown or washed away at a moment.")[33]

This impoverishment of the object gives protection against any sense of overwhelming mystery. Determined that nothing shake its confidence in the adequacy of its own version of reality, this ego "considers in the object only what is measurable, numerable, and calculable. In this way it guarantees the certainty and exactness of its own thought."[34]

Here once again is a Faustian bargain. As usual, the payoff is in the form of power. For not only is the ego confirmed in the adequacy of its "objective" perspective, but it is rewarded by the enhanced capacity to manipulate and dominate. "The subject separates itself from the object in order to ensure its own mastery over it." As usual, the price paid is the wage of sin, the cost of separation. "Through [this dualistic philosophy] our human bond with the cosmos has vanished. And not vanished on its own; we ourselves have banished it."[35]

And as usual, the sinner is deluded about his place in the scheme of things. To gain the comfort of certainty, the ego mistakes its own small truth for God's truth. For the sake of control, it stands apart from the living whole of which the human being is but a small part. Standing astride a world he can see as only so much dead stuff for his manipulations, he imagines himself lord over his own Creation.

BACH AND BEYOND

My kids have long known I have a thing about Bach. When they were younger, sometimes when some great music was playing, I'd ask them, "Who wrote this piece?" I was trying to get them to really listen to the music. Other than the time my son guessed "Beetzart," they generally knew to guess Bach. But that was because they knew me, knew that it is usually Bach who gets me excited enough to call their attention to the music. Not because they knew Bach from Beetzart. To them, it was all still so much sound.

I didn't really *hear* Bach until I was fifteen. I'd begun doing my homework to the Brandenburgs, liking the atmosphere they created. Then one night, the sound coming in through my ears blossomed in my mind like a rose. Not until my own mind had matured to a certain depth and complexity, it seems, could it even register an image of Bach's crystalline structures of energy. Suddenly, there stood Bach, like some huge organ pipe with a bit of the cosmic wind streaming through, singing.

It's a good thing for geniuses like Bach that we don't remain children. A Bach or a Shakespeare already stands head and shoulders above the rest of us. If we were any shorter, such great artists would be talking only to themselves. The mathematicians talk about the monkeys at the typewriter—asserting that given enough time one by chance would write *Hamlet*. Imagine, though, how lonely it would be to be a baboon who had the understanding to write *Hamlet*.

Regrettably, something of the sort does happen. Mozart in his time was not as well regarded as the mediocrity Salieri. By his contemporaries, Bach was not considered the equal of some other composer, whose work now interests only musical historians. And nobody bought van Gogh. But, fortunately I guess, even a transcendent genius like Bach is still a human being. And what one human being can express, there will be others who can understand.

All this leads me to wonder: What would be beyond Bach? Even Bach must have his limits. Even though none of us has encountered a consciousness superior to the human, our daily experience compels us to recognize how limited is the human mind. We just don't comprehend all we see. And who knows what we don't see?

Which makes me wonder, What would music be like that was as far over Bach's head as one of his fugues is over the head of a two-year-old? What would it sound like, and what would be our reaction to it? Would it be just so much sound and fury? Or would it be something that, though far beyond our comprehension, we would still find a source of beauty and joy?

Come to think of it, we do face that issue—when we walk out into the world, a world not made by any human mind—and encounter the coming of spring across a valley, or the smile on a sweet woman's face, or the opening of a rose.

Even the creative creature is not the Creator. To recognize that there are realities that far transcend us, sources of value greater than our selfish concerns, wholes of which we humans are but parts—these humbling but fundamentally enriching truths are at the core of our spiritual traditions. No vision of reality that neglects these truths will serve us well.

NOTES

CHAPTER 1. A QUESTION OF PURPOSE (pp. 15–33)

1. Oscar Wilde, "The Magnet," in Borges and Bioy Casares, eds., *Extraordinary Tales*.

2. The question of institutional remedies for problems induced by the structure of the system, addressed in some measure in my book *The Illusion of Choice*, will not be a focus here.

3. Scitovsky, *Joyless Economy*.

4. As it turns out, judging from various survey data, Americans don't *feel* very rich in material terms. Having now more than three times as much wealth per person as we did in the 1950s, in constant dollars, Americans have less sense of material satisfaction. Only a small portion even of the wealthy feel they are "living the American dream."

5. Tocqueville, *Democracy in America*, II, p. 145.

6. J. B. S. Haldane, in Pulliam and Dunford, *Programmed to Learn*, p. 98.

7. Williams, *Dream Worlds*, p. 225; internal quote is from Paul Leroy-Beaulieu.

8. Cf. Horowitz, *Morality of Spending*, p. xxvii.

9. See Mises, *Anti-Capitalistic Mentality*.

10. See Mandeville, *Fable of the Bees*, p. 333.

11. Williams, *Dream Worlds*, p. 224.

12. Ernest Dichter, quoted in Gold, *Advertising, Politics, and American Culture*, p. 52.

13. Cavanaugh, *Following Christ in a Consumer Society*.

14. Lynn, R. "Anxiety and Economic Growth."

15. Marchand, *Advertising the American Dream*, p. 11.

16. John Adams, in Bowen, *Miracle at Philadelphia*, p. 195.

17. Freud, *Civilization and Its Discontents*, 1961, pp. 70–71.

CHAPTER 2. EVERYTHING MONEY CAN BUY (pp. 34–61)

1. Slater, *Wealth Addiction*, p. 6.

2. *ABC News*, July 16, 1990.

3. Frank, *Choosing the Right Pond*, p. 15.

4. Heilbroner, *Quest for Wealth*, p. 32.

5. Ibid., p. 33.

6. Rite of Hospitalers, quoted in Seward, 1972, p. 21.

7. Matthew 6:24, KJV.

8. Paul Samuelson, quoted in Etzioni, *The Moral Dimension*, p. 24.

9. Browning and Browning, quoted in ibid., p. 24.

10. C. B. MacPherson, quoted in Parel and Flanagan, *Theories of Property*, p. 5.

11. Jeremy Bentham, quoted in ibid.

12. Jeremy Bentham, quoted in ibid.

13. Mises, *Anti-Capitalist Mentality*, pp. 11, 10.

14. Ibid., p. 15.

15. Schudson, *Advertising, the Uneasy Persuasion*, p. 235, italics in original.

16. Clark, *Want Makers*, p. 143.

17. These will be explored in the next book in this series, *Filling a Sieve*, on the psychological and spiritual bases of the materialism of our civilization.

18. Csikszentmihalyi and Rochberg-Halton, *Meaning of Things*, p. 239.

19. Adam Smith, quoted in Galbraith, *Affluent Society*, p. 139.

CHAPTER 3. LIMITED LIABILITY (pp. 63–92)

1. John Locke, *An Essay Concerning the True Original, Extent, and End of Civil-Government*, no. 93.

2. On some of the differences between the "natural and the unnatural," see chapter 6 of my earlier book *The Parable of the Tribes*, "Systems of Nature and of Civilization."

3. Francis Edgeworth, quoted in Schwartz, *Battle for Human Nature*, p. 54.

4. Friedman and Friedman, *Free to Choose*, p. 27.

5. Smith, *Wealth of Nations*, p. 14.

6. See chapter 4, "Human Nature and the Evaluation of Civilization," in my book *The Parable of the Tribes*.

7. Schudson, *Advertising, the Uneasy Persuasion*, p. 221.

8. Ryan, "Distrusting Economics," p. 26.

9. Ibid.

10. MacPherson, *Political Theory of Possessive Individualism*, p. 3.

11. Ibid. My next book, *Filling a Sieve*, will explore some of the psychological dimension of the radical avoidance of a sense of debt, which is inseparable at its root from the sense of guilt.

12. Robert Bellah, in *Habits of the Heart*, explores as illustrative of a wider phenomenon in our society the worldview of a woman psychotherapist. Though she works to help others, her understanding of "personal responsibility" leads to an "inability to make legitimate demands on others . . . even in the closest, most committed relationships." In this world, "in the end you really are alone."

13. Kendall, "Social Contract."

14. Smith, *Wealth of Nations*, 1937, p. 423.

15. Shi, *Simple Life*, p. 83.

16. Philip Greven, quoted in Shi, *Simple Life*, p. 83.

17. Friedman and Friedman, *Free to Choose*, p. 215.

18. Leonard Bushkoff, review of *Casey: From the OSS to the CIA*, by Joseph Persico, in *Christian Science Monitor*, January 1991.

19. Williams, *Dream Worlds*, p. 398. Williams argues instead for a position she terms "solidarist austerity," which she describes as "rejecting the moral assumption that the individual consumer has the right, if not the duty, to maximize his own material self-interest" (p. 398). She favors the revival of "sumptuary laws," laws, like those in early capitalist England and Puritan America, limiting the conspicuous display of wealth, and the placing of much greater limitations on consumption that has an adverse impact on scarce natural resources.

20. The reporter on "All Things Considered" (September 15, 1989) says, "Crack is a capitalism problem," speaking of the burgeoning market in the dangerous, cocaine-derived drug, a market that flourishes in those areas of American society where there is no other avenue of economic opportunity open to those ambitious to get ahead.

21. *Good Money* 6 (May/June 1988), no. 3, p. 1.

22. Ibid.

23. Ibid.

24. Polanyi, *Great Transformation*, p. 57.

25. Quoted in Bellah, *Broken Covenant.*

26. Bellah et al., *Habits of the Heart*, p. 6.

27. Verlyn Klinkenborg, review of *Killing Mr. Watson*, by Peter Matthiessen, *The New Republic*, November 5, 1990, p. 43.

28. Quoted in Bellah et al., *Habits of the Heart*, p. 264.

29. Edward Bok, quoted in Shi, *Simple Life*, p. 218.

30. Ibid.

31. Schwartz, *Battle for Human Nature*, p. 18.

32. Ibid., pp. 148, 149.

33. Ibid., p. 18.

CHAPTER 4. GUIDING VOICES (pp. 93–165)

1. I remember the day in 1969 that a California Highway Patrolman gave me a ticket because I wore a beard. That is not what the ticket said, of course, but from the circumstances it was clear to me and to the three other people in my car that my appearance, which identified me as being on the rebellious side of the cultural conflict then ongoing, was the real reason for the ticket.

2. Christopher Lasch, quoted in Waterman, *Psychology of Individualism*, p. 75.

3. Robert Hogan, quoted in ibid., p. 73.

4. Edward Sampson, quoted in ibid., p. 8.

5. Waterman, p. 74.

6. Edward Sampson, quoted in ibid., p. 79.

7. Waterman, p. 78.

8. Ibid.

9. Wallach and Wallach, quoted in ibid.

10. For a course in the history of Western philosophy, I wrote a paper searching for the foundation of value in answering the question, How should we live our lives? One idea I arrived at in the process that felt important to me was the discovery that even the existence of a God telling us what we should or should not do would not in itself establish what was good. God, after all, might turn out to be all-powerful but not all-good. What if he were a brutal tyrant? I asked. Would that make what he commanded good, and not just expedient, to obey?

11. Quoted in Andrzejewski, *Military Organization and Society*, p. 131.

12. Nikolaus Zinzendorf, quoted in Weber, *Protestant Ethic and the Spirit of Capitalism*, p. 168.

13. Ben Franklin, quoted in Van Doren, *Benjamin Franklin*, 1938, p. 69.

14. R. E. Money-Kyrle, quoted in Fornari, *Psychoanalysis of War*, p. 100.

15. Bell, *Cultural Contradictions of Capitalism*.

16. Norton, *Personal Destinies*, p. 5.

17. Ibid., pp. 4, 8, italics added.

18. Ibid., p. 16.

19. Ibid., p. 5.

20. Waterman, *Psychology of Individualism*, p. 16.

21. Pindar, quoted in Norton, *Personal Destinies*, p. 16.

22. Ibid., p. 8.

23. Theodore Adorno, quoted in Levin, *Pathologies of the Modern Self*, p. 19.

24. J. Sulzer's "Essay on the Education and Instruction of Children," appearing as epigraph in Alice Miller, *For Your Own Good*.

25. Clark, *Want Makers*, p. 198, 199.

26. Giedion, *Mechanization Takes Command*, p. 98.

27. Andren et al., *Rhetoric and Ideology in Advertising*, p. 137.

28. Rowe, "Gauging the Impact of Advertising."

29. Tracy Westen, quoted in Jonathan Rowe, "Advertising and Children's TV."

30. Jerry Mauder, quoted in Rowe, "Gauging the Impact of Advertising."

31. Margarita Laski, quoted in Marchand, *Advertising the American Dream*, p. 265.

32. Marchand, p. 265.

33. See Marchand, *Advertising the American Dream*, pp. 282, 265.

34. The process has evidently now come full cycle. The other day I saw a T-shirt emblazoned with the question, What is God like? Below this question were a series of answers drawing upon the familiar world of products and their slogans. "God is like magic tape," the shirt said, "you can't see it, but you know it's there." "God is like Coke, He's the real thing." "God is like United Airlines, He offers the friendly skies." "God is like Tide, He gets the stains out." And on went the list.

35. Ernest Calkin, quoted in Marchand, *Advertising the American Dream*, p. 24.

36. Wickse, *About Possession*, pp. 92–93.

37. Rousseau, quoted in ibid., p. 93.

38. Linden, *Affluence and Discontent*, p. 15.

39. Ibid., p. 14.

40. Ibid., p. 17.

41. Ibid.

42. Preston, *Great American Blow-up*, p. 4.

43. Ibid., pp. 4, 23, 26.

44. Ibid., pp. 26, 27.

45. Ibid., pp. 26, 27, 29.

46. Ibid., p. 26.

47. Quoted in Clark, *Want Makers*, p. 186.

48. Center for Science in the Public Interest, News Release, September 4, 1988.

49. Marchand, *Advertising the American Dream*, p. 3.

50. Schudson, *Advertising, the Uneasy Persuasion*, p. 240.

51. Potter, *People of Plenty*, p. 177.

52. Norton, *Personal Destinies*, p. 24.

53. Ibid., p. 43.

54. Samuel Butler, quoted in W. H. Auden and Louis Kronenberger, *The Viking Book of Aphorisms* (Middlesex: Penguin Books, 1966), p. 367.

55. Waterman, *Psychology of Individualism*, pp. 156, 157

56. Ibid., pp. 156–57.

57. Ibid., p. 157.

58. There is a dream told by the Jungian psychologist Maria von Franz that I in turn have retold more than once because its lesson seems to me so important. A woman dreams that two figures break into her house, apparently wanting "to torment me and my sister." In the midst of this threatening scene, one of the criminals "makes a sketch on the wall, and when I see it, I say (in order to seem friendly) 'Oh! But this is well drawn!' Now suddenly my tormentor has the noble head of an artist, and he says proudly, 'Yes, indeed.'" About this dream, von Franz says that "the dream reveals that the veiled burglars are actually disguised artists, and if the dreamer recognizes their gifts (which are her own) they will give up their evil intentions." In Jung et al., *Man and His Symbols*, p. 203.

59. Norton, *Personal Destinies*, p. 77.

60. Quoted in Bellah et al., *Habits of the Heart*, pp. 290–91.

61. Stein, "Farmer and Cowboy."

62. R. H. Tawney, quoted in Norton, *Personal Destinies*, p. 43.

63. Schwartz, *Battle for Human Nature*, p. 149, italics in original.

64. Gendlin, "Philosophical Critique of the Concept of Narcissism," p. 267 (italics added). Freud, quoted in ibid., p. 262.

65. Ibid., p. 264.

66. Ibid., p. 266.

67. Ibid., p. 266.

CHAPTER 5. THE WAGES OF SIN (pp. 166–201)

1. Csikszentmihalyi and Rochberg-Halton, *Meaning of Things*, p. 40.
2. Richard Wilhelm, trans., *I Ching*, p. 48.
3. Bateson, *Steps to an Ecology of the Mind*, p. 493.
4. Brown, *Life Against Death*, pp. 218–19.
5. Abercrombie, *Sovereign Individuals of Capitalism*, p. 8.
6. Berry, *Home Economics*, p. 168.
7. On *The MacNeil-Lehrer News Hour*, November 24, 1988.
8. Ibid.
9. Klein, *Envy and Gratitude*, p. 181.
10. Polanyi, *Great Transformation*, p. 178.
11. On this, see chapter 3, "Missing Our Connections," in Schmookler, *Illusion of Choice*.
12. Frank, *Choosing the Right Pond*, p. 149.
13. Ibid.
14. Ibid., pp. 150–51.
15. Ibid., p. 151.
16. Ewen, *All Consuming Images*, pp. 21, 22.
17. Marshall Sahlins, on the "original affluent society," in *Stone-Age Economics*.
18. *Time* magazine, April 24, 1989, pp. 59, 64.
19. Ibid., p. 59.
20. Gardner, "Rent-a-Family—The Latest Service Industry."
21. Csikszentmihalyi and Rochberg-Halton, *Meaning of Things*, pp. 230–31, 242–43.
22. Ibid., p. 149.
23. Novak, *Spirit of Democratic Capitalism*, p. 351.
24. *Wall Street Week*, June 9, 1989.
25. Clark, *Want Makers*, p. 257.
26. Quoted in ibid., p. 283.
27. Warren Breed and James Defoe, quoted in Rowe, "Gauging the Impact of Advertising."
28. *Boston Globe*, March 2, 1989.
29. Elderkin, "Baseball Brew."
30. Ibid.
31. Berry, *Home Economics*, p. 54.
32. Ibid., pp. 54–55.

33. Ibid., p. 60.

34. Ibid., p. 55.

FINALE (pp. 202–231)

1. Maurice Merleau-Ponty, quoted in Wickse, *About Possession*, p. 45. Wickse identifies this as Merleau-Ponty's articulation of the Cartesian position.

2. Carpenter, *Oh, What a Blow That Phantom Gave Me!* p. 17.

3. Will, "Real Game."

4. Campbell, *The Romantic Ethic and the Spirit of Consumerism*, p. 48.

5. Kingsley Amis, from *Lucky Jim*, quoted in McCracken, *Culture and Consumption*, p. 126.

6. McCracken, p. 127.

7. Ibid., p. 79, italics added.

8. Ibid., p. 89.

9. Quoted in Gold, *Advertising, Politics, and American Culture*, p. 51.

10. Ibid.

11. Cavanaugh, *Following Christ in a Consumer Society*, p. 23.

12. "A Jumpin' Night in the Garden of Eden." Produced and edited by Michael Goldman. First Run Features, 1989.

13. Percy, *Message in the Bottle*, p. 56.

14. Ibid., pp. 55–56.

15. Carpenter, *Oh What a Blow That Phantom Gave Me!* p. 96.

16. Ibid.

17. Ibid.

18. Rosalind Williams, "Corrupting the Public Imagination."

19. Carpenter, *Oh What a Blow That Phantom Gave Me!* p. 97.

20. Schumacher, *Small Is Beautiful*, p. 7.

21. Carpenter, *Oh What a Blow That Phantom Gave Me!* p. 97.

22. Hein Piet, *Grooks.*

23. Percy, *Message in the Bottle*, p. 56.

24. Slater, *Wealth Addiction*, p. 28.

25. Ibid.

26. Axelrod, *The Evolution of Cooperation*, p. 117.

27. Guenon, *Reign of Quantity*, p. 125.

28. Moffett, "Israel Urges End to Nomadic Life."

29. Berry, "Profit in Work's Pleasure."

30. Rezzori, "A Stranger in Lolitaland," p. 218.
31. Percy, *Message in the Bottle*, pp. 46, 47.
32. Barrett, *Illusion of Technique*, p. 191.
33. Rezzori, "A Stranger in Lolitaland," p. 218.
34. Ibid.
35. Ibid.

BIBLIOGRAPHY

Abercrombie, Nicholas. *The Sovereign Individuals of Capitalism*. London: Allen & Unwin, 1986.

Abramowitz, Moses. "Economic Growth and Its Discontents." In Boskin, *Economics and Human Welfare*.

Andren, Gunnar, Lars O. Ericcson, Ragnar Ohlsson, and Torbjorn Tannsjo. *Rhetoric and Ideology in Advertising: A Content Analytical Study of American Advertising*. Stockholm: LiberForlag, 1978.

Andrzejewski, Stanislaus. *Military Organization and Society*. London: Routledge and Kegan Paul, 1954.

Appadurai, Arjun, ed. *The Social Life of Things: Commodities in Cultural Perspective*. Cambridge: Cambridge Univ. Press, 1986.

Arnold, Thurman W. *The Folklore of Capitalism*. New Haven: Yale Univ. Press, 1937.

Axelrod, Robert. *The Evolution of Cooperation*. New York: Basic Books, 1984.

Barber, Benjamin. "What Do 47-Year-Olds Know?" *New York Times*, December 26, 1987.

Barfield, Owen. *Saving the Appearances: A Study in Idolatry*. London: Faber and Faber, 1957.

Barol, Bill. "The Eighties Are Over." *Newsweek*, January 4, 1988.

Barrett, William. *The Illusion of Technique: A Search for Meaning in a Technological Civilization*. Garden City, NY: Anchor Press, 1978.

Bateson, Gregory. *Steps to an Ecology of Mind*. New York: Ballantine Books, 1972.

Belk, Russell W. "Cultural and Historical Differences in Concepts of Self and Their Effects on Attitudes Toward Having and Giving." Manuscript.

———. "Materialism and Status Appeals in Japanese and US Print Advertising." *International Marketing Review*, Winter 1985.

———. "Materialism: Trait Aspects of Living in the Material World." *Journal of Consumer Research* 12 (December 1985).

———. "Possessions and the Extended Self." Manuscript.

————. "Third World Consumer Culture." *Research in Marketing.* Supplement 4, 1988.

————. "Worldly Possessions: Issues and Criticisms." Manuscript.

Belk, Russell W., and Richard W. Pollay. "Images of Ourselves: The Good Life in Twentieth-Century Advertising." *Journal of Consumer Research* 11 (March 1985).

Belk, Russell W., and Melanie Wallendorf. "The Sacred Meaning of Money." Manuscript.

Bell, Daniel. *The Cultural Contradictions of Capitalism.* New York: Basic Books, 1976.

Bellah, Robert N. *The Broken Covenant: American Civil Religion in Time of Trail.* New York: Harper & Row, 1976.

Bellah, Robert N., et al. *Habits of the Heart: Individualism and Commitment in American Life.* Harper & Row, New York: 1985.

Berle, Adolf A., and Gardiner C. Means. *The Modern Corporation and Private Property.* New York: Harcourt, Brace and World, 1968.

Berman, Marshall. *All That Is Solid Melts into Air: The Experience of Modernity.* New York: Simon & Schuster, 1982.

Berry, Wendell. *Home Economics.* San Francisco: North Point Press, 1987.

————. "The Profit in Work's Pleasure." *Harper's Magazine*, March 1988.

Block, Walter, Geoffrey Brennan, and Kenneth Elzinga, eds. *The Morality of the Market: Religious and Economic Perspectives.* Vancouver: The Fraser Institute, 1985.

Blum, Jeffrey D. *Living with Spirit in a Material World.* New York: Fawcett Columbine, 1988.

Borges, Jorge Luis, and Adolfo Bioy Casares, eds. *Extraordinary Tales.* New York: Herder and Herder, 1971.

Bornemann, Ernest. *The Psychoanalysis of Money.* New York: Urizen Books, 1976.

Boskin, Michael J., ed. *Economics and Human Welfare.* New York: Academic Press, 1979.

Boston Globe. "Madonna Sells Her Soul for a Song." March 2, 1989.

Bowen, Catherine Drinker. *Miracle at Philadelphia.* Boston: Little, Brown, 1986.

Braudel, Fernand. *Capitalism and Material Life, 1400–1800.* London: Fontana/Collins, 1974.

Brennan, Geoffrey. "Markets and Majorities, Morals and Madness." In Block, *Morality of the Market.*

Brooks, John. *Showing Off in America.* Boston: Little, Brown & Company, 1981.

Brown, Norman O. *Life Against Death,* Middletown, CT: Wesleyan Univ. Press, 1985.

Brownstein, Ronald, and Nina J. Easton. "The New Status Seekers." *Los Angeles Times Magazine,* December 27, 1987.

Butterfield, Stephen T. "Keeping a Short Bridge: Buddhist-Christian Dialogue." *The Sun,* October 1988.

Cabot, Robert, and Robert Fuller. "Empire's End, Russia's Rebirth." *Harvard Magazine,* May/June 1991.

Campbell, Colin. *The Romantic Ethic and the Spirit of Consumerism.* New York: Basil Blackwell, 1987.

Carnegie, Andrew. *The Gospel of Wealth.* Cambridge: Harvard Univ. Press, 1962.

Carpenter, Edmund. *Oh, What a Blow That Phantom Gave Me!* New York: Holt, Rinehart & Winston, 1973.

Cavanaugh, John Francis. *Following Christ in a Consumer Society.* Maryknoll, NY: Orbis Books, 1981.

Cawelti, John G. *Apostles of the Self-Made Man.* Chicago: Univ. of Chicago Press, 1965.

Center for Science in the Public Interest, "Kids Are as Aware of Booze as Presidents, Survey Finds." News Release, September 4, 1989.

Clark, Eric. *The Want Makers: The World of Advertising: How They Make You Buy.* New York: Viking, 1988.

Collett, Lily. "Step by Step: A Skeptic's Encounter with the Twelve-Step Program." *Utne Reader,* November/December 1988.

Collett, Merrill. "Bolivia Blazes Trail . . . to Where?" *Christian Science Monitor,* July 10, 1989.

Collins, Ronald K. L., and Michael F. Jacobson, "Commercialization Versus Culture." *Christian Science Monitor,* September 19, 1990.

Corporate Examiner. Vol. 16, no. 8–9. New York: Interfaith Center on Corporate Responsibility, 1987.

Csikszentmihalyi, Mihaly, and Eugene Rochberg-Halton. *The Meaning of Things: Domestic Symbols and the Self.* Cambridge: Cambridge Univ. Press, 1981.

Daly, Herman E. "The Economic Growth Debate: What Some Economists Have Learned But Many Have Not." *Journal of Environmental Economics and Management* 14 (1987):323–36.

————. *Steady-State Economics: The Economics of Biophysical Equilibrium and Moral Growth.* San Francisco: W. H. Freeman, 1977.

Darman, Richard. *Keeping America First: American Romanticism and the Global Economy.* Washington, DC: Office of Management and Budget, 1990.

Doi, Ayako. "'America-Bashing,' Japanese Style." *Washington Post,* July 6, 1989.

Douglas, Mary, and Baron Isherwood. *The World of Goods.* New York: Basic Books, 1979.

The Economist. "Voting with Your Wallet." April 15, 1988.

Elderkin, Phil. "Baseball Brew." *Christian Science Monitor,* July 27, 1988.

Elgin, Duane. *Voluntary Simplicity: An Ecological Lifestyle That Promises Personal and Social Renewal.* New York: Bantam Books, 1987.

Ellul, Jacques. *Money and Power.* Downers Grove, IL: Inter-Varsity Press, 1984.

"Ethics and Corporate Goals." *Good Money: The Newsletter for Socially Concerned Investors,* May/June 1988.

Etzioni, Amitai. *The Moral Dimension: Toward a New Economics.* New York: The Free Press, 1988.

Ewen, Stuart. *All Consuming Images: The Politics of Style in Contemporary Culture.* New York: Basic Books, 1988.

Ewen, Stuart, and Elizabeth Ewen. *Channels of Desire: Mass Images and the Shaping of American Consciousness.* New York: McGraw-Hill, 1982.

Faber, M.D. *Culture and Consciousness: The Social Meaning of Altered Awareness.* New York: Human Sciences Press, 1981.

Fallows, James. "America's Secret Weapon Is America." *Washington Post*, March 26, 1989.

———. "Japan: Playing by Different Rules." *Atlantic*, September 1987.

———. *More Like Us: Making America Great Again*. Boston: Houghton Mifflin, 1989.

Festinger, Leon, Henry W. Riecken, and Stanley Schachter. *When Prophecy Fails*. New York: Harper & Row, 1956.

Findhorn. "The Individual and the Collective." Conference Newsletter, Findhorn Community, Findhorn, Scotland, October 21, 1988.

Flanagan, T. E. "Hayek on Property." In Parel and Flanagan, *Theories of Property*.

Fornari, Franco. *The Psychoanalysis of War*. Garden City, NY: Auction Books, 1966.

Foster, Richard J. *Money, Sex and Power: The Challenge of the Disciplined Life*. San Francisco: Harper & Row, 1985.

Fowler, Jan. "Deep Ecology I: Relation to Image Finding." *Path Words*, Sevenoaks Pathwork Center, Madison, Virginia, December 1987.

Fox, Richard Wightman, and T. J. Jackson Lears, eds. *The Culture of Consumption: Critical Essays in American History*. New York: Pantheon Books, 1983.

Francis, David R. "As the Economy Goes, so Goes the Nation, This Analyst Indicates." *Christian Science Monitor*, February 16, 1988.

Frank, Robert H. *Choosing the Right Pond: Human Behavior and the Quest for Status*, New York: Oxford Univ. Press, 1985.

Freedman, Jonathan L. *Happy People*. New York: Harcourt Brace Jovanovich, 1978.

Freud, Sigmund. *Civilization and Its Discontents*. New York: W. W. Norton, 1961.

Friedman, Milton, and Rose Friedman. *Free to Choose*. New York: Harcourt Brace Jovanovich, 1980.

Galbraith, John Kenneth. *The Affluent Society*. Boston: Houghton Mifflin, 1971.

Gardner, Marilyn. "Rent-a-Family—The Latest Service Industry." *Christian Science Monitor*, May 16, 1989.

Gendlin, Eugene T. "A Philosophical Critique of the Concept of Narcissism: The Significance of the Awareness Movement." In Levin, *Pathologies of the Modern Self.*

Gibbs, Nancy. "Workers Are Weary, Parents Are Frantic, and Even Children Haven't a Minute to Spare." *Time Magazine*, April 24, 1989.

Giedion, Siegfried. *Mechanization Takes Command: A Contribution to Anonymous History*. New York: W. W. Norton, 1948.

Gold, Philip. *Advertising, Politics, and American Culture: From Salesmanship to Therapy*. New York: Paragon House, 1987.

Goldberg, Jeffrey. "Free Market Economics, Old Testament Morality." *Washington Post*, October 23, 1988.

Goodman, Ellen. "Families Under Separate Roofs." *Washington Post*, September 8, 1990.

———. "Mortality Is Not the Option of Choice." *Baltimore Sun*, April 29, 1988.

Grossman, Richard. "Growth as Metaphor, Growth as Politics." *The Wrenching Debate Gazette*, July 1985.

Guenon, Rene. *The Reign of Quantity and the Signs of the Times*. London: Luzac and Company, 1953.

Heilbroner, Robert L. *The Quest for Wealth*. New York: Simon & Schuster, 1956.

Henderson, Hazel. *Paradigms in Progress: Life Beyond Economics*. Indianapolis: Knowledge Systems, 1992.

———. *Politics of the Solar Age*. Indianapolis: Knowledge Systems, 1988.

Hendin, Herbert. *The Age of Sensation*. W. W. Norton, New York: 1975.

Herndon, Nancy. "Local Land Trusts Flex New Muscle." *Christian Science Monitor*, June 7, 1989.

Hiatt, Fred, and Margaret Shapiro. "Japan's New Era: Sudden Riches Creating Conflict and Self-Doubt." *Washington Post*, February 11, 1990.

Hoffman, Eva. *Lost in Translation: A Life in a New Language*. New York: E. P. Dutton, 1989.

Hollis, Martin, and Edward J. Nell. *Rational Economic Man: A Philosophical Critique of Neo-Classical Economics.* Cambridge: Cambridge Univ. Press, 1975.

Hollowell, Peter G. *Property and Social Relations.* London: Routledge & Kegan Paul, 1982.

Hook, Sidney, ed. *Human Values and Economic Policy: A Symposium.* New York: New York Univ. Press, 1967.

Horney, Karen. *The Neurotic Personality of Our Time.* New York: W. W. Norton, 1937.

Horowitz, Daniel. *The Morality of Spending: Attitudes Toward the Consumer Society in America, 1875–1940.* Baltimore: Johns Hopkins Univ. Press, 1985.

Hostetler, John A. *Amish Society,* Baltimore: Johns Hopkins Univ. Press, 1968.

Hughes, John. "Moscow's Consumer Revolution." *Christian Science Monitor,* September 15, 1989.

Johnson, Don Hanlon. "The Possibility of a Social Body." Manuscript.

Joll, James. "The Cost of Bigness." *New York Review of Books,* February 4, 1988.

Jung, Carl G., et al. *Man and His Symbols.* Garden City, NY: Doubleday, 1964.

Kaiser, Robert G. "Beyond the Summit: The New Red Revolution." *Washington Post,* May 29, 1988.

Kassiola, Joel Jay. *The Death of Industrial Civilization: The Limits to Economic Growth and the Repoliticization of Advanced Industrial Society.* Albany: State Univ. of New York Press, 1990.

Kendall, Willmoore. "Social Contract." *International Encyclopedia of Social Sciences.* New York: Macmillan, 1967.

Kennedy, Paul. *The Rise and Fall of the Great Powers: Economic Change and Military Conflict from 1500 to 2000.* New York: Vintage Books, 1987.

Klein, Melanie. *Envy and Gratitude.* New York: Delacorte Press, 1975.

Klinkenborg, Verlyn. Review of *Killing Mr. Watson,* by Peter Matthiessen. *The New Republic,* November 5, 1990.

Laszlo, Ervin. *The Inner Limits of Mankind: Heretical Reflections on Today's Values, Culture and Politics.* Oxford: Pergamon Press, 1978.

Lears, Thomas Jackson. *No Place of Grace: Antimodernism and the Transformation of American Culture 1880–1920*. New York: Pantheon Books, 1981.

Leiss, William. *The Limits to Satisfaction: An Essay on the Problem of Needs and Commodities*. Toronto: Univ. of Toronto Press, 1976.

Levin, David Michael. *The Body's Recollection of Being*. London: Routledge and Kegan Paul, 1985.

———. "Clinical Stories: A Modern Self in the Fury of Being." In Levin, *Pathologies of the Modern Self*.

———. "Psychopathology in the Epoch of Nihilism." In Levin, *Pathologies of the Modern Self*.

Levin, David Michael, ed. *Pathologies of the Modern Self: Postmodern Studies on Narcissism, Schizophrenia, and Depression*. New York: New York Univ. Press, 1987.

Levy, Frank, and Richard C. Michel. "Why America Won't Save." *Washington Post*, February 4, 1990.

Liedloff, Jean. *The Continuum Concept: Allowing Human Nature to Work Successfully*. Reading, MA: Addison-Wesley, 1985.

Linden, Eugene. *Affluence and Discontent: The Anatomy of Consumer Societies*. New York: Viking Press, 1979.

Linder, Staffan Burenstam. *The Harried Leisure Class*. New York: Columbia Univ. Press, 1970.

Lindgren, Henry Clay. *Great Expectations: The Psychology of Money*. Los Altos, CA: William Kaufmann, 1980.

Lowen, Alexander. *Depression and the Body*. New York: Coward, McCann & Geoghegan, 1973.

Lynn, Kenneth S. *The Dream of Success: A Study of the Modern American Imagination*. Boston: Atlantic Monthly Press, 1955.

Lynn, R. "Anxiety and Economic Growth," *Nature* 219 (1968).

McCracken, Grant. *Culture and Consumption: New Approaches to the Symbolic Character of Consumer Goods and Activities*. Bloomington: Indiana Univ. Press, 1988.

McKendrick, Neil, John Brewer, and J. H. Plumb. *The Birth of a Consumer Society: The Commercialization of Eighteenth-Century England*. Bloomington: Indiana Univ. Press, 1985.

MacPherson, C. B. *The Political Theory of Possessive Individualism: Hobbes to Locke.* Oxford: Clarendon Press, 1962.

———. "Property as Means or End." In Parel and Flanagan, *Theories of Property.*

Mandeville, Bernard. *The Fable of the Bees.* In *Eighteenth-Century Poetry and Prose,* 2d ed., edited by Louis I. Bredvold, Alan D. McKillop, and Lois Whitney. New York: The Ronald Press, 1956.

Marcel, Gabriel. *Being and Having: An Existentialist Diary.* New York: Harper & Row, 1965.

Marchand, Roland. *Advertising the American Dream: Making Way for Modernity, 1920–1940.* Berkeley and Los Angeles: Univ. of California Press, 1985.

Marx, Leo. *The Machine in the Garden: Technology and the Pastoral Ideal in America.* New York: Oxford Univ. Press, 1964.

Milbrath, Lester W. *Envisioning a Sustainable Society: Learning Our Way Out.* Albany: State Univ. of New York Press, 1989.

Miller, Alice. *The Drama of the Gifted Child.* New York: Basic Books, 1981.

———. *For Your Own Good.* New York: Farrar, Straus, Giroux, 1984.

———. *Thou Shalt Not Be Aware: Society's Betrayal of the Child.* New York: Farrar, Straus, Giroux, 1984.

Mises, Ludwig von. *The Anti-Capitalistic Mentality.* New York: Van Nostrand Reinhold, 1956.

Mishan, Ezra J. *The Economic Growth Debate.* London: George Allen & Unwin, 1977.

———. "Religion, Culture and Technology." In Block, *Morality of the Market.*

Moffett, George D., III. "Israel Urges End to Nomadic Life." *Christian Science Monitor,* October 31, 1989.

Montagu, Ashley. *The American Way of Life.* New York: G. P. Putnam's Sons, 1967.

———. *Touching: The Human Significance of the Skin.* New York: Harper & Row, 1978.

Montagu, Ashley, and Floyd Matson,. *The Dehumanization of Man.* New York: McGraw-Hill, 1983.

Morishima, Michio. *Why Has Japan 'Succeeded'? Western Technology and the Japanese Ethos.* Cambridge: Cambridge Univ. Press, 1982.

Morris, David. "Two Million Tons of Rock Salt." *Washington Post,* January 17, 1988.

Mukerji, Chandra. *From Graven Images: Patterns of Modern Materialism.* New York: Columbia Univ. Press, 1983.

Norton, David L. *Personal Destinies: A Philosophy of Ethical Individualism.* Princeton, NJ: Princeton Univ. Press, 1976.

Novak, Michael. "Overview." In Block, *Morality of the Market.*

———. *The Spirit of Democratic Capitalism.* New York: Simon & Schuster, 1982.

Parel, Anthony, and Thomas Flanagan, eds. *Theories of Property: Aristotle to the Present.* Waterloo, Ontario: Wilfrid Laurier Univ. Press, 1979.

Percy, Walker. *The Message in the Bottle.* New York: Farrar, Straus & Giroux, 1975.

Perrin, Pat, and Wim Coleman. "Is Addiction Actually a Misguided Move Toward Wholeness?" *Utne Reader,* November/December 1988.

Piet, Hein. *Grooks.* Garden City, NY: Doubleday, 1969.

Polanyi, Karl. *The Great Transformation.* New York: Farrar and Rinehart, 1944.

Popper, Frank J., and Deborah Epstein Popper. "Saving the Plains: The Bison Gambit." *Washington Post,* August 6, 1989.

Potter, David M. *People of Plenty: Economic Abundance and the American Character.* Chicago: Univ. of Chicago Press, 1954.

Preston, Ivan L. *The Great American Blow-up: Puffery in Advertising and Selling.* Madison: Univ. of Wisconsin Press, 1975.

Pulliam, H. Ronald, and Christopher Dunford. *Programmed to Learn: An Essay on the Evolution of Culture.* New York: Columbia Univ. Press, 1980.

Reich, Robert B. "Who Is Us?" *Harvard Business Review,* January-February 1990.

Repetto, Robert. "No Accounting for Pollution." *Washington Post,* May 28, 1989.

Reuss, Ronald. "U.S. Faces Challenge to Maintain Its Standard of Living." *Piper Market Digest.* Minneapolis: Piper, Jaffray and Hopwood, March 1990.

Rezzori, Gregor von. "A Stranger in Lolitaland." In Talese, *Best American Essays 1987.*

Rowe, Jonathan. "Advertising and Children's TV." *Christian Science Monitor,* January 29, 1987.

———. "Gauging the Impact of Advertising." *Christian Science Monitor,* January 28, 1987.

Rudmin, Floyd W. "The Meaning and Morality of Voluntary Simplicity." Manuscript.

Ryan, Alan. "Distrusting Economics." *New York Review of Books,* May 18, 1989.

Sagoff, Mark. "Property Rights and Environmental Law." *Philosophy and Public Policy,* Spring 1988.

Sahlins, Marshall. *Culture and Practical Reason.* Chicago: Univ. of Chicago Press, 1976.

———. "Social Science, Or the Tragic Western Sense of Human Imperfection." Manuscript.

———. *Stone Age Economics.* Chicago: Aldine Atherton, 1972.

Sampson, Edward E. "The Challenge of Social Change for Psychology." *American Psychologist,* June 1989.

Satin, Mark. "Breaking the Hold of Television Advertising." *New Options,* December 26, 1988.

Schaef, Anne Wilson. *When Society Becomes an Addict.* San Francisco: Harper & Row, 1987.

Schama, Simon. *The Embarrassment of Riches: An Interpretation of Dutch Culture in the Golden Age.* New York: Alfred A. Knopf, 1987.

Schmookler, Andrew Bard. *The Illusion of Choice: How the Market Economy Shapes Our Destiny.* Albany, NY: State Univ. of New York Press, 1993.

———. *Out of Weakness: Healing the Wounds that Drive Us to War.* New York: Bantam Books, 1988. (Indianapolis: Knowledge Systems, 1990).

———. *The Parable of the Tribes: The Problem of Power in Social Evolution*. Berkeley and Los Angeles: Univ. of California Press, 1984.

———. *Sowings and Reapings: The Cycling of Good and Evil in the Human System*. Indianapolis: Knowledge Systems, 1989.

Schudson, Michael. *Advertising, the Uneasy Persuasion: Its Dubious Impact on American Society*. New York: Basic Books, 1984.

Schumacher, E. F. *Small Is Beautiful*. New York: Harper & Row, 1973.

Schwartz, Barry. *The Battle for Human Nature: Science, Morality and Modern Life*. New York: W. W. Norton, 1986.

Scitovsky, Tibor. *The Joyless Economy: An Inquiry into Human Satisfaction and Consumer Dissatisfaction*. New York: Oxford Univ. Press, 1976.

Scott, William B. *In Pursuit of Happiness: American Conceptions of Property from the Seventeenth to the Twentieth Century*, Bloomington: Indiana Univ. Press, 1977.

Seward, Desmond. *The Monks of War*. Suffolk: Paladin, 1972.

Shi, David E. *The Simple Life: Plain Living and High Thinking in American Culture*. New York: Oxford Univ. Press, 1985.

Simons, Marlise. "West Germans Get Ready to Scrub the East's Tarnished Environment." *New York Times*, June 27, 1990.

Slater, Philip. *Earthwalk*. New York: Bantam Books, 1980.

———. *The Pursuit of Loneliness*. Boston: Beacon Press, 1970.

———. *Wealth Addiction*. New York: E. P. Dutton, 1980.

Smith, Adam. *The Wealth of Nations*. New York: The Modern Library, 1937.

Stein, Howard F. "Farmer and Cowboy: The Duality of the Midwestern Male Ethos." Manuscript.

Talese, Gay, ed. *The Best American Essays 1987*. New York: Ticknor and Fields, 1987.

Taylor, Paul. "For Disconnected Americans, Citizenship Fades." *Washington Post*, May 6, 1990.

Thevenin, Tine. *The Family Bed*. Wayne, NJ: Avery Publishing Group, 1987.

Thoreau, Henry David. *Walden and Other Writings*, New York: Bantam Books, 1962.

Tocqueville, Alexis de. *Democracy in America*. New York: Random House, 1945.

Tournier, Paul. *The Meaning of Persons*. New York: Harper & Brothers, 1957.

Trump, Donald, with Tony Schwartz. *Trump: The Art of the Deal*. New York: Random House, 1987.

Van Doren, Carl C. *Benjamin Franklin*. New York: Greenwood, 1938.

Veblen, Thorstein. *The Theory of the Leisure Class*. Boston: Houghton Mifflin, 1973.

Ward, Geoffrey C. "Tiger in the Road!" In Talese, *Best American Essays 1987*.

Waterman, Alan S. *The Psychology of Individualism*. New York: Praeger, 1984.

Weber, Max. *The Protestant Ethic and the Spirit of Capitalism*. New York: Charles Scribner's Sons, 1958.

Weil, Andrew. Tape of lecture on addiction and drugs.

Wickse, John R. *About Possession: The Self as Private Property*. University Park, PA: Pennsylvania State Univ. Press, 1976.

Wilhelm, Richard, trans. *The I Ching*. Princeton, NJ: Princeton Univ. Press, 1967.

Will, George. "Bombarded by Ads." *Washington Post*, December 20, 1987.

———. "The Real Game: The Commercials." *Washington Post*, January 28, 1990.

Williams, Rosalind. "Corrupting the Public Imagination." *Christian Science Monitor*, March 20, 1981.

———. *Dream Worlds: Mass Consumption in Late Nineteenth-Century France*. Berkeley and Los Angeles: Univ. of California Press, 1982.

Williamson, Judith. *Consuming Passions: The Dynamics of Popular Culture*. London: Marion Boyars, 1986.

Wolfe, Alan. *America's Impasse: The Rise and Fall of the Politics of Growth*. New York: Pantheon Books, 1981.